# Learning by Doing

## Concepts and Models
## for Service-Learning
## in **Accounting**

D.V. Rama, volume editor

Edward Zlotkowski, series editor

A PUBLICATION OF THE

**AAHE**
AMERICAN ASSOCIATION
FOR HIGHER EDUCATION

Published in cooperation with KPMG Peat Marwick Foundation

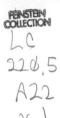
## Special Acknowledgment

AAHE is grateful to the KPMG Foundation
for its generous support in helping to make possible
widespread distribution of this volume.

**Learning by Doing: Concepts and Models for Service-Learning in Accounting**
**(AAHE's Series on Service-Learning in the Disciplines)**

D.V. Rama, *volume editor*

Edward Zlotkowski, *series editor*

Opinions expressed in this publication are those of the contributors and do not necessarily represent those of the American Association for Higher Education or its members.

### About This Publication

This volume is one of eighteen in AAHE's Series on Service-Learning in the Disciplines to be released during 1997-1999. Additional copies of this publication, or others in the series from other disciplines, can be ordered using the form provided on the last page or by contacting:

AMERICAN ASSOCIATION FOR HIGHER EDUCATION
One Dupont Circle, Suite 360
Washington, DC 20036-1110
ph 202/293-6440 x11, fax 202/293-0073
www.aahe.org

ISBN 1-56377-008-3
ISBN (18 vol. set) 1-56377-005-9

# Contents

# Foreword

KPMG is pleased to support the American Association for Higher Education and the American Accounting Association's Teaching and Curriculum Section by providing funding to help distribute *Learning by Doing*. To quote the Teaching and Curriculum Section:

> *In our efforts to engage students in their learning of accounting, many of us have become interested in new learning strategies that have the power to help students become active, lifelong learners and better appreciate the broad, social significance of their work as accounting professionals. This volume on service-learning in accounting illustrates a specific active-learning strategy that many have found to be a useful, even powerful, teaching tool.*

Another publication that relates to a broader definition of learning is the Accounting Education Change Commission monograph *Intentional Learning: A Process for Learning to Learn in the Accounting Curriculum*, by Marlene C. Francis, Timothy C. Mulder, and Joan S. Stark (American Accounting Association, 1995).

KPMG is a national supporter of Students in Free Enterprise (SIFE), and one of the papers in *Learning by Doing* captures the way SIFE students have engaged in service-learning. We are also pleased to sponsor Beta Alpha Psi, The National Accounting Fraternity, and the Golden Key National Honor Society. All three of these organizations have programs for student members that offer significant opportunity for service-learning, much of which is directed toward student involvement in the broader community.

KPMG supports these types of activities, which cause students to work together in teams and bring their talents to bear on curricular and extracurricular projects.

— KPMG Peat Marwick Foundation

# About This Series

by Edward Zlotkowski

The following volume, *Learning by Doing*, represents the fifth in a series of monographs on service-learning and the academic disciplines. Ever since the early 1990s, educators interested in reconnecting higher education not only with neighboring communities but also with the American tradition of education for service have recognized the critical importance of winning faculty support for this work. Faculty, however, tend to define themselves and their responsibilities largely in terms of the academic disciplines/interdisciplinary areas in which they have been trained. Hence, the logic of the present series.

The idea for this series first surfaced approximately four years ago at a meeting convened by Campus Compact to explore the feasibility of developing a national network of service-learning educators. At that meeting, it quickly became clear that some of those assembled saw the primary value of such a network in its ability to provide concrete resources to faculty working in or wishing to explore service-learning. Out of that meeting there developed, under the auspices of Campus Compact, a new national group of educators called the Invisible College, and it was within the Invisible College that the monograph project was first conceived. Indeed, a review of both the editors and contributors responsible for many of the volumes in this series would reveal significant representation by faculty associated with the Invisible College.

If Campus Compact helped supply the initial financial backing and impulse for the Invisible College and for this series, it was the American Association for Higher Education (AAHE) that made completion of the project feasible. Thanks to its reputation for innovative work, AAHE was not only able to obtain the funding needed to support the project up through actual publication, it was also able to assist in attracting many of the teacher-scholars who participated as writers and editors.

Three individuals in particular deserve to be singled out for their contributions. Sandra Enos, former Campus Compact project director for Integrating Service and Academic Study, was shepherd to the Invisible College project. John Wallace, professor of philosophy at the University of Minnesota, was the driving force behind the creation of the Invisible College. Without his vision and faith in the possibility of such an undertaking, assembling the human resources needed for this series would have been very difficult. Third, AAHE's endorsement — and all that followed in its wake — was due largely to AAHE vice president Lou Albert. Lou's enthusiasm for the monograph project and his determination to see it adequately supported have been critical to its success. It is to Sandra, John, and Lou that the monograph series as a whole must be dedicated.

Another individual to whom the series owes a special note of thanks is Teresa Antonucci, who, as AAHE project assistant, has helped facilitate much of the communication that has allowed the project to move forward.

## The Rationale Behind the Series

A few words should be said at this point about the makeup of both the general series and the individual volumes. At first glance, accounting may seem like an unusual choice of disciplines with which to link service-learning. However, "natural fit" has not played a determinant role in helping decide which disciplines/interdisciplinary areas the series should include. Far more important have been considerations related to the overall range of disciplines represented. Since experience has shown that there is probably no disciplinary area where service-learning cannot be fruitfully employed to strengthen students' abilities to become active learners as well as responsible citizens, a primary goal in putting the series together has been to demonstrate this fact. Thus, some rather natural choices for inclusion — disciplines such as anthropology, geography, and religious studies — have been passed over in favor of other, sometimes less obvious selections. Accounting represents the first volume that emphatically demonstrates service-learning's broad educational relevance.

If a concern for variety has helped shape the series as a whole, a concern for legitimacy has been central to the design of the individual volumes. To this end, each volume has been both written by and aimed primarily at academics working in a particular disciplinary/interdisciplinary area. Many individual volumes have, in fact, been produced with the encouragement and active support of relevant discipline-specific national societies. About this Accounting volume, the Teaching and Curriculum Section of the American Accounting Association says: "In our efforts to engage students in their learning of accounting, many of us have become interested in new learning strategies that have the power to help students become active, lifelong learners and better appreciate the broad, social significance of their work as accounting professionals. This volume on service-learning in accounting illustrates a specific active-learning strategy that many have found to be a useful, even powerful, teaching tool."

Furthermore, each volume has been designed to include its own appropriate theoretical, pedagogical, and bibliographical material. Especially with regard to theoretical and bibliographical material, this design has resulted in considerable variation both in emphasis and in level of discourse. Thus, for example, a volume such as Accounting necessarily contains more introductory and less bibliographical material than does Composition — simply because there has been less written on and there is less familiarity with service-learning in accounting. However, no volume is meant to provide a detailed introduction to service-learning *as a generic concept*. For material of this nature, the reader is referred to such texts as Kendall's *Combining Service and Learning: A Resource Book for Community and Public Service* (NSIEE, 1990) and Jacoby's *Service-Learning in Higher Education* (Jossey-Bass, 1996).

I would like to conclude with a note of special thanks to D.V. Rama, editor of this Accounting volume. Dr. Rama's enthusiasm for this project — long before it developed momentum within the accounting community — is a testimony to her foresight and her commitment to the kind of reforms envisioned by the Accounting Education Change Commission. Her colleagues, in service-learning as well as in accounting, owe her a gesture of genuine thanks.

April 1998

# Introduction

## by D.V. Rama

Recent efforts toward curriculum reform in accounting have led to calls for the increased use of active-learning strategies, including those based on direct experience. Service-learning, a specialized form of experiential learning that links community service projects with the accounting curriculum, constitutes one such strategy. Service projects involving accounting assistance to low-income/disadvantaged individuals, nonprofits, and small businesses provide increased opportunities for incorporating direct experience into the accounting curriculum. In addition, solving real problems for individuals/organizations can provide a richer learning experience than even some traditional projects in the private sector.

One key goal recently emphasized by accounting educators is lifelong learning. Lifelong learners are independent, confident, reflective, motivated, flexible, interpersonally competent, and confident. The Accounting Education Change Commission (AECC)[1] has advocated the use of "reflective practice" for developing these qualities. Service-learning explicitly seeks to incorporate such reflective practice into the accounting curriculum.

The present volume has two main objectives: (1) to develop a theoretical framework for service-learning in accounting consistent with the goals identified by accounting educators and the recent efforts toward curriculum reform, and (2) to describe specific implementations across the accounting curriculum. Hence, the book is organized into two separate though clearly related sections.

Part 1's first essay provides an introduction to the idea of service-learning, the differences between service-learning and community service, and a broad overview of how service-learning can be integrated into accounting. In the second essay, Bremser focuses on the service component of service-learning and describes a variety of community projects that would be appropriate for service-learning programs in accounting. Weis, in the third chapter, focuses on the other component of service-learning — reflection. Reflection, a key component of all experiential learning, is especially important in service-learning, and involves a critical examination of the service experience in light of particular learning objectives. Finally, Oddo highlights some key issues from a department chair's perspective. These include the need to promote faculty ownership of service-learning as well as student acceptance of this approach.

Part 2 describes specific implementations. These essays present different ways in which service-learning can be implemented in accounting and are intended to function as a resource for other accounting faculty in implementing service-learning projects in their courses. DeBerg's essay on service projects in introductory accounting demonstrates the feasibility of implementing service-learning projects early in the accounting curriculum. Pringle focuses on projects in an intermediate accounting course. Carr, Milani, and Oestreich et al. present three approaches to building a service-learning initiative around the Volunteer Income Tax Assistance (VITA) program. Michenzi and Lenk describe the integration of service-learning projects into an accounting information systems course, while Woolley outlines an initiative that involves a wide variety of technical skills. Ravenscroft discusses service-learning in the context of a capstone course focusing on ethics and social responsibility. Mech concludes the section on implementation approaches with the only example of an implementation not linked to a specific course.

The book concludes with my own summary of issues that emerge from this entire collection of case studies. Locatelli's afterword places the book in the still broader context of service-learning and the needs of the contemporary academy. A brief annotated bibliography rounds off the volume.

## Note

1. The Accounting Education Change Commission no longer exists. Any correspondence about AECC should go to: American Accounting Association, Attn: Craig E. Polhemus, Executive Director, 5717 Bessie Drive, Sarasota, FL 34233.

# Service-Learning: An Active-Learning Approach for Accounting Education

## by D.V. Rama

Recently, accounting programs across the country have begun to be changed to better prepare students for the accounting profession. In contrast to the traditional approach to accounting education, which stressed calculating one right answer, the new focus emphasizes dealing with unstructured problems and dealing with messy or incomplete data (Williams 1993). The Accounting Education Change Commission (AECC) notes that students should be active participants in the learning process and not passive recipients of information. Such active learning calls for different instructional approaches from the traditional lecture format. For example, Williams suggests the use of pedagogical strategies such as case studies and role plays to simulate the real world.

Zlotkowski (1996) notes that while such in-class activities are valuable, they can only approximate the complexity of real-world situations. Direct practical experience is probably the best way for students to learn how to deal with complex situations. Morton and Troppe (1996) note that approaches based on direct experience motivate lasting learning. In contrast, traditional "information-assimilation" models are more efficient but do not facilitate retention. The AECC, in Issues Statement No. 4 (1993), also underscores the importance of experiential learning as follows: "Students should seek opportunities to obtain firsthand knowledge of the business world and practice environment."

This essay examines the use of service-learning as a way of incorporating direct experience and promoting active learning in the accounting curriculum. Service-learning is a specialized form of experiential education that combines academic study and community service. Community service is described as providing services to improve the quality of life of the residents of a community, especially low-income individuals, or to solve specific problems facing a disadvantaged community. Kendall (1990) states:

> Service-learning programs emphasize the accomplishment of tasks [that] meet human needs in combination with conscious educational growth. . . . They combine needed tasks in the community with intentional learning goals and with conscious reflection and critical analysis. (20)

Recently, service-learning has been incorporated in many undergraduate programs. According to Campus Compact, about 91 percent of its more than 500 member institutions now offer service-learning courses (Zlotkowski 1996). Since several detailed descriptions of the service-learning movement are available (cf. Kendall 1990), this article does not focus on service-learning in general. Rather, the purpose of this essay is to explore the potential for integrating service-learning into the accounting curriculum. The motivation for this discussion is that until recently much of the momentum behind service-learning has been provided by academics tied to the social sciences and liberal arts (Zlotkowski 1996). It may be difficult to directly adopt in accounting the models of service-learning emerging from these disciplines. Further, it may be difficult for accounting educators to adopt a pedagogical approach based on an activity (community service) not intrinsically linked to business education (Zlotkowski 1996). Hence, a key objective of this paper is to examine the extent to which the goals and pedagogical strategies of service-learning overlap with the overall goals of accounting education. This article as well as the other articles in this volume are a first step toward developing a vision of service-learning that is congruent with the goals of accounting educators as well as the recent efforts toward curriculum reform in accounting.

The rest of this essay is organized as follows. While a detailed discussion of the service-learning movement is beyond the essay's scope, it is important to understand that service-learning is not identical to community service. The next section discusses some key differences between service-learning and community service. Next, the potential for using service-learning to enhance opportunities for "direct experiences" in the accounting curriculum is discussed. This is followed by a discussion of how the goals commonly articulated for service-learning are congruent with many of the goals of accounting education and the current efforts toward curriculum reform in accounting. The final section presents a summary.

## Service-Learning and Community Service

Before we can discuss the potential for integrating service-learning into the accounting curriculum, it is important to distinguish between the terms "community service" and "service-learning." Elsewhere in this volume, William Weis observes that while his accounting students participated extensively in community service through organizations such as Beta Alpha Psi, he moved toward service-learning as a vehicle to connect such service more directly with the curriculum. Kendall (1990) considers this integration to be critical, since the curriculum is the primary expression of the institution's view of what needs to be learned. Markus (cited in Morton and Troppe

1996: 22) asserts that "the kinds of service activities in which students participate should be selected so that they will illustrate, affirm, extend, and challenge material presented in readings and lectures."

The above discussion suggests that not all community service activities will be good service-learning projects for a particular discipline; rather, the service-learning paradigm implies that faculty and students must seek out the types of community projects that are closely tied to their educational goals. While general service activities may result in the development of some skills required by accountants, service-learning will be a significant pedagogy for accounting education only if accounting educators are able to select and carefully structure the service work according to the curriculum. The essays in this volume provide prototypes that show how community service can be linked specifically to the accounting curriculum.

Another defining characteristic that can be used to differentiate service-learning from community service is reflection. Reflection is an important component of experiential learning — enhancing both technical, discipline-specific goals and broader goals related to social awareness and civic responsibilities. Bringle and Hatcher (1995) define reflection as the "intentional consideration of the service experience in light of particular learning objectives" (115). David Kolb (1984) has developed one of the most widely accepted models of experiential learning that identifies concrete experience and reflective observation as two key steps in action-based learning. Service-learning is, of course, a subset of experiential learning. Hence, it is hardly surprising that the National Society for Experiential Education (1989) has formulated a set of "Principles of Good Practice in Student Community Service-Learning" that clearly describes the role of reflection in service-learning projects:

> The service experience alone does not ensure that either good service or good learning will occur. Both are improved by frequent opportunities for conscious reflection on the experience and critical analysis of the issues involved. This interplay of action and reflection on experience is central to service-learning. Seminars, carefully planned journals, discussions among service-learners, conversations with those being served, faculty conferences with students, debriefing sessions, analysis papers, public presentations, and creative artistic expressions are examples of reflective practice [that] can help the experience become much more than a one-time service opportunity.
>
> Students who engage in structured, conscious reflection and who explore the broader social issues behind community problems are more likely to appreciate the complexity of social problems. Research shows they are more likely to have a sense of social responsibility, more likely to commit to addressing these problems in their adult lives as workers and citi-

zens, and more likely to demonstrate political efficacy. They will also have practiced the reflective skills needed to be self-directed, lifelong learners. This "reflective learning component" is most useful when it is intentional, continuous throughout the experience, and evaluated.

This section ends with Bringle and Hatcher's (1995) definition of service-learning, which can serve as a good starting point for developing models of service-learning appropriate for accounting education:

> We consider service-learning to be a course-based, credit-bearing educational experience in which students (a) participate in an organized service activity in such a way that meets identified community needs and (b) reflect on the service activity in such a way to gain further understanding of course content, a broader appreciation of the discipline, and an enhanced sense of civic responsibility. (112)

# Expanding Experiential Learning Opportunities for Accounting Students

An important argument for integrating service-learning into accounting programs is that service-learning can be used to enhance the quantity and quality of experiential learning opportunities for accounting students. The AECC's Issues Statement No. 4 underscores the importance of experiential learning as follows:

> Students should seek opportunities to obtain firsthand knowledge of the business world and practice environment
> - Seek internships, cooperative work/study arrangements, and summer employment opportunities that are broadly relevant to your career choice. Students considering an accounting career should seek general business and organizational experience, not just accounting experience, because a key role of accounting is to support managerial decision making.
> - Seek campus opportunities to build communication and business skills — for example, serve as an officer of a campus organization. (433) [emphasis added]

Certain words in the AECC's description have been emphasized to show that in arguing for experiential education, AECC is not limiting itself to a single kind of accounting experience but is endorsing broader organizational experience that can help develop important skills required for the accounting profession. Service-learning projects can provide such broad organizational experiences to prepare students for that profession.

Thus, one practical argument for service-learning is that it can increase the number and kind of experiential learning opportunities available to students. In an essay elsewhere in this volume, Janice Carr notes that traditional internships are usually available only to top students. Further, not all internships are paid, and some internship programs may delay graduation. Service-learning programs can create opportunities for more students to participate in experiential learning activities, since a variety of community-based projects can be integrated into the accounting curriculum to reinforce technical accounting skills and to develop general business skills as well as a deeper sense of social responsibility.

Service projects through student organizations (e.g., through a student chapter of the Accountants for the Public Interest [see Wayne Bremser's essay] and Project Empowerment [see Timothy Mech's] provide yet another way for increasing learning opportunities based on direct experience for accounting students. This approach is consistent with AECC's suggestion that students "seek campus opportunities to build communication and business skills — for example, serve as an officer of a campus organization." This alternative is particularly attractive, because the increasing complexity of accounting knowledge limits the time available to integrate direct experience into accounting courses. In adopting this approach to service-learning, instructors should consider the differences between community service and service-learning discussed in the previous section. To be called service-learning, these projects should be selected and designed in such a way that they (1) meet a community need, (2) enhance understanding of material learned in accounting courses, (3) help in developing a broader appreciation of the accounting profession, (4) help in promoting a sense of civic responsibility, and (5) develop communication, teamwork, and interpersonal skills. Faculty advisers have an important role to play in realizing the educational potential of these community projects and making them into service-learning projects. One limitation of this approach, compared with course-linked projects, is that it may be difficult to implement structured reflection, given the fact that the sponsored projects are outside the curriculum and its structures.

## Enhancing the Quality of Experiential Learning

Service-learning can also be used to improve the *quality* of "experiences" for accounting students. For example, service-learning projects in accounting often involve doing work for nonprofit organizations. Working with nonprofits can offer significant development opportunities for business professionals. In a recent *Wall Street Journal* article, Isenberg (1993) notes that "the beauty of nonprofit volunteer work is that it gives operating experience relevant to corporate management but gives it much faster." He suggests that the business and the nonprofit communities can forge a strategic alliance that is beneficial to both as follows:

*Nonprofits today need people with real insights into budgeting and cash flows, people who understand how to utilize information systems and create human resource programs.*

*On the other side of the alliance, corporations have promising young managers who don't get a chance to practice those skills because they are not yet high enough on the management hierarchy. Nonprofit organizations provide corporate volunteers a chance to put their skills to work immediately. (1)*

Similarly, a strategic alliance between business schools and the nonprofit community can be beneficial to both. Service-learning offers some unique benefits over strategies such as case studies and even some traditional business internships. For example, the AIS (accounting information systems) course I taught had traditionally required students to document and analyze accounting systems in a real business. Most of these studies were not conducted to meet specific needs of the organization. In contrast, the service projects I incorporated in later semesters were driven by specific needs of requesting nonprofits. The issues involved in addressing the real needs of multiple users of AIS provided some unique opportunities for learning that I had not found in my traditional course project. Thus, one student who worked on a billing project for an AIDS program remarked that if she had to do the project again she would interview counselors in addition to the project director. During the course of the project, she had come to realize that while the project director supported the project on improving billing procedures/documents, the counselors might not support the recommendations if the latter involved more record keeping on their part. In this way, she came to realize that involving affected users early in systems development was essential to project success. While such issues should always be emphasized in an AIS course, direct experience can help students understand these issues much better than class discussions alone.

Other types of service-learning projects, such as the ones based on the Volunteer Income Tax Assistance (VITA) program, which involve working with individuals in the community rather than with nonprofit organizations, offer similar advantages [for more, see the essays by Janice Carr and Ken Milani]. Thus, accounting educators should consider integrating service-learning into the curriculum as a means of increasing the quality of opportunities for learning based on direct experience.

# Service-Learning and Accounting Education: Shared Goals

This section provides justification for integrating service-learning in accounting by examining the common goals of service-learning and accounting education. First, the key objectives of accounting education are briefly discussed. Service-learning is then shown to be an appropriate pedagogical approach for accounting education, since it is geared toward the accomplishment of similar goals.

## Goals of Accounting Education

Recently, accounting educators and professionals have identified several goals for accounting programs. For example, in a recent study conducted by the Institute of Management Accountants (IMA 1996), 800 management accountant respondents were asked to rate (on a scale of 1 to 5) the importance of knowledge, skills, and abilities (KSAs) to the competent performance of their work as corporate accountants. This study was conducted by IMA to help accounting educators design or revise curricula to better prepare students for careers in management accounting by giving them skills that meet the needs of corporate America. Respondents gave highest ratings to work ethic (mean 4.67), analytical/problem-solving skills (4.66), interpersonal skills (4.64), and listening skills (4.58). KSAs such as writing skills (4.32), familiarity with business processes (4.32), leadership skills (4.30), and speaking/presentation skills (4.11) also received mean ratings greater than 4. Similarly, a recent study by Brigham Young University (Francis, Mulder, and Stark 1995: 2) lists 27 competencies organized into the following categories: (1) communication skills, (2) information development and distribution skills, (3) decision-making skills, (4) knowledge of accounting, auditing, and tax, (5) professionalism, and (6) leadership development. It is important to note that only four of these 27 competencies are related to a direct knowledge of accounting. The monograph also points out that while many of these competencies can be gained in general education, they may not be developed adequately in our graduates unless they are also included in the accounting curriculum.

Udpa (1996) makes a similar argument for moving from a narrow technical focus in accounting education to a broad-based approach that develops the types of competencies identified above. He uses the term "liberal" accounting education to describe such an educational approach. He asserts that the main objectives of liberal education are "the cultivation of intellectual skills, development of students' ability to communicate their thoughts effectively, both orally and in writing, and a deep understanding of the ethical and social problems that exist in the society in which they function" (3). Udpa further argues that since accounting is a professional service activity, our graduates must be prepared to deal with moral and ethical conflicts, uncertainties and ambiguities in their environment, and interaction with diverse cultural and ethnic communities. Thus, accounting educators must be committed to liberal learning to ensure the effective development of accounting professionals.

The recent discussion of the goals of accounting education has been accompanied by a corresponding discussion of the pedagogical approaches that will support these goals. The liberalization of the accounting curriculum as suggested above calls for a range of pedagogical strategies rather than traditional lectures. So AECC's Position Statement No. 1 states:

> Students must be active participants in the learning process, not passive recipients of information. They should identify and solve unstructured problems that require the use of multiple information sources. Learning by doing should be emphasized. Working in groups should be encouraged.

Service-learning has significant potential for accounting education since it has all the attributes suggested in the above description. Next we examine the common goals of service-learning and accounting education to provide further support for the use of service-learning in accounting.

## Lifelong Learning

Given the complexity of the accounting profession and the practice environment, accounting educators and professionals are increasingly emphasizing lifelong, independent learning as an important goal of accounting education. A recent American Accounting Association monograph on intentional learning (Francis, Mulder, and Stark 1995) identifies learning qualities desired of future accountants as their being (1) independent, (2) confident, (3) reflective/self-aware, (4) curious/motivated, (5) flexible, and (6) interdependent/interpersonally competent. It further states that the qualities required to be independent learners are not automatically acquired and that students must practice the process of independent learning throughout the accounting curriculum. Accordingly, instructors must adopt active-learning approaches that can develop such independent learning capabilities rather than following the traditional instructional approaches that view students as "empty vessels" to be filled with academic content.

A key question for accounting educators then is, What types of learning approaches can help students become independent learners? According to the AAA monograph, one key element in the learning process involves the use of "reflective practice" as advocated by Schön. Schön (cited in Francis, Mulder, and Stark 1995) has suggested that effective professional practice requires good judgment and the ability to make wise decisions in a variety of complex situations. He has further proposed the "reflective practicum" as an effective way to develop such judgment and decision-making skills. The monograph underscores the importance of reflective practice as follows: "Professional training, then, must include opportunities to apply and adapt knowledge and to reflect on practice as one engages in the process" (10).

Experiential learning approaches, including service-learning, provide precisely such opportunities for reflective practice that can enable students to develop the types of independent learning capabilities identified above. Whether students work on tax problems for low-income individuals or help nonprofits in setting up accounting systems, they have to seek information and solve problems independently. Students also have to be flexible in dealing with clients and their problems — a situation quite different from the structured learning situations typically encountered in classrooms. As many of Janice Carr's students remarked, such opportunities for applying their knowledge in real-life situations help them in developing confidence in their abilities. Further, the need to interact with clients, supervisors, team members, reviewers, etc. can develop interpersonal competencies. Thus, service-learning encourages self-management of learning in a variety of ways and is an appropriate strategy for developing independent learning capabilities.

## Reinforcement of Technical Knowledge

As noted in the section on community service and service-learning, the service-learning approach seeks to illustrate, affirm, extend, and challenge material discussed in a discipline. Thus, accounting educators should seek service projects that can reinforce technical knowledge. Also, the application of technical knowledge to unstructured real-world problems can improve students' understanding of the material as well as their retention. The implementation section of this volume (Part 2) provides examples of how service activities can be structured to reinforce technical material covered in courses, such as accounting information systems or taxation.

In addition to technical accounting knowledge, service projects can also be used to reinforce technical skills related to the use of information technology. For example, students often have to use spreadsheet or database packages in implementing systems for nonprofit organizations. In their essay in Part 2, Oestreich, Venable, and Doran describe the use of collaborative technology classrooms, Internet newsgroups, electronic mail, electronic conferencing, and electronic filing technologies in their service-learning implementation.

## Communication and Interpersonal Skills

Service-learning projects offer numerous opportunities to interact with people of diverse socioeconomic, ethnic, and educational backgrounds, thus helping students develop interpersonal, teamwork, and communication skills. In her program, Carr structures VITA projects in a way that requires extensive interaction with the community, other students, and accountants. The requirement that students have to market the program to the community is another interesting strategy by means of which communication skills are developed in her course. Similarly, Curtis DeBerg's project (described in Part 2) involves extensive interaction with teachers and students in high schools. Accounting systems projects usually require students to interview various users.

Reflective assignments can provide still other opportunities for developing communication skills. In his essay, William Weis describes the use of debriefing sessions for discussing the service experience. Alternatively, students can be required to make a presentation to the class or to write journals and prepare detailed reports. Students working on a systems design project can write a report to the project director discussing the problems in the existing system and their recommended solutions. Such assignments can help in preparing students for the kinds of writing that will be required of them as professionals.

## Ethical and Moral Development

Another common goal for service-learning relates to ethical and moral development. Ethical development is increasingly recognized as one of the goals of business and accounting education. Susan Ravenscroft's essay discusses the limitations of traditional instructional approaches to ethics education and identifies service-learning as an important alternative. She gives examples of how service-learning has been used to enhance ethics instruction in a variety of disciplines.

One such example is the use of service-learning in a college ethics course (Boss 1994). Boss examined the effect of service-learning projects on moral development. Both a control group and the experimental group engaged in discussions of moral issues in the course. However, only the experimental group had to complete 20 hours of community service and reflect on the moral issues encountered during their work. The results of this study support the hypothesis that students who engage in community service will make greater gains in moral reasoning than students who engage in academic discussion of similar issues without the practical experience. Thus, service-learning could be an effective strategy for ethics instruction in accounting.

## Social Responsibility and Community Involvement

A related goal emphasized by service-learning programs is social responsibility and community involvement. Giles and Eyler (1994) note that one of the most frequently expressed goals of service-learning is the development of social responsibility in adolescents. They further state that "student volunteers in community settings have a more complex understanding of social problems and how communities are organized to meet needs and are less judgmental about their clients' need for service" (329). William F. Buckley (cited in Zlotkowski 1996), the noted conservative author, stresses the importance of nurturing an ongoing civic disposition and solidarity with one's fellow citizens.

The accounting service projects described in this volume share such objectives. For example, one goal stated by Alfred Michenzi is that "this service to others might blossom into future involvement in community service once the students graduate and launch their careers" [see p. 133]. Giles and Eyler (1994) note that service involvement is affected by efficacy (belief that one can make a difference by participating in such activities). Service projects in technical disciplines such as accounting can play a unique role in promoting a sense of efficacy. Students become aware that the technical skills of their chosen discipline enable them to provide a unique set of skills/knowledge that can be very valuable to the community. In his essay, Weis describes how "students spoke genuinely of their need and desire to serve, of their growing sense of personal confidence and personal efficacy in the act of providing real assistance to people who needed help, and of their awakening to the reality of coping with the demands of subsistence on incomes that many had thought were well below levels where this was possible" [see p. 40].

To support such goals, service projects should involve some discussion of social problems and the ways in which communities and human service agencies meet these needs. Michenzi organized a presentation by a social worker, who discussed the problems faced by human service agencies in meeting social needs with limited staff and funds — as well as the importance of volunteers. Similarly, students providing tax assistance to low-income individuals [see Carr's and Milani's essays] became more aware of problems facing such individuals, as well as the cultural/linguistic barriers affecting them in an increasingly diverse society.

While the articles in this volume have successfully integrated such notions of social responsibility and community involvement with essentially technical accounting projects, some accounting educators may understandably argue that solving social problems and promoting community involvement cannot be the primary justification for service projects in the accounting curriculum. While notions of community involvement and civic responsibility are integral to service-learning, the primary justification for making service-learning part of accounting education is that service-learning does indeed help in developing skills identified by the accounting profession itself as of critical importance.

# Service-Learning in Accounting: Action and Reflection

The previous section discussed the shared goals of accounting education and service-learning. Next, the broad issues related to the design of action and reflection components for service-learning projects in accounting are discussed. Details of projects for specific areas/courses are available in the essays in the implementation section of this volume (Part 2).

## Designing the Action Component

Wayne Bremser, a member of the board of directors of Accountants for the Public Interest (API), describes in his essay three categories of service engagements — working with individuals, nonprofits, and small businesses. The first type of project follows the typical model used in liberal arts disciplines where service activities involve face-to-face interaction with low-income or disadvantaged individuals, such as a service project in a sociology course that requires students to serve meals in a homeless shelter and record their observations and interactions. Some of the service projects described in this volume [see essays by DeBerg, Pringle, Carr, Milani, and Oestreich et al.] follow this approach. Carr and Milani have built their service-learning programs around the VITA program. Lynn Pringle's students organized budgeting and money management workshops for individuals at homeless shelters and a program for unemployed teenage mothers. DeBerg's students teach accounting to at-risk students in middle schools.

Although projects such as these can provide powerful learning experiences, one must be careful lest an overly restrictive interpretation of community needs excludes projects of particular value to business disciplines. An alternative model of service-learning in accounting would focus on helping nonprofits to provide services in an efficient and effective manner. Such projects may or may not involve direct contact with disadvantaged populations. For instance, an accounting systems project for an AIDS counseling program may require interaction only with employees working for the program rather than with the clients being counseled. Bremser describes several types of projects for accounting students in nonprofit settings and describes resources that can be used in such projects.

The essay by James Woolley is valuable for several case studies describing such projects in a capstone course. Service-learning projects were implemented as part of an effort to integrate various subjects, including financial, tax, managerial, systems, and auditing. Ethical and social issues associated with the accounting profession were included in the integration. Alfred Michenzi's students "participate in a meaningful academic activity by [helping] not-for-profit agencies . . . in the solution of their business and accounting problems" [see p. 133]. In her essay, Margarita Lenk provides another example of projects involving nonprofits in an accounting information systems course. Given the limited funds and staff available to many nonprofits, such service projects can certainly help the community.

Yet another approach involves working with government agencies. Niagara University [see Alfonso Oddo in this volume] provides service-learning opportunities for students through the economic development project and the Niagara Falls budget project, which aim at developing strategies "to stimulate the economy, create jobs, and develop entrepreneurial opportunities for community residents" [see p. 56]. Finally, service projects can sometimes involve business settings. Susan Ravenscroft's students worked with clients assigned by the local community development board through its program for helping low-income people to become entrepreneurs. In her essay, Ravenscroft offers three arguments to justify inclusion of this work in a service-learning program: (1) The businesses were started by economically disadvantaged individuals to whom these businesses represented an alternative to continued government support; (2) these businesses could not survive without some help; and (3) small businesses are important to the local community, since they are likely to hire from the area and to contribute to programs in the local community. Furthermore, reflection on personal responsibility and ethics is emphasized in her projects.

To summarize, accounting service-learning projects can serve individuals, nonprofit organizations, government agencies, or small businesses. Bremser emphasizes the need for service-learning programs to establish criteria for deciding which projects will be accepted. API's affiliates provide services to those who cannot pay, and deciding whether an organization can or cannot pay involves some judgment. Gathering client information as suggested by Bremser can help in selecting appropriate service-learning projects.

## Reflection

As noted previously, critical reflection is essential to enhance learning from service projects.[1] Students' participation in community projects such as the VITA program must be accompanied by appropriate reflective exercises before they can be considered service-learning.

Indeed, the reflection component should consist of both technical and social components. The technical component could be implemented in the form of reports, essays, and presentations. For example, students designing an accounting system for a nonprofit organization could be required to present their design to users in the form of a report. They could also be asked to present their report to the class. Adding a social component to the reflective process turns the service activity into a multidimensional learning experience. Ravenscroft emphasizes personal responsibility and ethics in reflection. Lynn Pringle's students reflect on the complexities of the welfare system while teaching budgeting and money management skills at homeless shelters and a program for unemployed teenage mothers. Students at Niagara University [see Oddo] develop a better understanding of the problems facing the elderly while participating in the tax assistance program.

## Summary

Recent efforts toward curriculum reform in accounting have led to calls for the increased use of pedagogical strategies based on direct experience. This paper has discussed how service-learning projects that link community service projects with the accounting curriculum constitute one such strategy. Service projects involving accounting assistance to low-income/disadvantaged individuals, nonprofits, or small businesses provide increased opportunities for incorporating direct experience into the accounting curriculum. In addition, solving real problems for individuals/organizations can provide a richer learning experience than even some traditional business projects.

An examination of the common goals of service-learning and accounting education provides further support for incorporating service-learning in accounting programs. The essays in this volume have identified several goals for service-learning in accounting, including reinforcing technical knowledge, developing communication and interpersonal skills, and furthering ethical and moral development, as well as the importance of a sense of community involvement and social responsibility. Finally, a key goal emphasized recently by accounting educators is lifelong learning. Lifelong learners are independent, confident, reflective, motivated, flexible, interpersonally competent, and confident. AECC advocates the use of "reflective practice" for developing these qualities. The notion of reflective practice is also at the heart of service-learning, making it a potentially significant strategy for accounting education.

### Note

1. A study by Boss (1994) provides empirical support for the importance of reflection in achieving the goals of service-learning. Boss examined the effect of service-learning projects in a college ethics course on moral development. Moral development was measured by the Defining Issues Test (DIT). The results of the study supported the hypothesis that students who engage in community service will make greater gains in moral reasoning than those students who engage in academic discussion of similar issues without the practical experience. Further, she found that prior community service experience had no significant effect on students' pretest DIT scores, suggesting that both the service and structured reflection on these activities are important in enhancing moral reasoning. Thus, research provides important support for the idea

that reflection is an essential component for achieving the goals of service-learning — both technical, discipline-specific goals and broader goals related to social awareness and civic responsibilities.

## References

Accounting Education Change Commission. (Fall 1993). "Improving the Early Employment Experience of Accountants." Issues Statement No. 4. *Issues in Accounting Education* 8(2): 431-435.

Boss, J.A. (1994). "The Effect of Community Service Work on the Moral Development of College Ethics Students." *Journal of Moral Education* 23(2): 183-197.

Bringle, Robert, and Julie Hatcher. (Fall 1995). "A Service-Learning Curriculum for Faculty." *Michigan Journal of Community Service–Learning* 67(2): 112-122.

Francis, Marlene C., Timothy C. Mulder, and Joan S. Stark. (1995). *Intentional Learning: A Process for Learning to Learn in the Accounting Curriculum*. Accounting Education Series, no. 12. Sarasota, FL: American Accounting Association.

Giles, D.E., Jr., and J. Eyler. (1994). "The Impact of a College Community Service Laboratory on Students' Personal, Social, and Cognitive Outcomes." *Journal of Adolescence* 17(4): 327-339.

Institute of Management Accountants. (February 1996). "Practice Analysis of Management Accounting." Working Draft. Montvale, NJ: IMA.

Isenberg, Howard. (September 13, 1993). "Nonprofit Training for Profitable Careers." *The Wall Street Journal*, 1.

Kendall, Jane C. (1990). "Combining Service and Learning: An Introduction." In *Combining Service and Learning: A Resource Book for Community and Public Service*, edited by Jane C. Kendall and Associates, pp. 1-33. Raleigh, NC: National Society for Internships and Experiential Education.

Kolb, D.A. (1984). *Experiential Learning: Experience as the Source of Learning and Development*. Englewood Cliffs, NJ: Prentice-Hall.

Morton, Keith, and Marie Troppe. (1996). "From the Margin to the Mainstream: Campus Compact's Project on Integrating Service With Academic Study." *Journal of Business Ethics* 15(1): 21-32.

National Society for Experiential Education. (Summer 1989). "Principles of Good Practice in Combining Service and Learning." *Voluntary Action Leadership*.

Udpa, Suneel. (1996). "Accounting as a Liberal Discipline." Presentation at the national meeting of the American Accounting Association, Chicago, IL.

Williams, Doyle Z. (August 1993). "Reforming Accounting Education." *Journal of Accountancy*: 76-82.

Zlotkowski, Edward. (January 1996). "Opportunity for All: Linking Service-Learning and Business Education." *Journal of Business Ethics* 15(1): 5-19.

# Service-Learning:
# The Accountants for the Public Interest Perspective

by Wayne G. Bremser

Domestic violence, substance abuse, crime, child abuse are serious social problems. Toxic waste, air and water pollution threaten our environment. There are no easy answers to solving these problems. We cannot rely on the government to do the job. Politicians concerned with budget deficits are cutting back social programs. Volunteers willing to give to the community will be an integral part of America's efforts to combat social problems.

Accounting professionals have an important role to play in the country's efforts to solve social problems. There are opportunities and needs for accounting professionals at all levels to make significant contributions of their time and talent. Professional accounting organizations, including the American Institute of Certified Public Accountants (AICPA), Institute of Management Accountants, and state CPA societies, have recognized their role in promoting community service. They encourage members to volunteer their services to help those less fortunate. A spirit of giving back to the community is growing. These opportunities extend to accounting students, who are preparing for entry-level positions.

There is a need for pro bono accounting services to be provided to individuals, nonprofit organizations, and small businesses that cannot afford to pay for these services. Accountants for the Public Interest (API) has played an important role in mobilizing accounting professionals toward meeting this need. This article describes API's activities and programs. API and API affiliates across the country are important resources for professors involved in service-learning programs.

## Pro Bono

In 1973, API was formed in San Francisco, California. Initially, API's activities focused on public issues work. Professional accountants in the San Francisco Bay area had volunteered their time to study important public concerns, such as funding of the airport. The founders recognized the need to expand pro bono accounting across the country. Local affiliates were formed in several major cities. Over the years, API and its affiliates have provided thousands of volunteer hours to individuals, nonprofit organizations, and small businesses.

## Changing the Image

API's mission is to enhance and increase the availability of pro bono accounting services to organizations and individuals who otherwise would not have access to needed professional assistance, and to improve the image of the accounting professional. By acting for the public good *(pro bono publico)*, accountants can improve their image.

API has three basic goals. The first goal is to design, identify, and support public service accounting organizational structures, which involve accountants in effective public service activities. This includes stimulating commitment to public service through encouragement of community service activities within accounting firms, companies, and associations. API has supported individual public service accounting organizations and volunteer units within accounting associations. For example, API and its affiliates have worked with state CPA societies and student organizations. API and its affiliates have developed tools and client service packages for use by various organizations.

API's second goal is to promote volunteer accounting services and link the commitment of accounting professionals and organizations with the needs of the community. This includes fostering the involvement of accountants with public boards, commissions, and advisory bodies. There is a tremendous need for volunteer accounting services. API and its affiliates facilitate the delivery of such services. There are many accountants who would be willing to provide volunteer services, but they have not been asked or directed toward the need. Conversely, there are many individuals and organizations in need of service, but they are unaware that there are public service accounting organizations to provide the needed services.

The third basic goal is to acquire resources for pro bono services. Resources are needed at the national and local levels. At the national level, API has received resources from the AICPA and the Big Six accounting firms, which evidences the profession's commitment to pro bono accounting. Numerous foundations, CPA firms, corporations, and individuals have provided in-kind and financial contributions to support API. Similarly, these groups have supported API's affiliates at the local level.

## Affiliate Network

API's local affiliates are very visible in their communities. Affiliates work with community service organizations to identify individuals and organizations in need of pro bono accounting assistance. They work with local accounting firms and professional organizations to identify volunteers. A listing of API affiliates is presented at the end of this chapter.

The volunteer accounting services provided by affiliates range from a narrow focus to a wide spectrum. Some affiliates focus on only one type of service, usually assistance in tax return preparation. Several affiliates provide a full range of volunteer accounting services to individuals, nonprofit organizations, and small businesses. Some affiliates have a broader mission, and accounting services are just one of many types of services provided to the community.

# Service Opportunities

We can look at the types of engagements that API's affiliates perform to get insight into the opportunities for accounting students in a service-learning activity. When you talk about community service activities, most people think of nonprofit organizations. Nonprofits play an important role in mobilizing volunteer efforts to meet the needs of the community. Many accountants and accounting students have volunteered for nonprofit organization activities. Their experience may involve hands-on services that directly benefit program beneficiaries. These tasks might include cleaning up a neighborhood, serving meals to the homeless, or fundraising. These nonprofits need volunteers for many different types of tasks. However, each of these organizations also needs accounting expertise.

The level of accounting expertise needed depends upon the size and complexity of the organization. Small nonprofits often operate initially with just a checkbook and an envelope to keep copies of receipts. As the organization grows, needs change. Four basic types of accounting service opportunities will accompany growth — accounting systems design, tax and regulatory compliance, preparing for an audit, and financial management.

## Accounting Systems Design

Volunteer accountants can perform a valuable service to small nonprofits that need help in designing and implementing effective accounting systems. The typical small nonprofit that asks for help from an API affiliate is doing the best it can to get along with limited financial resources. It feels that it cannot spare the resources to pay for accounting expertise, and quite often it has waited too long to ask for help. Members of the board of directors may have attempted but failed to find someone with accounting training to help. The small nonprofit probably heard about the API affiliate through the network of nonprofits in the community. The API affiliate performs the critical roles of reaching out to the community with an offer of help and identifying willing accounting volunteers.

A direct-assistance engagement to help a small nonprofit with an accounting system usually lasts from three to six months. The volunteer accountants must gather information about the organization to get an understanding of its mission and its finances. This involves a review of the current bookkeeping system and supporting documentation, if any. The design of the new system often involves setting up a cash receipts and disbursement journal and instructing the person who will maintain the books, who often is a volunteer. The system will also involve documentation, reconciling bank accounts, and sometimes an accounts payable ledger. If there are employees, a payroll system will be designed and instructions on it and payroll responsibilities provided. As the organization becomes more complex, there is also a need for more extensive financial controls to ensure that resources are used for authorized purposes. There may also be a need to computerize the accounting system.

## Tax and Regulatory Compliance

Internal Revenue Service regulations present a challenge to small nonprofits. The first hurdle is applying for tax-exempt status with the IRS. Volunteer accountants can help by assisting with the financial pages of Form 1023. Most organizations exempt under Paragraph 501(C)(3) or Paragraph 501(C)(4) must file a federal information return — Form 990 or 990-EZ when gross receipts exceed $25,000 per year. The nonprofit must have adequate books and records to support this filing. Volunteer accountants may either prepare a Form 990 or review one prepared by the organization.

Nonprofit organizations must also be concerned with state regulatory requirements. Reporting requirements vary widely among states. Studies have shown that fundraising abuses are the primary concerns of most state regulatory commissions. Some states accept Form 990 as a report of the nonprofit's financial operations. The amount of contributions received by the nonprofit usually dictates the degree of reporting. After reaching a certain level, the state may require that financial statements be reviewed by a CPA. At some higher level, an audit will be required.

## Preparing for an Audit

Unfortunately, many small nonprofits reach the threshold for a review or audit and get sticker shock. After realizing that they have a responsibility for such a review, they ask a CPA to bid on the engagement only to find out that the cost is much more than they can afford. A major reason for the high cost is that the organization's books and records are in poor shape. API affiliates do not perform audits or reviews of financial statements. However, volunteers do help small nonprofits prepare their books and records so that a reasonable audit fee can be negotiated. The volunteer may instruct the organization's treasurer on how to prepare financial statements.

## Financial Management

Small nonprofits also need help with financial management. Volunteers can assist an organization in its planning by translating its statement of goals and objectives into an annual budget. A budget prepared in appropriate detail will help the small nonprofit take a realistic view of its limited resources. This is an important step in setting priorities. Educating the nonprofit's management on essential budgeting techniques can help avoid cash management problems. The control aspects of a budgeting system can be built into the accounting system. Reports can be designed to show actual versus budgeted revenues and expenses on a monthly or quarterly basis, depending upon the organization's needs.

Many nonprofits will ask the volunteer accountant who provides direct assistance in designing their accounting system to be on the board of directors. Finding an accountant to volunteer as a director is complex, because there is a long-term commitment involved and responsibilities extend beyond financial matters. Community Accountants, the API affiliate in Philadelphia, Pennsylvania, publishes *Board Room News*, which periodically lists nonprofits seeking accountants for their boards. Exhibit 1 (on the next page) lists selected board of directors opportunities from the December 1995 issue. The purpose of listing such organizations in an article on service-learning is to provide insight into the missions of small nonprofits and their related budgets. This shows that there is a wide range of opportunities to help.

# API Publications

Several publications are available from API that would be excellent references for accounting students and faculty in a service-learning program. API's affiliates discovered through experience that many accountants were willing to volunteer to help nonprofits, but they lacked current familiarity with nonprofit accounting. To fill this void, API has published several useful books on nonprofit accounting and related management issues. All are available from API at a modest cost. These publications are described below to provide insight on how they could be useful in a service-learning project in an accounting course.

## Accounting Guide

The core publication on nonprofit accounting is entitled *What a Difference Nonprofits Make: A Guide to Accounting Procedures*. This publication is a "must have" reference for an accounting service-learning project involving a nonprofit organization. It provides an important introduction to the nature of the nonprofit sector. This includes a realistic perspective on what one can expect when one works with a nonprofit. The publication makes the point that nonprofit managers know a great deal about factors related to the organization's mission, but usually little about financial planning and account-

**Exhibit 1**

---

## Board of Directors Opportunities

**Maternal and Child Health Consortium of Chester County**

Mission: Enhance the availability and accessibility of services to women, children and families. Programs include advocacy, education of low-income women, prenatal education. Incorporation: 1994

Budget: $200,000

**YWCA of Greater West Chester**

Mission: The empowerment of women and elimination of racism; programs include mentoring, Home share, and Mother's Center. Incorporation: 1960

Budget: $132,000

**Agape Campfire Program for Girls and Boys**

Mission: Provide clubs and camping to teach youth in the Greater Philadelphia five-county area self-reliance. Incorporation: 1975

Budget: $230,000

**Big Sisters of Philadelphia**

Mission: Reach at-risk girls and their families through casework and one-to-one volunteer mentoring to enable the girls and their families to achieve positive choices in life. Incorporation: 1961

Budget: $1.8 million

**Southwest Germantown Performing Arts Center**

Mission: Provide music, drama, dance, and writing classes to low-income children in Lower Germantown. Incorporation: 1993

Budget: $5,000

**Women's Alliance for Job Equity**

Mission: Improve economic and workplace conditions for women through direct service, public education, and peer support. Incorporation: 1979

Budget: $118,000

---

From the December 1995 *Board Room News,* a publication of Community Accountants, Philadelphia, PA.

ing matters. It also provides an orientation to the role of the nonprofit in our society. The various tax-exemption provisions that apply to nonprofits are explained, and the procedures for achieving nonprofit status are described.

Sound advice on maintaining professional standards is presented in the accounting guide. The accountant's role as a volunteer in various tasks is identified. Since volunteers may work with members of the board of directors, or even become a member of the board, the guide provides an overview of the board's role in nonprofits. Emphasis is placed on fiscal responsibilities and financial matters that are commonly discussed at board meetings.

The guide provides a clear and concise explanation of accounting methods and tax compliance for nonprofit organizations. This includes control features of an accounting system, timing and measurement of contributions, and preparing financial statements. Material on budgeting in nonprofit organizations contains helpful advice on estimating revenues and expenses. A sample Form 990 is provided in the guide with advice on some of the trickier issues.

## Audit Guide

API's *What a Difference Preparation Makes: A Guide to the Nonprofit Audit* was written for the small nonprofit organization. The purpose of this guide is to provide practical advice to management and staff of nonprofits in preparing for an audit. Since it was written as a practical guide, technical language is avoided wherever possible. The basic idea behind this publication is to help nonprofits be better prepared for audits so they can keep down audit fees. If a nonprofit's books and records are not ready for an audit, the CPA will have to charge for accounting services to get them ready. Given this orientation, the audit guide is excellent for a service-learning course. A service-learning project designed to help a nonprofit implement an accounting system with appropriate internal and management controls will be very beneficial in providing insight into the practical issues of management control systems.

The audit guide provides an overview of nonprofit accounting and auditing issues, including a discussion of whether an audit is actually needed. The guide's basic position is that an audit should be a positive experience for a nonprofit and not a disruption of mission-seeking activities. Unexpected audit costs and disruptions may result if —

1. Management and staff do not have a basic understanding of accounting for nonprofits.

2. Personnel are not adequately trained in accounting functions, or these functions are understaffed.

3. The nonprofit has a deficient accounting system.

4. The internal controls are poorly designed or not followed.

5. Audit service procurement is poorly planned.

6. Nonprofits are unaware of cost-saving opportunities in preparing and participating in the audit process.

To help nonprofits avoid these pitfalls, the audit guide provides information on the operation of a basic accounting system, including the question of whether a cash or accrual accounting system should be followed in keeping the books. The guide describes basic methods of internal control for nonprofits and provides examples of practical applications of internal controls.

When service-learning projects include preparing the nonprofit for audit, students have to be prepared for questions about selecting and engaging an auditor. The audit guide provides a step-by-step approach to engaging an auditor. It outlines the type of information that the auditor wants about a nonprofit organization, information that a student group could help assemble. It provides guidance on how to negotiate a fee and what to expect in an auditor's proposal and engagement letter. Cost-saving tips are provided on many important aspects of engaging an auditor and preparing for the auditor's visit. The guide's appendix contains a glossary, sample accountant's reports, sample requests for audit services, a sample engagement letter, and sample retention times for nonprofit records. The audit guide was funded by the W.K. Kellogg Foundation.

## Guides to Nonprofit Management

In 1995, API published *What a Difference Understanding Makes: Guides to Nonprofit Management*. This guide, a collection of five booklets on important topics affecting nonprofit management, was also funded by the W.K. Kellogg Foundation.

In recent years, there has been a trend toward greater public accountability for nonprofits. As a result, nonprofits have more extensive disclosure obligations. "Making Public Disclosures" is a booklet designed to prepare nonprofits to fulfill their disclosure obligations. Students in a service-learning environment should understand the nonprofit's obligations. A basic concept promoted by the guide is that voluntary disclosures present an opportunity for nonprofits to enhance their credibility. Stakeholders are likely to be impressed by a nonprofit's efforts to be very open about its operations. The booklet provides guidance to the nonprofit organization in fulfilling state and federal disclosure requirements. Finally, it provides insight into the related topics of interpreting financial information and conflicts of interest. These are issues that may be encountered by students in a service-learning project.

In June 1993, the Financial Accounting Standards Board issued Statements 116 and 117, which mandated significant changes in nonprofit accounting. These statements require a fundamental change in accounting for contributions, both restricted and unrestricted. "Tracking Special Monies" provides guidance in implementing the new standards with regard to contributions. It is very possible that students may encounter questions related to special monies in a nonprofit service-learning project.

Two other of the booklets are concerned with tax issues. The first, "Classifying 501(C) Organizations," covers how nonprofit entities are classified under the Internal Revenue Code. The second, "Filing Nonprofit Tax Forms," outlines various compliance requirements; it includes some preparation and planning tips. "Selecting Computer Software" is the fifth booklet; it helps assess various software options. The five booklets that make up the series can be purchased as a set or individually.

### National Connections

In 1996, API launched its site on the World Wide Web. Its address is *http://www.accountingnet.com/asso/api/index.html*. The API website promises to be an up-to-date resource for nonprofit organizations and volunteer accountants. The API website greets one with "Make an offer that can't be refused." One can click on this and find out about becoming a volunteer with API. One is also greeted with "an offer you won't want to refuse." Clicking on this provides information to nonprofits on how a volunteer accountant can help. The website also allows one to email API with questions.

The AICPA Public Service Committee funded API's *National Directory of Volunteer Accounting Programs*. The basic purpose of the directory is to list providers so that nonprofits needing assistance can identify volunteer programs. Accounting professionals can consult the directory to identify organizations that can channel their volunteer efforts toward deserving organizations. The directory is updated periodically.

Such a national directory can be a valuable resource to a service-learning program. Faculty can consult it to identify programs in the region. Faculty members will find that the people involved in these programs will be glad to answer questions, providing a valuable resource base. After an accounting service-learning program has been established, it should be publicized. An easy way to do this is to request that API list the program in the next edition of the directory.

## Accounting Students for the Public Interest

API has always welcomed accounting educators and students to participate in the pro bono accounting cause. In 1974, I was one of five accounting educators on the board of directors of Community Accountants in Philadelphia. I worked with a student from the University of Pennsylvania to help a small minority business in West Philadelphia on a case in 1975. Over the years, API affiliates have been receptive to working with accounting students. Generally, the experience seems to be that students can provide enthusiasm, energy, and skills to appropriate case assignments. However, they do need some structure provided by working with a professor or practitioner volunteer.

After years of positive experiences with student volunteers, the API board of directors voted to establish student chapters in 1995. The concept was that these chapters, through their activities, would encourage community service activities by accounting students on college and university campuses. This would help to instill a sense of "giving back" to one's community as a lifelong commitment. The new program was designated Accounting Students for the Public Interest (ASPI). API's expectation is that ASPI chapters will enable accounting students to learn firsthand about accounting needs in local communities. It provides a structure for students to work with a faculty adviser and local area CPA volunteers (where appropriate) to provide pro bono accounting services to economically disadvantaged individuals, small businesses, and nonprofit organizations.

As of this writing, ASPI is in a formative stage. API is seeking foundation funding to promote the program, provide resources, and subsidize member dues. An ASPI chapter can exist as a separate group or incorporate as part of an existing accounting society or Beta Alpha Psi chapter. Each ASPI chapter must have a faculty adviser and be endorsed by the college or university. Students must have attained at least sophomore status and be in good academic standing. The school must be regionally accredited.

API currently will supply advice and technical assistance to any students or faculty member who wishes to establish an ASPI chapter. API stands ready to provide assistance to student chapters in the following ways:

• technical assistance with chapter grant proposals and program ideas, including endorsements by API;

• liaisons and contacts with API affiliates and other volunteer accountants;

• two free copies of API publications and additional copies available at reduced prices;

• awards for and recognition of outstanding student volunteers;

• publicity through national media coverage on ASPI student activities;

• copies of API newsletters.

With regard to the last item, API newsletters provide coverage of the world of pro bono accounting. The newsletters provide exciting stories of how volunteer accountants help deserving individuals and organizations. They also provide ideas on how student chapters might reach out to the community.

# Working With Students in a Service-Learning Project

Service-learning programs can benefit by looking at some of the techniques used by API affiliates in working with clients. While API affiliates are autonomous, they continually share ideas and information, and operate in a similar fashion. There are pitfalls in providing pro bono accounting services. However, sound operating procedures can minimize the chances of unforeseen problems.

It is essential to have a clear statement of the types of volunteer services you want to provide and to whom you want to provide them. API's affiliates provide services to those who cannot afford to pay. These include individuals, nonprofits, and small businesses. Occasionally, API is approached by an organization that can afford to pay but is trying to get something for free. Unfortunately, there are also a few small nonprofit organizations that exist essentially to profit their directors. Deciding whether an organization or individual has the ability to pay requires some judgment. While a service-learning program may have somewhat different criteria, similar judgment will be necessary. To make such decisions, one must first gather essential information. A useful strategy is to have an application form. Exhibit 2 (on the next page) displays the type of information that should be gathered from a nonprofit organization applying for services. The application form should be carefully designed to fit the program criteria. The amount of information gathered should be commensurate with the extent of the engagement. If a nonprofit organization needs accounting system work that may involve 50 to 100 hours of assistance, it is worth the time and effort to gather sufficient information to make sure there really is a need. Also, the information in the application form will be helpful in completing the engagement. Since a service-learning program can be expected to evolve over time, client screening criteria must be regularly adjusted.

Another dimension of the project is the commitment of the client. If the client really needs help, the client should be willing to spend the time and effort needed to provide adequate information. Many API affiliates also require a token fee, such as $25, to show that a client is serious about need. One also wants the client's expectations to be very clear. In a service-learning program, clients should realize that students will probably have scheduling constraints. Afternoon or evening meetings may be necessary, and students' lives are sometimes complicated by exams and term papers. Students, in turn, must have a clear understanding of the expectations and requirements of the project.

An engagement letter is a very useful tool for documenting the scope of the project. A nonprofit organization's board and staff may have unrealistic expectations of what is to be provided. API affiliates and service-learning

**Exhibit 2**

## Nonprofit Organization Application for Service

In order to make an informed decision about whether a nonprofit
organization meets the criteria for receiving volunteer accounting services,
the following information is very useful:

Organization Name
Organization Address
Telephone
Client Representative Present
History and Mission
Key Management Personnel:
      President
      Treasurer
      Executive Director
      Number of Board Members
Brief Description of Programs
501(C)(3) Status
Incorporation Date
Budget for Current Year:
      Gross Income
Fiscal Year:
      Total Expenses
Number of Employees
Description of Present Bookkeeping System
Financial Data From Previous Year
Gross Income
Total Expenses
Current Period Funding:
      Source
      Amount
      Restrictions
Litigation Against the Organization
Previous and/or Current Accountant
Volunteer Services Requested

programs have encountered this many times. Thus, the engagement letter should carefully outline the services to be performed and who is to perform them. It should also state who is to pay for expenses incurred and identify the client's responsibilities. A sample engagement letter is contained in API's publication *What a Difference Nonprofits Make: A Guide to Accounting Procedures*.

Problems with clients should be expected in service-learning programs. There have been instances where students have gone to a client's offices to work — and found no one there. In another case, a student went to the organization's treasurer's residence to get the books, and the treasurer refused to hand them over. Apparently, there was a disagreement at a recent board of directors meeting, and the outcome was never communicated to the student. In another situation, the students were told to leave and come back at another time because they were interrupting office activities. Fortunately, these types of situations are not very common, but one does have to be prepared for them. At the outset, the client's commitment to the project must be explicitly established, with all client responsibilities articulated. Some API affiliates have client responsibilities outlined in the engagement letter, and make it clear that the engagement will be terminated if the client does not meet these responsibilities.

An important question that often arises is whether students have the capability and the time to perform accounting services. Whether one is paid or not, one must not perform accounting or consulting services for which one is not qualified or is unwilling to acquire the necessary knowledge base. Many assignments require accounting skills that a junior- or senior-level accounting major would possess. Since skills vary among students, the service-learning program must make sure that the appropriate skills exist or can be acquired by a student. It should also provide a reference library for technical questions. One of the benefits of a service-learning program is that it affords students the opportunity to research real-world problems.

Implementing a computerized accounting information system can be an especially exciting project. Accounting students are likely to think that this is a logical step for most organizations. The students are computer literate and have, possibly, considerable experience using computers. However, small nonprofits have limited computer capabilities. While the nonprofit's office might have a computer for word processing, using it for data entry may cause a problem. Currently, a volunteer may keep the books and records. This volunteer may or may not be computer literate, and the volunteer may not want to go to the office to do the work. Still another question concerns who will resolve technical problems after the service-learning project is over. The client must understand the limits of the students' commitment and the possible pitfalls a computerized accounting system may create once they are gone.

Consultation and review are two important concepts for student service programs. Students need a practitioner or professor to be available to ask for advice. For example, if they have doubts as to whether or not something should be recorded as a contribution, they should be able to ask someone with experience and technical knowledge. Some service-learning projects may include the preparation of financial statements and a Form 990. These should be reviewed.

## Pro Bono Accounting and Career Advancement

Community service activities can be an important aspect of a career advancement plan. One has only to look at CPA firm partners, who routinely volunteer their time to good causes. CPAs often are members of boards of directors or are presidents of nonprofit organizations. They are busy people, and they carefully select the causes they support. They get a great deal of satisfaction from the good that comes from their efforts. However, they also acknowledge there are benefits over and beyond a good feeling. By participating in service projects, they learn new skills. A CPA may also make important contacts with other board members, and gain new clients as a result.

Service-learning experiences can be the foundation for making community service activities a habit. A positive service-learning experience results in a student's being receptive to volunteering or desiring to volunteer throughout the stages of his or her career. It is important for a service-learning program to give students the message that there are tangible benefits both to the volunteer and to the community from the former's continuing in community service. They should be encouraged to seek out opportunities once they become entry-level accountants. By participating in a service-learning program in their early career stages, accounting students will become part of a network. This will open up opportunities for them to be on boards of directors of small nonprofits four to seven years after graduation. At a later career stage, such activities may open up regional and national opportunities.

## Conclusion

Pro bono accounting has made substantial progress since 1973 when API was formed. The accounting profession has demonstrated a willingness to embrace its pro bono responsibilities. API and its affiliates have provided resources to identify needs within the community and mobilize willing volunteers.

Service-learning programs have a key role to play in the pro bono accounting movement. In my opinion, the richest opportunities for service-learning are with nonprofit organizations. Students have the opportunity to learn skills and see the needs that exist in the community. Positive service-learning programs can instill a sense of "giving back" to one's community as a lifelong commitment.

# Accountants for the Public Interest
## Affiliate Offices

## CALIFORNIA

Clearinghouse for Volunteer
Accounting Services
31971 Quartz Lane
Castaic, CA 91384
TEL: (805) 295-8912
FAX: (805) 295-8333

## CONNECTICUT

Community Accounting Aid and
Services, Inc.
1800 Asylum Avenue, 4th Floor
West Hartford, CT 06117
TEL: (203) 241-4984
FAX: (203) 241-4907

## DISTRICT OF COLUMBIA

Support Center of Washington
Volunteers for Community Service
2001 O Street, N.W.
Washington, DC 20036
TEL: (202) 833-0300
FAX: (202) 857-0077

Community Tax Aid, Inc.
P.O. Box 33704
Washington, DC 20033
TEL: (202) 338-4722

## FLORIDA

FL Assn. of Nonprofit Organizations
7480 Fairway Drive, Ste. 206
Miami Lakes, FL 33014
TEL: (305) 557-1764
FAX: (305) 821-5228

## GEORGIA

Nonprofit Resource Center
The Hurt Building, Suite 220
Atlanta, GA 30303
TEL: (404) 688-4845
FAX: (404) 521-0487

## ILLINOIS

CPAs for the Public Interest
222 S. Riverside Plaza, 16th Floor
Chicago, IL 60606
TEL: (312) 993-0407 ext. 243
FAX: (312) 993-9432

## INDIANA

Quality for Indiana Taxpayers, Inc.
P.O. Box 441070
Indianapolis, IN 46204
TEL: (317) 226-7168
FAX: (317) 226-6270

## MARYLAND

Maryland Association of Nonprofit
Organizations
190 W. Ostend St., Suite 201
Baltimore, MD 21230
TEL: (410) 727-6367, (800) 273-6367
FAX: (410) 727-1914

## MASSACHUSETTS

Support Center of Massachusetts
Accounting Assistance Program
41 Winter Street, Suite 55
Boston, MA 02108
TEL: (617) 338-1331
FAX: (617) 338-4975

Community Tax Aid, Inc.
711 Atlantic Avenue, 4th Floor
Boston, MA 02111
TEL: (617) 451-0927
FAX: (617) 482-2028

## MICHIGAN

Accounting Aid Society
One Kennedy Square, Suite 2026
719 Griswold
Detroit, MI 48226
TEL: (313) 961-1840
FAX: (313) 961-6257

## MINNESOTA

Minnesota Accounting Aid Society
1806 South Riverside Avenue
Minneapolis, MN 55454
TEL: (616) 288-9476
FAX: (612) 636-8772

## NEW JERSEY

API - New Jersey
Turnpike Plaza, Suite 302-N
197 Route 18 South
East Brunswick, N.J. 08816
TEL: (908) 249-7565
FAX: (908) 249-8158

## NEW YORK

Support Center of New York
API-Accounting Aid Program
305 7th Avenue, 11th Floor
New York, NY 10001
TEL: (212) 924-6744
FAX: (212) 924-9544

Community Tax Aid, Inc.
176 E. 85th Street, 4C
New York, New York 10025
TEL: (212) 686-0550
FAX: (212) 686-0560

## PENNSYLVANIA

Community Accountants
1420 Walnut Street
Suite 411
Philadelphia, PA 19102
TEL: (215) 893-9333
FAX: (215) 893-9339

Western Pennsylvania Community
Accountants, Inc.
213 Bishop Boyle Center
120 E. 9th Avenue
Homestead, PA 15120
TEL: (412) 462-9722
FAX: (412) 462-3275

## RHODE ISLAND

Support Center of Rhode Island
Volunteer Accounting Program
10 Davol Square, 3rd Floor
Providence, RI 02903-4752
TEL: (401) 861-1920 or 861-1921
FAX: (401) 273-0540

## VERMONT

Vermont Accountants for the Public
Interest
P.O. Box 5777
Burlington, VT 05402-5777
TEL: (804) 270-5344
FAX: (804) 273-1741

## VIRGINIA

Virginia Society of CPAs
Public Service Volunteer Program
P.O. Box 4620
Richmond, VA 23058-4620
TEL: (804) 270-5344
FAX: (804) 273-1741
Street Address: 4309 Cox Rd.
Glen Allen, VA 23060

## WISCONSIN

Wisconsin Institute of CPAs
Public Interest Committee
235 N. Executive Drive, Suite 200
P.O. Box 1010
Brookfield, WI 53008-1010
TEL: (414) 785-0445, (800) 772-6939
FAX: (414) 785-0838
Southern Chapter - Madison
Southeast Chapter - Milwaukee

—

## COLLEGE/UNIVERSITY STUDENT CHAPTERS

Prof. Peter Vico, Faculty Adviser
Lincoln University Accounting Club
Dept. of Econ. and Business Admin.
Lincoln University, PA 19352
TEL: (610) 932-8300
FAX: (215) 932-8317

# "What I Do, I Understand":
## Service-Learning in Accounting Curricula

by William L. Weis

Thirty years ago, when I was an undergraduate studying accounting at Bowling Green State University, those in the antiwar movement commonly referred to any business school as the "School of Guns and Money." It was a popular view that when business students weren't being taught how to make profits from waging war in Vietnam, they were being taught how to profit from oppressing and exploiting the poor and disadvantaged. And as for academic rigor, it was easier for athletes to maintain academic eligibility by majoring in business than in physical education. And one thing a business school was certainly *not* known for was commitment to serving the needs of people in the community, much less an emphasis on educating business students to embark upon lives of service to others.

To say that such a business school image has been eliminated in the ensuing three decades would be a stretch, although the business school is no longer the first choice of athletes seeking an easy way to maintain academic eligibility. Certainly only the severely reality-challenged still think that business schools advocate war as good-business politics. As for failing to serve the needs of the community — well, not much has changed.

When I began teaching at Seattle University in 1973, the last thing I would have considered as a course requirement or option for my MBA students in financial accounting was a service project. That remained true for nearly 20 years.

Then, when I was chairing the accounting program, one day an undergraduate accounting major dropped by my office and asked me if I wanted to help recruit volunteers for an upcoming American Cancer Society "Candlelight Challenge" fundraiser. As it turned out, our Beta Alpha Psi (BAP) chapter had agreed to provide logistical support for this 24-hour run-a-thon, including solicitation of participants, registration, collection of donations, all accounting functions, setup, takedown, traffic control, and first-aid support. We had about 25 active students in the organization, who collectively worked more than 800 hours to organize and direct this project.

Recently thereafter our BAP faculty adviser left, and I inherited the job.

I was about to learn something surprising and endearing about our accounting students. At my first meeting with the officers of our BAP chapter, a student was asked to report on the "soup kitchen" project he was chairing. He proceeded to lay out the schedule of past and future commitments our accounting students had made to the operations of a local soup kitchen that provided dinners to predominantly homeless families five evenings a week. As it turned out, our students had undertaken the responsibility of providing workers every Friday for two work shifts: one for preparing and serving the dinners, and the other for cleanup.

It seemed as if every accounting student that I was acquainted with was on the schedule. Many were working four hours every Friday. The chair of the program had scheduled helpers every Friday of the year, including holiday breaks, during the summer, and during final examination weeks. About 20 students had committed nearly 1,000 hours to the soup kitchen that year. Even the program chair was at the kitchen nearly every Friday.

There were additional commitments I discovered our accounting majors had made: to the refugee's "First Thanksgiving" dinner, to the Yesler Terrace Senior Citizens' Christmas party, to the Christmas Adopt-a-Family program, to sponsoring quarterly blood drives, to tutoring, to the campus literacy campaign. I struggled to relate what I was seeing to my experience as an undergraduate student 30 years earlier, when "service" was never mentioned, though we memorized ultimatums about keeping only "irreproachable associates." I never quite knew what that meant, but I think the student who organized our soup kitchen volunteers and spent nearly every Friday of his school career serving the homeless was what they had in mind by "reproachable" — a bitingly sarcastic guy who gave more in volunteer service to his community in one year than most of us do in a lifetime. I was beginning to believe that our university's mission statement urging "preparation for service" meant something more to our accounting students than just innocuous, obligatory verbiage.

In 1991, I attended a week-long service-learning symposium at Stanford University sponsored by Campus Compact with funding support from the Ford Foundation. This conference particularly emphasized the value and importance of the reflection process in service-learning. I recall one prominent service-learning guru asserting that *all* learning derived from experience comes from *reflection* on the experience — *none* from the experience alone. I suppose on one level of interpretation I agreed: We learn only by being conscious of what we are doing — by thinking and abstracting and rendering meaning to our life experiences. But unless we are truly sleepwalking, we can never avoid at least some reflection on what we do, with or without a guided reflection process.

I did agree, though, that our experiences can provide for richer, deeper, more meaningful learning when we engage in conscious, deliberate, even exhaustive reflection, particularly when shared with others engaged in similar service experiences. It was through my efforts to bring this reflective component to our only attempt at service-learning in our accounting curriculum that I found how influential service-learning could be in that environment.

## Our Program's Best Learning Experience

Of course, none of these student activities quite fit the mold of "service-learning in accounting," because they weren't connected to the requirements of a course, didn't apply accounting skills, and, most important, didn't employ a structured reflection process to amplify and deepen the learnings from the service experiences. Although we never thought of it as "service-learning," for nearly two decades we had included a substantial service requirement in our second course in income taxation. The course is elective for our accounting majors and addresses primarily corporate and partnership tax accounting issues. The service component, however, draws upon the students' prerequisite education in individual income taxation, which is further augmented by a tax preparation workshop prior to the commencement of service. Each student enrolled in the course must commit to working at least one 3- to 4-hour shift per week (nearly 40 hours total, in addition to preliminary training and testing) at our inner-city Seattle site in the IRS's Volunteer Income Tax Assistance (VITA) program.

Each tax season, our VITA service provides free tax preparation for more than 1,000 taxpayers by offering tax consultation and return preparation sessions beginning in late January and ending just before April 15. Students (who include BAP volunteers not enrolled in the class) must complete a return-preparation training program in early January and pass an obligatory test for all VITA volunteers. The program is highly structured and professionally administered by our students, with review and oversight provided by alumni, faculty, and IRS representatives.

Needless to say, our VITA program is a major service to the Seattle central area. In terms of value of services provided, some 40 students contribute between $90,000 and $100,000 annually in free tax consultation and return preparation: about 25 returns per student. Since all returns are computer-checked for arithmetic accuracy and subject to professional review for tax-policy compliance, the quality of the client service is very high.

After the Campus Compact workshop at Stanford, I encouraged my faculty colleague teaching the second tax class to incorporate a structured reflection process after the VITA program was over. Ideally, I had wanted to encourage a reflection period after each VITA session. Practically, however, this was difficult because of the substantial time and stress already imposed on the participants. An evening at our VITA site can be as exhausting as it is educational — especially as the sessions get closer to April 15.

We scheduled the first post-tax-season reflection period after the VITA project the following year, in early May. We invited the director of our campus volunteer center, as well as the VITA coordinator with the Seattle office of the IRS, to come and help lead the reflection process. Although only half of the students who participated in the VITA project attended, the ensuing discussion was more rewarding and enlightening than any of us could have hoped for.

Students spoke genuinely of their need and desire to serve, of their growing sense of personal confidence and personal efficacy in the act of providing real assistance to people who needed help, and of their awakening to the reality of coping with the demands of subsistence on incomes that many had thought were well below levels where this was possible.

> Every night I looked squarely in the face of deprivations that I never had to deal with. It made me feel both good and guilty when my clients were genuinely thankful for the little help I gave them — you know, a client raising a family on an $11,000 income.

> It was the first time that I've felt, "Wow, these are real clients and I can actually give them professional service." That's a lot different [from] taking an accounting test!

> One of my goals this year was to do some community service. I felt I really did that the last couple months. But I didn't realize I would learn so much. Honestly, I've learned more from VITA than from all the other accounting courses I've taken.[1]

It was clear to me after this reflection period that the only service-learning activity in our accounting curriculum was perceived by our students as the flagship learning experience in that curriculum. After that, I queried alumni who had participated in VITA, and the response was unanimous. The 10 weeks of VITA constituted the singular highlight of their accounting studies at Seattle University.

> We learned to actually do some accounting. We learned about client service. We saw difficult, angry clients. We saw thoughtful, thankful clients. We served clients with special problems. We insisted on quality.

> I've been coming back to help now for five years, and I think it's the best thing I can do as an alumnus of SU. It was the best learning experience I had while I was there.

Being on hand at the formal reflection session for VITA completely changed and informed my appreciation for the importance of that program. I realized that this activity, which I had unconsciously neglected and casually dismissed as just another volunteer opportunity, was, in fact, the best learning experience of our accounting program. I began to ask myself whether there were other opportunities to enhance our students' learning experience in our accounting program through service-learning.

## Experience With Service-Learning in an MBA Course

A totally unconnected diversion of my professional activities laid a foundation for the next steps in the development of the service-learning component of our accounting curriculum. As our BAP adviser, I initiated a series of annual Leadership Conferences for BAP chapters in the five-state Northwest Region. Several of those conferences were held at a camp in Idaho that had a challenge-course infrastructure on the premises (sometimes referred to as "ropes courses"). I inquired of the camp directors as to how the challenge-course activities were normally incorporated in camp and conference programs. Their explanation introduced me to what many regard as the *other* major genre in experiential education — outdoor experiential-based training (OEBT), or outdoor programs that focus on problem-solving and team-building activities. When I first incorporated a half-day of OEBT activities into the Leadership Conferences, that component of the weekend retreat immediately became the highest-rated activity of the weekend. In fact, all 55 respondents in the first year gave the OEBT module a 5 on a scale of 0 to 5!

Impressed by this result, I invested the time and training necessary to lead and facilitate outdoor experiential activities on my own, rather than relying on outside providers. After a few years of experience with this very rewarding methodology, I offered an elective course (nonaccounting) to our MBA students that utilized OEBT for leadership and team development. The course instantly became the highest-rated, most oversubscribed course in our MBA program.

This experience offered me a couple of advantages in pursuing my interest in expanding our service-learning opportunities for both our accounting and our MBA students. First, I not only had to concentrate my personal training and education upon facilitation skills but, through my classes and leadership workshops, I logged hundreds of hours as an actual "processor" of experiential activities.[2]

Second, the MBA course offered a chance to experiment with service-learning in our MBA program. Since a major focus of the OEBT course is on leadership and team-building skills, I decided to offer a group service-project option. As an alternative to writing "application papers" to synthesize course learning and plan a strategy for incorporating that learning into their work settings, students could collaborate, as a whole or in teams comprising at least eight students,[3] to find and implement meaningful service projects involving a minimum of 10 hours of service by each student. Due to our emphasis on team effectiveness, the project needed to accommodate the entire team working together. The only other restriction was that the project meet a social service need, excluding beneficiaries such as theaters, performance groups, and churches.[4] It was my decision, albeit arbitrary, to focus our service efforts on critical human needs (i.e., shelter, food, health care, protective services) rather than on artistic and religious institutions.

Writing an application paper was clearly the easiest and least time-consuming way to complete the course. The service project involved a good deal more time in planning, organizing, and delivering the service. Nevertheless, virtually every student in each of the six classes that I've taught with the service option has chosen the service project. This is particularly noteworthy in that most of our MBA students are fully employed professionals with demanding work responsibilities, family responsibilities, as well as academic responsibilities.

The number of students opting for service-learning over a much less demanding paper assignment was not the only indication that service-learning is effective. In addition to the verbal processing that followed every activity, students recorded their reflections in written journals to further enhance their learning from each experience. This gave fairly extensive feedback on the quality of the service-project option as perceived by the students.

The feedback was more than encouraging. Most students felt the service project should be *required* and that to have opted for the application paper would have seriously reduced their learning in the course. Since our project was a direct application of the team-building aspects of the course, the service project offered an opportunity for the group to coalesce and collaborate on a "real" work goal. In addition, transforming a homeless shelter from a state of badly deferred maintenance into a showcase was meeting a vital community need. Further, a dozen volunteers accomplishing in one day a task that might otherwise require several days of skilled labor reinforces the fact that time spent in an effective team-building program is time well spent; the whole can become greater than the sum of its parts.

## Service-Learning in Accounting Courses

After the resounding success of service-learning in the MBA leadership course, I began to ask myself whether a similar benefit from service-learning could accrue to accounting students taking the first financial accounting course. Clearly, it would not be achieved as easily. Though the application of general teamwork skills can be exercised in virtually any environment, the same cannot be said for the application of accounting skills. For a service-learning opportunity to be appropriate for a beginning class in financial accounting, it must involve accounting. And the needs of the clients served must fall within the scope of what can reasonably be expected from students in beginning accounting.

So my first step toward service-learning in my introductory accounting course was taken apprehensively. I had visions of thoroughly frustrated students suffering with thoroughly frustrated clients with thoroughly dashed hopes and expectations. But since I had become a believer in service-learning, I decided to add an "experiential" requirement to the course. However, the required experiential component did not *mandate* service — the service-project element was optional. Students were warned that I would *not* bail them out of trouble they might encounter while serving a client. I expected this warning would be discouraging to some.

The experiential project involved the use of MYOB[5] accounting software, which each student was required to purchase (the educational rate was approximately $40). Each student was to pretend to start a small business and to contrive a set of reasonably diverse transactions for the first three months of the entity's operations. The transactions needed to meet a reasonable level of complexity to utilize the power of the MYOB system[6] and lead to a mixed and varied set of adjustments at the end of the three-month period. In other words, I wanted students to set up an accounting system on MYOB, tailor it for their business, and use it to process business transactions, make adjustments and closings, and prepare financial statements.

For the service-project option, students could, individually or in collaboration with other students, find a nonprofit organization that needed some accounting systems work and provide for that need. In explaining this option, I emphasized that I would be flexible in my approval of a service-project proposal because I realized that clients' needs for accounting assistance could vary greatly.

Ideally, students might find an organization that was in need of a complete, from-scratch, accounting system — but that was unlikely. Other possibilities were clients with a manual bookkeeping system that would like to convert to MYOB or with an unsophisticated software accounting system that might benefit from conversion to a more powerful yet inexpensive software such as MYOB. Of course, I knew other possibilities existed so I was willing to consider almost any proposal. I also provided a grade-weight incentive for trying the service-project option, expecting that it could consume many hours of false-start time and tons of frustration.

The results of the experiment were far more positive than I could have imagined. About a third of my students chose the service-project option, some working in groups of up to four. They served 10 nonprofit organizations during fall 1995. In several cases, the students not only created or converted the client accounting systems but also wrote user-friendly manuals for client personnel and gave hands-on training to those who would be maintaining the systems.

It became clear to me during postexperience reflection sessions that students who had opted for the service-learning opportunities learned more from those experiences than they would have learned by doing the make-believe projects. Although frustrations were at times great, in the end the students felt that they had learned more from dealing with real clients in service situations than they had learned in other courses where opportunities for practical application were not offered.

## Processing the Service Experience

Processing and debriefing students' service experiences is an art that is best honed by practicing. I use the traditional processing elements in guiding reflection on all experiential learning activities, whether they be service projects or OEBT challenges. Those elements are briefly named the "what," the "so what," and the "now what" building blocks of an effective group debriefing.

In the "what" phase, I encourage participants to simply recount the details of their experience. "Tell me about your project" is a fairly typical prompt for beginning that discussion. In accounting service projects, the number of students on a service team is typically small, usually two or three. When the groups are small, I recommend bringing two or three groups together for a collective debriefing of several projects. In this way, other students are informed of the service that their colleagues have performed, and benefit from hearing of other experiences and perspectives.

Once the details of the service project have been explained, I move to the "so what" phase of the debriefing, asking questions that probe for learnings and epiphanies. In this phase, it may be particularly helpful to ask students individually what the experience taught them and what meaning they personally ascribe to the service endeavor. Asking a general question of the group may prove too intimidating for the more introverted students, who often have reflected most deeply on the experience and have the most profound thoughts and observations to share. I generally spark a more interesting discussion when I begin with "Monica, looking back over the time you spent working with the food bank, what do you feel you have learned?" rather than asking the group, "What have you learned from this experience?"

Finally, when the discussion on immediate learnings from the experience seems complete, I move to the "now what" phase. In experiential training, this is the all-important transference of concepts from the experiential laboratory — in this case, from the service project — to the students' other lives in the workplace, in the family, and in other community groups. A question such as "How will this service experience affect your future plans and activities?" will generally help students make the transition from the previous discussion of meaning to a discussion of how to further that learning in their future lives. For some, the service project will be their first exposure to community service, and its personal value to them often inspires a commitment to incorporate service in their life schedules. For others, the experience informs their attitudes toward community service organizations and alters their intentions to support similar causes, whether that takes the form of additional time in service, personal contributions, or political and community-based advocacy.

Once again, leading an effective reflection discussion is an art that can be improved by practice. It's vitally important to remember that this reflection process is crucial to a service-learning pedagogy. It should not be slighted or abridged just because it's difficult and uncomfortable for the instructor. It's well worth investing in the time, and if necessary the training, to develop effective processing skills.

## Why Incorporate Experiential Learning in Your Accounting Classes?

Why should you incorporate experiential learning in your classes? Because experience is the best teacher, and it works! In addition:
- Students learn more and what they learn, they learn better.
- It strengthens students' interpersonal and teamwork skills.
- Students enjoy it and are enthusiastic about it.
- Students feel an extra sense of pride of accomplishment.
- It complements the service mission of your college or university.

So in other words, you can do a better job teaching your students and help the community at the same time. As examples of the type of nonprofit organizations your students can help, some of the organizations my students have worked with are listed in the table that follows.

## Questions and Answers to Help You Get Started

- **Question:** *At what level of accounting courses is service-learning possible?*
Service-learning is possible at any level, depending on the maturity of your students. I include a service-learning option in the first financial accounting course for MBA students. Although my MBA students are beginners in accounting, they typically have business experience, such as design-

## Organizations Students Have Worked With

| Beneficiary Organization | Type of Organization |
|---|---|
| Denny Place Teen Shelter | A residential shelter for teens who have left their homes |
| Emerald City Outreach Ministries | A center for basic skills training for adults in transition |
| Sojourner Place | A residential shelter for abused women |
| Belltown Theatre Center | A central area performance center |
| Seattle Style Basketball Academy | A supervised recreational and job skills training program for at-risk youth |
| St. Mary's Food Bank | A neighborhood food bank |
| Chinatown/International District BIA | An agency to assist business development in the International District |
| HOPE | An equestrian stable for physically and mentally challenged children and adults |
| DOVIA of King County | A central coordinating agency for volunteer-based organizations |
| Little Bit Therapeutic Riding Center | An equestrian riding facility for physically and mentally challenged children |
| St. Francis House | A food and clothing distribution center in the central area |
| Sacred Heart Shelter | A residential shelter for homeless families |
| Children's Home Society of Washington | A residential facility for children without families |

| | |
|---|---|
| St. James Family Kitchen | A central-area soup kitchen for families, women, children, elderly men |
| King County Literacy Coalition | A coordinating agency for literacy training for adults and children |
| Providence Place | A full-service distribution and training center for adults in transition |
| The Benefit Gang | An organization that encourages voluntarism among young adults by providing volunteer support, education, and quality volunteer opportunities with nonprofit agencies |
| ProHomo Vocce | A Seattle Choral Group dedicated to developing and performing original local music |

ning aircraft for Boeing or software for Microsoft. They are savvy, smart, and learn fast.

At the undergraduate level, we offer a less sophisticated service-learning experience with our VITA program for students who have completed a first course in individual income taxation and a training session in tax preparation. Most of our VITA volunteers are traditional undergraduate students, yet the structure and the culture of the VITA program help them grow in sophistication, confidence, and demeanor. They deliver outstanding service to our 1,100 tax "clients" every year. We have not yet, however, attempted to incorporate service-learning in our sophomore principles courses.

- **Question:** *How do students find community service opportunities?*

Students find community service opportunities by taking personal initiative to search out appropriate clients and needs, but they can be helped in this process. If your campus has a volunteer center that maintains working relationships with organizations in your community, by all means use it. I invite personnel from our volunteer center to visit my classes, distribute the list of our organization affiliations, offer advice for finding and approaching service organizations, and make themselves accessible for future follow-up.

Our MBAs frequently work with the community resources manager in the local United Way office, who has helped link students with a number of organizations through the United Way's Management Assistance Program. Additionally, many large companies have community outreach programs that place volunteers. We have served several clients who were found through the Boeing Company's volunteer matching service.

- **Question:** *How can we make the experience less daunting for our students?*

In my MBA financial accounting class, where I know the students will be stretching themselves if they find a service client, I ask students to self-categorize themselves according to what special skills and backgrounds they might bring to a consulting team. Basically, I ask them to place themselves into one or more (or none) of the following groupings:

- *Nerds* — Those who have strong computer skills.
- *Bean Counters* — Those who have had some previous background in accounting, perhaps having worked some with an accounting system or having taken courses in accounting.
- *Groupies* — Those who are adept at organizing a group, getting people together, communicating with team members, etc.
- *Do-Gooders* — Those who have experience as community volunteers and possible connections to nonprofit organizations from that background. They also know something about how to approach and interact with social-service providers.
- *Poets* — Those skilled in report writing, document preparation, manu-

al preparation, written communications in general.

These preliminary groupings seem to make the task of forming service-project teams much easier. I distribute this listing of "consultants" along with a class roster with phone numbers and addresses, and encourage students to call people who might be interested in contributing their specialties to their group.

It also seems to make matching students to projects much simpler. For example, one organization in fall 1995 was particularly interested in the services we could provide but didn't even have a computer yet. They had even delayed the acquisition of one because they weren't sure what they should get. So, in addition to the installation of and conversion to an MYOB-based system, the organization required consultation on the selection of appropriate hardware. A third of the class were certifiable "nerds," and it was an easy thing to pair them with the organization as a result of the preliminary groupings. For the organization, a more expert level of hardware consultation could not have been purchased at any price!

• **Question:** *How can I minimize the students' possible frustration with service-learning?*

As one step to help minimize frustration, stress flexibility. Let students know that prospective nonprofit clients will have widely differing accounting needs, and that the important thing is to find clients with needs that can be met reasonably. That will mean that the level of actual *accounting* sophistication that students will provide can vary from training client employees to entering basic accounting transactions, to setting up a reasonably sophisticated accounting system from scratch. Emphasize to the students that they may not be able to control the needs and expectations of their clients, but the important thing is to gain practical knowledge from determining what those needs and expectations are and from helping to meet them.

• **Question:** *What are the likely inhibitors to success in service-learning?*

I spend time identifying potential inhibitors at the outset of most experiential training programs involving groups. Inhibitors are those things that may prevent a group from achieving its goals — for example, fatigue, resentment, or alienation.

Lack of *vision* is the biggest inhibitor to initiating service-learning — vision of community service needs. I have heard some argue that it is easy for schools such as Seattle University to do service because in Seattle there are many needs, but there are few needs in smaller cities or towns. The reality is, the era when all the needs in *any* community are fully met is not here now, will not be here tomorrow, and will never exist. One does not appreciate the extent of community needs until one looks for them. They are everywhere!

# Conclusion

We often see the volumes of experiential-learning theory reduced to three snippets from an ancient Chinese proverb:

*What I hear I forget.*
*What I see I remember.*
*What I do I understand.*

Today the two most widely discussed genres of experiential education embodying this proverb are OEBT and service-learning, both of which are often combined in adventure-based programs and in leadership and team-building courses such as the one I teach to our MBA students. The expansion of service-learning throughout the U.S. collegiate milieu and throughout disparate academic curricula (from social work to biology) can be credited largely to the Campus Compact movement and to the Ford Foundation's investment in stimulating awareness of service-learning possibilities in higher education.

My perspective in writing this article is that of a veteran accounting instructor and academic program administrator who has seen firsthand the benefits that service-learning can bring to a course and to a program. I have chosen to share my own successes with service-learning in the hope that the "already convinced but inexperienced" will be further encouraged and empowered to take the next step.

No doubt many believe the jury is still out on whether service-learning activities are appropriate and effective in the education of accounting students. If you've not yet experimented personally with a service component in your accounting classes but feel that such an initiative *might* work for you, I hope you'll take the risk. You can then judge for yourself whether the risk was worth it for you and for your students. I think you will find the answer to be a resounding "yes!" as it was for me.

## Notes

1. This comment had every participant in the room nodding in agreement.

2. For some help with the art of processing, I would recommend reading *Processing the Adventure Experience* by Nadler and Luckner (Dubuque, IA: Kendall/Hunt Publishing Co., 1992), or *Islands of Healing* by Schoel, Prouty, and Radcliffe, available from Project Adventure in Hamilton, MA, ph 508/468-7981. These discussions pertain specifically to OEBT-type programs, but the processing suggestions transfer well into the service-learning arena.

3. The course is limited to 24 students for reasons of safety and practicality in using OEBT methods.

4. But not excluding church-affiliated social service entities such as homeless shelters, soup kitchens, or food banks.

5. Mind Your Own Business™, a product of Bestware.

6. For example, the business had to buy and sell inventory as well as deliver services.


## Additional Readings

A good starting place for those needing some theoretical rationale is a compendium of articles published by the Association for Experiential Education, *The Theory of Experiential Education,* 2d ed., edited by Richard Kraft and Mitchell Sakofs. It can be ordered through the AEE at Box 249-CU, Boulder, CO 80309. For an application-based, albeit psychological, discussion of transference issues around experiential education, you might find interesting Stephen Bacon's *The Conscious Use of Metaphor in Outward Bound,* available from the Colorado Outward Bound School, 945 Pennsylvania St., Denver, CO 80203-3198.

# Service-Learning in Accounting:
## A Department Chair's Perspective

by Alfonso R. Oddo

Accounting is a service profession. How can accounting education best prepare students for careers in the accounting profession? Boyer and Hechinger (1981) urged that colleges must not only teach and conduct research, but they must also involve students in service to society. Incorporating service-learning as an integral part of the accounting curriculum can enhance the education of accounting students. The process of integrating service-learning into the accounting curriculum begins with an expression of the importance of service-learning in the mission statement of the university.

## Service-Learning at Niagara University

The mission of an academic department must necessarily be an extension of the university mission. Service-learning as a part of the university mission will be presented first, followed by service-learning in the Department of Accounting.

### The University Mission

Niagara University has a long tradition of learning through service to the poor and homeless. Its mission, according to the 1996-98 undergraduate catalogue, states that:

> Niagara University feels called to emulate the altruistic spirit of Vincent de Paul. It seeks to instill in its students a deep concern for the rights and dignity of the human person, especially for the poor, the suffering, the handicapped, and the outcast. It expects that the same concerns will inspire and motivate its faculty and staff in the educative process. (7)

Perhaps one example of how the curriculum seeks to "inspire and motivate" faculty and students to serve the poor is the freshman writing course, which is a one-semester required course in the general-education component of the curriculum. Faculty from all departments and various academic disciplines are invited to teach the writing course around a theme based on the interests and expertise of the faculty. One section of the writing course, Writing and Thinking About the Poor, was inspired by a commencement address to Niagara University graduates given by Mother Teresa. She reminded us that we do not have to go to the gutters of Calcutta to serve the poor; the poor are with us always, in our families, friends, neighbors, and strangers — anyone who hungers for love. And so, this writing course asks students to identify "their poor," and to think and write about ways to help them. Class discussions and presentations help students to broaden their understanding of the poor.

Another required course in the general-education component of Niagara University's curriculum is the university studies course, which provides opportunities for interdisciplinary collaboration. Team taught by two faculty members from different disciplines, these courses explore issues from the different perspectives of the participating teachers, and, according to the catalogue, "attempt to integrate the contribution of several disciplines to a problem, issue, or theme from life" (53). For example, one course investigates The Art of Mathematics/The Mathematics of Art.

When service-learning is incorporated into a university studies course, students begin to see the complexity of real-world issues. A course entitled Prison Literacy Tutoring deals with the problem of illiteracy and its relationship to poverty, racism, and crime. Students spend one-half day per week in prison tutoring an inmate, and participate in class discussions that contrast the diverse views of prisoners, correctional officers, reading tutors, and others. Service-learning courses provide excellent opportunities for both faculty and students to bring the mission alive in the community.

## The Department of Accounting Mission

What impact does the accounting profession have on the community it serves? How should accounting education prepare students for careers in the accounting profession? How can service-learning bring accounting into the community in a concrete, active way? Perhaps one of the challenges facing administrators of accounting programs is to address these questions as part of the process of developing a mission statement for the Department of Accounting.

At Niagara University, the Department of Accounting supports the mission of the university by educating accounting students in the spirit of Vincent de Paul. For example, the Department of Accounting promotes social responsibility by:

1. providing a value-based, ethics-centered business education that incorporates the Vincentian tradition;

2. providing students with opportunities for extracurricular and practical interaction with the business community on a local, regional, national, and international level; and

3. reinforcing the accounting program with internships and community service experiences.

## The Scholarship of Service-Learning

Boyer (1990) notes that "all too frequently, service means not doing scholarship but doing good" (22). Boyer goes on to say that "to be considered *scholarship,* service activities must be tied directly to one's special field of knowledge and relate to, and flow directly out of, this professional activity" (22). Hence, by incorporating service-learning into the mission of the Department of Accounting, service activities are part of the professional education process, and students learn accounting and social responsibility through service activities tied directly to the curriculum. As an expression of the mission of the Department of Accounting, service-learning activities are indeed *scholarship.*

Moreover, service-learning is linked directly to accounting practice. For example, one of the service-learning projects our students are involved in is a tax counseling for the elderly program. Since tax services are an important part of the professional services provided by accounting firms, the tax counseling for the elderly program enables students to gain valuable experience in professional tax services.

Thus, service-learning activities are tied directly to accounting practice and are an integral part of the educational programs in the College of Business and the Department of Accounting. In addition to the tax counseling for the elderly program, other service-learning projects include the economic redevelopment project for the Niagara Falls area, the city of Niagara Falls budget project, and participation in the Boys' Club, the YMCA, and the Police Athletic League. As a first step in extending accounting education into the community, the tax counseling for the elderly program was incorporated into the accounting curriculum.

## The Tax Counseling for the Elderly Program

One service-learning course at Niagara University is Intermediate Accounting, a required course for all accounting majors. As part of the Intermediate Accounting course requirements, students learn about income taxes, pass an IRS written test, and then prepare tax returns for low-income and elderly taxpayers in the community. The IRS provides all materials for the tax training, which is taught by the Intermediate Accounting instructor with assistance from other interested faculty. The tax training requires about eight hours of instruction, and is done during regularly scheduled class meetings in the Intermediate Accounting course. Students then work two to four hours per week during tax season doing tax returns both on campus and at various sites in the community.

Learning is measured in several ways. First, all students must pass an IRS written test to demonstrate that they are qualified to prepare tax returns. Next, throughout the semester, class discussions are held to give students an opportunity to reflect on what they are doing, how the community is affected by their service, what the students have learned from the community, and how their experience is related to and enhances their careers and their personal lives. Finally, students write a term paper at the end of the semester to reflect on their experiences in the service-learning program. Class discussions and term papers are evaluated by the instructor as part of the course grade for Intermediate Accounting.

In addition to the students who are required to participate in the tax program as a component of the accounting course, some students do taxes to fulfill service-learning requirements in other courses. This is a good way to promote service-learning both within the College of Business and across the university. Students in the tax program participate in the classroom reflection discussions in the accounting course as well as in their required "home" courses. Thus, students and faculty learn about a wide variety of service-learning experiences throughout the campus, and they tend to share their ideas with others. And students themselves are often the best salespersons for service-learning. For example, many students in the tax program are "repeat customers"; that is, having participated in the tax program as a service-learning requirement, they freely volunteer to serve again in subsequent years, and they recommend it to other students.

## Other Service-Learning Programs

Niagara University recognizes its place in the local community. Students, faculty, administrators, and staff each contributes their unique talents to enhance the quality of life in the local community, and to grow and learn in the process of serving. Two projects of critical importance to the future of the Niagara Falls community are the economic redevelopment project and the city of Niagara Falls budget project. Economic redevelopment of the Niagara Falls area is a challenging issue, rich in learning opportunities for our students. City officials, students, faculty, and other university representatives are pooling resources to formulate strategies and implement action plans to stimulate the economy, create jobs, and develop entrepreneurial opportunities for community residents. The city of Niagara Falls budget project involves a proposal developed by the university to help guide local government officials in the budgetary decision process.

The university also participates in various service activities of the Boys' Club, the YMCA, and the Police Athletic League. For example, the dean of the College of Business serves as a judge in the annual youth scholarship competition of the Police Athletic League. Association with these and other local community organizations can lead to service-learning opportunities directly related to accounting scholarship. Students have researched, evaluated, and implemented computerized accounting systems for local businesses and nonprofit organizations, assessed the tax implications of alternative business projects, and helped small business entrepreneurs decide on the most advantageous form of business organization. In the process of working with community organizations, students have learned valuable lessons in team building, group decision making, and social responsibility.

# Role of the Department Chair

## Faculty Involvement

It is essential for the department chair to encourage other faculty, accounting faculty as well as faculty from other disciplines, to get involved in service-learning. Faculty should not feel that they must add a complete service-learning component to their courses all at once. Like so many things in life, it is important to begin with small steps. For example, faculty can invite their students to participate in established service-learning activities such as the tax program, and then conduct discussions in their own classrooms to enable students to reflect on their experiences. In this way, faculty can gradually learn about some existing service-learning programs, and begin to form ideas *of their own*. Faculty *ownership* of service-learning is essential to implementing service-learning on a department-wide basis. That is, faculty themselves must see the value of service-learning and develop their own ideas for service-learning opportunities.

Also, the department chair can invite faculty to contribute their expertise to existing service-learning programs. Faculty from the Department of Accounting and other departments have been involved in the tax program. Accounting faculty have served as guest lecturers in the tax training course and as mentors to students to answer tax questions during the tax season. Service-learning offers many opportunities for interdisciplinary collaboration. Marketing faculty, with the assistance of faculty from the Communications Studies Department, have helped to promote the tax program both on campus and in the community. And Religious Studies faculty have worked with agencies for the elderly in the community to identify needs and to coordinate the placement of students to address those needs.

## Community Involvement

Bringle and Hatcher (1996) recommend that community representatives need to be involved in planning service-learning programs. And Muse (1990) notes that university and community partnerships can strengthen the economic development of the region. At Niagara University, two examples come to mind that illustrate some ways to involve the community in planning. At the university level, the president of the university formed a task force consisting of community leaders and university faculty and administrators to seek ways to stimulate economic development in the city of Niagara Falls, New York, and to engage our university community in service-learning projects.

At the departmental level, representatives of the local chapter of the American Association of Retired Persons were invited to visit our campus to help coordinate and plan our students' involvement in tax services to the elderly. The local office of the Internal Revenue Service is involved in planning and implementing the tax program, as well as in recognizing our students for their service in the program. At the end of tax season, an IRS representative presents a certificate of appreciation to each student at the annual accounting society banquet, which is attended by students, faculty, university administrators, accounting professionals, and members of the local community. Moreover, since many faculty are already involved in community service, the department chair can ask faculty to invite their contacts in the community to attend departmental meetings to discuss ways in which service-learning projects can serve community needs.

Students and the people they serve in the community both benefit from service-learning endeavors. Bringle and Kremer (1993) found that, compared with a control group, students who had visited home-bound elderly persons were significantly more positive toward the elderly and in their views of their own aging. In our tax program, students who had visited homes for the elderly to prepare tax returns experienced firsthand some of the realities of life for the elderly — loneliness, dependence on others — as well as the more positive aspects of aging, such as wisdom, understanding, and freedom to travel. And perhaps the elderly can learn from the students as well, especially that the students care about them and sincerely want to help. Bringing the young and old together pays dividends to both, and can help to bridge the generation gap. In addition to serving elderly persons, our students also do taxes for low-income families. The students have become more aware of the problems and dignity of the poor, and have realized the great satisfaction that can come from helping people even in small ways. Similarly, Giles and Eyler (1994) note that students became less likely to blame social service clients for misfortunes.

## Faculty Concerns

Zlotkowski (1996) emphasizes the need to help faculty broaden their perspectives to see how service-learning enhances learning. What are some of the concerns that faculty may have about service-learning, and how can the department chair address these concerns and help faculty to embrace service-learning as an important resource in educating students?

Perhaps one meaningful way in which accounting department chairs can facilitate the implementation of service-learning on a wider scale is for department chairs to use their contacts with accounting firms to ascertain what views they have on the value of service-learning to a student's education. This information can be gathered through informal contacts, surveys, and by associations with business leaders on advisory boards and professional organizations. Accounting firms and other business professionals have indicated their support of service-learning by hiring service-learning students for internships, co-ops, and entry-level positions. Department chairs need to clearly communicate to accounting faculty the importance that employers place on service-learning. With this knowledge, accounting faculty may be more inclined to incorporate service-learning into their courses.

Faculty sometimes feel that they can't fit service-learning into an already crowded syllabus. This is a common, but inaccurate, perception that service-learning is an additional discrete topic that requires more time, and must necessarily displace other essential topics in the course. If faculty view service-learning in this light, then it will be difficult to get faculty to embrace service-learning as a component of their courses. Service-learning will be seen as an intrusion in the course, rather than a means of enhancing the education of the students. We need to see service-learning as an opportunity to integrate classroom theory with the reality of accounting as a service profession. The challenge for the department chair is to help faculty to appreciate service-learning as a highly effective way to achieve course objectives. Service-learning is one of many learning strategies we can use in our courses to realize the course objectives and to enhance the education of our students.

Related to the concern that service-learning cannot be "squeezed" into the already crowded syllabus is the pressure that faculty often feel to get through the syllabus — "It doesn't matter whether students actually learn anything, so long as we cover all the topics." The answer to this apprehension is: Less is more and more is less. If we cover fewer topics but cover them well, students will understand and retain more knowledge than if we rush through more topics and students retain less. In other words, it is better for students to retain eight out of 10 topics than to retain five out of 25.

Another constraint that faculty, and especially department chairs, must deal with is limited faculty resources — "We barely have enough faculty to teach our real courses, and we certainly cannot afford to add new service-learning courses without sufficient faculty to teach them. And where would these service-learning courses fit in the curriculum?" One response to this issue is that service-learning does not have to involve the addition of a "new" course that must "fit" into the curriculum. Just as service-learning should not be viewed as a discrete topic within a course, service-learning need not be a separate course in the curriculum. The mission of the Department of

Accounting, as defined by the accounting faculty, is implemented through its curriculum, which includes various courses and learning experiences designed to accomplish the mission. So the challenge for the department chair is to allocate scarce faculty resources in a manner that most effectively accomplishes the mission of the department. Service-learning is one of many means of extending the learning that takes place in the existing "real" courses.

Faculty sometimes feel that they are not qualified to incorporate service-learning into their courses. Since service-learning is new to many faculty, it is understandable that they may feel the need to have special training to deal with the demands of service-learning experiences. It seems that there are at least two ways to address this anxiety. First, faculty should be asked to deal only with those areas that they feel comfortable with. If faculty are qualified to teach the course content, then service-learning is simply another way to deliver the content. All faculty have unique talents, and they should be encouraged to extend these talents into the service-learning arena. Second, the department could sponsor service-learning workshops conducted by service-learning "experts" or simply organize periodic informal discussion groups where faculty could gather to discuss issues and share experiences. Farmer (1990) suggests that faculty with experience in service-learning should meet one on one with interested faculty. The department chair could arrange such meetings at the academic department level.

Even if all of the concerns discussed above are resolved, faculty may feel that they don't have time to adequately manage the field experiences of service-learning. While proper supervision and control of field experiences are important, faculty need not make regular field visits. As long as students clearly understand their responsibilities and have access to sufficient guidance from the faculty member, most of the activities can be managed in the classroom as part of the reflective component of the course. For example, in the income tax program, the faculty member arranges tax assistance sites at local libraries and community centers, and schedules students to work during specified days and times. Then, in the classroom, students share their experiences and discuss any problems they may have encountered, and the faculty member can make suggestions and recommendations. Faculty can make periodic announced or unannounced field visits if they desire, but these are not required. And part of the service-learning experience is for students to assume responsibility for the success of the field experience, and to feel that they are in charge of the service-learning experience.

## Student Concerns

Students as well as faculty may experience some anxiety about service-learning as a required component of an academic experience — "Am I really learning? Shouldn't the teacher teach something to me rather than expect me to learn through service?" If the teacher is the only one dispensing knowledge in the course, then students can learn only what the teacher has to offer. But through service-learning, the community is the classroom, and students learn not only from the faculty member but also from the people they serve, from the experiences they live, and from each other in the reflective process.

Another way in which department chairs can promote service-learning among students is by helping students to understand the value of service-learning in getting a job. In cooperation with the career planning office, the department chair can show students that service-learning not only looks good on a resume but also develops social skills, organizational ability, and maturity, and teaches students appropriate dress and etiquette for business.

Faculty must also deal with the reality that students have only a limited amount of time to devote to community service. Many students must work to finance their education. Therefore, the scheduling of service-learning must be flexible enough to accommodate the students' class and work schedules. In the tax program, for example, the training and reflection are done during regular class meetings, and the students themselves indicate when they are available to prepare tax returns. In this manner, students' anxiety about not having enough time for service-learning is allayed.

Students, like faculty, sometimes feel that they are not qualified to engage in community service. This concern, I think, goes to the heart of service-learning as an educational strategy. Where do students learn? Only in the classroom, or in the classroom as well as in the community? Students should not feel that they need to be "experts" before they can provide useful community service. Service-learning provides opportunities to apply classroom learning in the community, and the experience of community service in turn enhances classroom learning. We need to help students understand that learning is a lifelong process, and that we don't suddenly become "qualified" by virtue of earning a degree. Indeed, service-learning is an essential part of becoming "qualified" to serve in the accounting profession.

Student learning can be measured and demonstrated by various outcome assessments. In addition to the IRS written test, classroom discussions, and term papers mentioned earlier, students check each other's work on-site to make sure that tax returns are accurately prepared, and tax returns are then sent to the local IRS office for further quality review. The IRS provides periodic reports on student performance, and the participating service-learning instructor reviews the reports with students.

Related to the issue of not being qualified is the concern some students have that their education is being shortchanged by service-learning. This notion probably stems from the fact that the classroom has been the traditional (and perhaps the only) model for learning. "When I'm in the class-room, I'm learning, but am I learning by performing community service?" The idea of active learning has certainly received a lot of attention lately. Is not service-learning a form of active learning? As long as community service is coupled with an opportunity for students and faculty to reflect on their experiences in classroom discussions, then service-learning is certainly a rich learning experience. Education is not shortchanged, but rather enhanced, by service-learning.

How does service-learning *enhance* the education of our students? Markus, Howard, and King (1993) found that service-learning students were significantly more likely to feel that they had performed to their potential, learned to apply principles, and developed a greater awareness of social problems than students in traditional discussion sessions. Students in our tax program echoed these feelings in their classroom reflections and in their term papers. Students indicated that service-learning helped them to vivid-ly see the connection between classroom learning and helping real people, to develop a keener awareness of the social problems of elderly persons and low-income families, and to more fully appreciate their role in business and society.

Similarly, research by Cohen and Kinsey (1994) shows that service-learn-ing "is an effective means of teaching that increases student understanding of complex material." Our experience in the tax program supports this find-ing. Students were able to learn and apply complex tax rules better and faster through service-learning than in the traditional classroom setting. Perhaps this is because service-learning students (1) see at the outset the "big picture" of how their classroom learning will be applied, and (2) have an opportunity to quickly apply their learning by preparing real tax returns.

## Conclusion

To make service-learning a part of accounting education at the college level requires the cooperation and support of many constituencies, including uni-versity administration, staff, faculty, students, community leaders, and par-ticipating community agencies. It begins with an expression of the impor-tance of service-learning in the university mission statement, and is sup-ported by the mission statements of individual academic departments. Ser-vice-learning is carried out through the curriculum, both in general educa-tion courses and in courses within the academic major. Perhaps the primary role of the department chair in implementing a department-wide service-learning program in accounting is to help faculty to appreciate the value of community service as an effective learning strategy in educating students for the accounting service profession. If faculty and students see service-learning as a means of *enhancing* accounting education, then service-learning will be *mainstreamed* into the accounting curriculum.

## References

Boyer, E.L. (1990). *Scholarship Reconsidered: Priorities of the Professoriate*. Princeton, NJ: Carnegie Foundation for the Advancement of Teaching.

————, and F.M. Hechinger. (1981). *Higher Learning in the Nation's Service*. Washington, DC: Carnegie Foundation for the Advancement of Teaching.

Bringle, R.G., and J.A. Hatcher. (1996). "Implementing Service-Learning in Higher Education." *Journal of Higher Education* 67(2): 221-239.

Bringle, R.G., and J.F. Kremer. (1993). "An Evaluation of an Intergenerational Service-Learning Project for Undergraduates." *Educational Gerontologist* 19: 407-416.

Cohen, J., and D. Kinsey. (Winter 1994). "'Doing Good' and Scholarship: A Service-Learning Study." *Journalism Educator*: 4-14.

Farmer, D.W. (1990). "Strategies for Change." In *Managing Change in Higher Education*, edited by D.W. Steeples, pp. 7-17. San Francisco: Jossey-Bass.

Giles, D.E., Jr., and J. Eyler. (1994). "The Impact of a College Community Service Laboratory on Students' Personal, Social, and Cognitive Outcomes." *Journal of Adolescence* 17: 327-339.

Markus, G.B., J.P.F. Howard, and D.C. King. (1993). "Integrating Community Service and Classroom Instruction Enhances Learning: Results From an Experiment." *Educational Evaluation and Policy Analysis* 15: 410-419.

Muse, W.V. (1990). "A Catalyst for Economic Development." *Metropolitan Universities* 1: 79-88.

Zlotkowski, E. (January/February 1996). "Linking Service-Learning and the Academy: A New Voice at the Table?" *Change* 28(1): 20-27.

# Service-Learning:
# A "Free Enterprise" Model for Accounting Faculty

by Curtis L. DeBerg

The Bedford Report (American Accounting Association 1986), the White Paper (Andersen et al. 1989), and the Accounting Education Change Commission (AECC 1990) all called for reforms in how courses are taught (pedagogy), what is taught (content), and the environment in which content and pedagogy are delivered (infrastructure). In 1992, the AECC emphasized that the first course in accounting should be given special attention because this course provides students with their first exposure to accounting:

> The first course [has] significance for those considering a career in accounting and those otherwise open to the option of majoring in accounting. The course shapes their perceptions of (1) the profession, (2) the aptitudes and skills needed for successful careers in accounting, and (3) the nature of career opportunities in accounting. These perceptions affect whether the supply of talent will be sufficient for the profession to thrive. For those who decide to major in accounting or other aspects of business, the course is an important building block for success in future academic work. (1-2)

Student organizations such as Beta Alpha Psi provide one avenue for students to practice skills that are difficult to teach in a traditional, lecture-based classroom. Unfortunately, eligible students have already selected accounting as a major, and must have outstanding academic credentials. What is lacking, I believe, is a student organization whereby potential accounting majors can actively participate in meaningful projects related to accounting. These projects can be designed and implemented in collaboration with faculty advisers.

Well-conceived service-learning projects provide an avenue for instructors to enhance and enrich students' experiences. The AECC (1992) stated:

> Teachers of the first course in accounting should put a priority on their interaction among students. Students' involvement should be promoted by methods such as cases, simulations, and group projects. Emphasis should be on teaching the student to learn on his or her own. (4)

The purpose of this article is to describe a service-learning program at California State University–Chico in Principles of Accounting. Students self-select into groups and decide which projects to pursue, with the approval of the faculty adviser. A student organization, called Students in Free Enterprise (SIFE), provides a vehicle for the service program. Participating students gain the leadership experience of establishing free enterprise community outreach programs that teach others how market economies and business operate. This article explains SIFE's main projects at CSU–Chico, which involve teaching at-risk middle school students how math, English, and computer skills are relevant to everyday decisions.

This paper will first describe what SIFE is and how it fits into the service-learning program. The second section explains how the CSU–Chico SIFE team was created. The third section presents the details of the main SIFE project our students have undertaken. In the fourth section, I describe how a SIFE team's service-learning projects can be assessed for effectiveness. The fifth section presents reasons why an accounting faculty member, or any business faculty member, would want students to participate in service-learning projects. This section also includes a list of benefits for students and the community. The sixth section describes how a faculty member can get started if he or she wants to be a service-learning advocate. Finally, the paper concludes by offering a way for readers to subscribe to a network that brings accounting and other business faculty together to exchange project ideas, to discuss assessment issues, and to suggest ways of disseminating the most successful service-learning projects.

## Service-Learning and SIFE

Integrating service-learning projects into the business curriculum has been gaining support over the past several years. For example, the Wingspread Group on Higher Education (1993), a blue-ribbon commission of some of the leading educators and businesses in the United States, stated:

> There is no substitute for experience. Academic work should be complemented by the kinds of knowledge derived from firsthand experience, such as contributing to the well-being of others, participating in political campaigns, and working with the enterprises that create wealth in our society.

Others concur with the Wingspread commission. For example, Ernest Lynton, a leading education reformer, contends that the value of direct, unsimulated experience must not be overlooked: "Practical experience, design activities, and case studies constitute probably the best way for future practitioners to master the way of approaching and dealing with complex situations" (1993: 18-19). Zlotkowski (1996b) has echoed Lynton's call for practical experience, stressing the suitability of service-learning:

> Community-based projects can provide business students with a variety of technical opportunities. . . . At the same time, they can facilitate development of a variety of "soft" skills — without the addition of any new, inde-

*pendent curricular unit. Effective teamwork, cross-functional flexibility, interpersonal and communication skills, and multicultural sensitivity are just a few of the more important nontechnical skills community-based projects can naturally foster. (9)*

The SIFE organization, founded in 1975, provides one framework for a team of students on campus to begin their service-learning projects. SIFE is a nonprofit educational organization that works in partnership with business and higher education, providing college students with an opportunity to establish free enterprise community outreach programs that teach others how market economies and businesses operate. Each spring, participating SIFE teams compete against one another at one of 12 regional competitions throughout the United States. Winning teams at the regional competitions advance to a national competition held in Kansas City, Missouri, at the end of May (a later section provides additional details about these competitions).

The SIFE organization stresses that teaching free enterprise principles is its core mission. The primary goal of SIFE student teams is to teach others how market economies and businesses operate. This helps the students and those they teach use this knowledge to improve themselves and their communities.

To understand better how the SIFE organization is linked to service-learning, it is helpful to keep in mind a clear sense of what service-learning entails. According to the National and Community Trust Act of 1993, it is a "method under which students or participants learn and develop through active participation in thoughtfully organized service that is conducted in and meets the needs of a community, and is coordinated with the community and with an elementary school, secondary school, institution of higher education, or community service program."

Some faculty have been unwilling to integrate service-learning into their courses because there is too much emphasis on "service" and not enough on "learning." Zlotkowski (1996a) suggested that faculty must focus more on learning:

*Unless service-learning advocates become far more comfortable seeing "enhanced learning" as the horse pulling the cart of "moral and civic values," and not vice versa, service-learning will continue to remain less visible — and less important — to the higher education community as a whole than is good for its own survival. (24-25)*

The CSU–Chico SIFE team, created in fall 1993, has completed several service-learning projects. The most comprehensive service-learning project completed by the CSU–Chico SIFE team is linked directly to the objectives of Principles of Accounting. The issue is not whether students benefit more from exposure to accounting content or to moral and civic values. The goal is for students to simultaneously learn accounting concepts and develop moral and civic values. Students acquire a better understanding of accounting concepts by explaining them to others, and they develop a sense of civic responsibility by providing service to the community. Students' reflective essays provide evidence that both forms of growth occur.

I believe that the creation of a student organization that cuts across departmental and college boundaries helps overcome traditional barriers in the higher education community. Students from different disciplines can interact as team members on service-learning projects. For example, students majoring in English and communications work closely with business students, serving as authors and editors of the team's newsletter. Another example is students majoring in computer science and management information systems working closely with public school teachers to design relevant software to support lessons. A third example is public relations students who interview team members and author press releases to inform the public about their projects. Students can quickly see the benefits of developing a network inside and outside the college. For example, because many students have advanced skills and knowledge in some areas, such as computer skills, much of what they know can benefit other team members.

## How the CSU–Chico SIFE Team Was Created

I learned of the service-learning movement by attending a project director's meeting in fall 1992 for grants funded under the U.S. Department of Education's Fund for the Improvement of Postsecondary Education (FIPSE). CSU–Chico had earned a three-year grant to reengineer its Principles of Accounting courses in fall 1992. Many of the reforms outlined in our grant proposal were consistent with the community service grants made by FIPSE under its Innovative Projects for Community Service program.

How did an interest in community service evolve from the reforms taking place in undergraduate accounting programs? At the FIPSE meeting, I attended a few workshops featuring community service projects. There, I saw the parallels between the reforms called for by the AECC and service-learning. I became convinced that student learning could be enhanced greatly if business instructors could find ways for students to gain hands-on experience outside of class in ways that benefit the community and the students. Based on the success of many of the FIPSE projects, I could see how well-designed projects could strengthen the linkages among K-12, community colleges, the university, and the community.

At the FIPSE meeting in fall 1993, Alexander Astin was the keynote speaker. Astin, a leading expert on outcomes assessment, provided convincing evidence that the "traditional" educational model of higher education should be revised. He found that "the single most important environmental influence on student development is the peer group; by judicious and imaginative use of peer groups, any college or university can substantially strengthen its impact on student learning and personal development" (1993: xiii-xiv). He also found that students in similar circumstances, and with common needs and interests, have a greater likelihood of interacting and learning together. Because most students who enroll in introductory accounting are pursuing a business major, they share business as a common interest. The challenge for me, therefore, was to create a structure whereby students could develop peer groups outside of class by working together on projects (1) related to accounting (2) that could add value to the community.

Because the goal of each SIFE team is to create community outreach projects that help others understand how market economies and businesses operate, SIFE provided such a structure. A faculty member who chooses to start a SIFE team applies to become what is known as a "Samuel M. Walton Free Enterprise Fellow." The duties of the fellowship (which pays a $1,000 stipend) are to organize a student team, help it define its mission, goals, and strategies, and complete specific projects in various program areas. In fall 1993, I recruited 16 students who were former students in intermediate accounting or senior accounting theory, along with students from other disciplines. Because I was not teaching introductory accounting at the time, beginning students were not a primary recruiting pool.

In later semesters, students enrolled in Principles of Accounting were recruited for SIFE teams. The goal of the first two Principles courses, under the FIPSE-reengineered course structure, was to provide students with an understanding of the uses and limitations of accounting information in economic decision making in a variety of personal, business, and other organizational contexts. The course materials developed under the grant focused on real-world cases designed to help students become more effective decision makers using both quantitative and qualitative data. Because of this real-world, decision-oriented approach, I believed that the service-learning movement complemented the accounting education reform movement.

Since spring 1993, I have taught Introduction to Accounting I and II (primarily financial and managerial accounting, respectively), implementing a 10 percent service-learning bonus in both courses. Exhibit 1 contains an excerpt from the fall 1996 syllabus in Principles of Accounting I, including a schedule of how the course grade is determined and narrative describing the optional service-learning project. Note in the narrative how students are given maximum flexibility through the option of participating in SIFE or in one or more programs with Community Action Volunteers in Education (CAVE). CAVE is a community service student organanization that maintains

## Exhibit 1

---

# Principles of Accounting I
# Fall 1996

**Course Grade**

Your letter grade in this course will be determined according to the following weightings:

| | |
|---|---|
| Midterm Exam | 25% |
| Small group assignments and quizzes | 16 |
| Individual assignments and quizzes | 25 |
| Computer spreadsheet proficiency | 3 |
| Attendance and class participation | 6 |
| Final exam | 25 |
| Total | 100% |

Note: Optional bonus points may be earned by participating in a service-learning project (see below).

**Optional Bonus Points**

You can earn a bonus equal to 10 percent of the total points you accumulate in the course by taking part in a service-learning project. This will require you to participate in one of the following two options:

1. delivering "business literacy" lessons to middle school students in the Chico area as part of a student group called Students in Free Enterprise (SIFE). This will require about three hours of time, per week, for the two weeks beginning September 16. Thereafter, the project will take about 1-2 hours per week; or

2. participating in one or more programs with Community Action Volunteers in Education (CAVE). It is preferred that this service be related to accounting or some other business discipline, but it is not mandatory.

During the semester, you must keep a "log" describing what you did. You must log at least 30 hours of service in order to earn the bonus points. For your information, in Spring 1996, 115 students were enrolled in three courses where this service-learning option was available. Of these, 27 students (23%) chose to complete a CAVE project, while 6 students (5%) chose the SIFE track. Of the 33 students who participated, 25 had their grades raised at least one level. At the end of the semester, you must write a two-page summary (single-spaced) reflecting on your experience. The paper should describe the project, explain what you learned, offer recommendations to improve the project, and indicate whether or not you plan to continue with the project after the semester is over.

more than 20 projects (e.g., Adopted Grandparent Program, Adult Literacy Program, Teacher Aid Program). Students have the freedom to select a program that best meets their time schedules and interests; however, a student must document at least 30 hours of service in order to receive the bonus. Note that the offer of a 10 percent bonus resulted in 33 students out of 115 (29%) choosing to participate.

## A Close Look at One Comprehensive Project

In fall 1993, our new SIFE team decided to create a project that could be implemented during spring 1994. The project, which I conceived, was designed to involve university students in teaching "business literacy" skills to groups of 13- and 14-year-old students who were at risk of not doing well in high school. After meeting with the assistant superintendent of the school district, I was directed to Chico Junior High. Four teachers enthusiastically welcomed the idea of small teams of SIFE student "mentors" to begin teaching one or two lessons per week, starting in spring 1994. Then I began authoring a series of lessons, entitled Using Math to Make Business Decisions, and recruited the first team of 16 SIFE students. Accompanying the lessons is a manual of mentor/instructor guidelines, which details each lesson's learning objectives, suggestions for teaching, and reminders for homework assignment and collection.

Before the beginning of each semester, SIFE mentors who choose to work on the middle school projects meet with their assigned teacher and me to discuss scheduling, goals, expectations, and roles. Usually, two or three SIFE students are assigned, as a team, to become mentors to one class. Each teacher is allowed flexibility to determine how much the SIFE project will count toward the eighth graders' final grade.

The university students rely heavily on the teacher to encourage parent involvement and to help with discipline problems. Teachers are strongly encouraged to take on the role of "associate mentor" on SIFE day, thereby allowing the university students to forge a bond with the class with little interference from the teacher. Only when a class starts to get out of hand is the teacher expected to step in and get the class back on track.

Each team of SIFE students has one lead mentor, who is a veteran SIFE student who has taught in a previous semester. The lead mentor is responsible for making sure he or she and the other mentors are prepared for each day's lesson. This mentor is also in charge of how each lesson is to be delivered.

Because there are 23 lessons in a semester (each lesson is 56 minutes long), it is important that the teacher and the mentor team plan ahead. Usually, the first five lessons are taught consecutively during a full, one-week time slot early in the semester. In the next two months, one or two lessons are delivered each week. Near the end of the semester, the team will again teach several lessons consecutively. Introductory accounting students who choose this project usually log in more than the 30-hour minimum required of students who select a CAVE project, but they do so willingly because they see other benefits of belonging to SIFE (as indicated later in this essay).

## What Do SIFE Students Teach?

The 23 lessons are listed in Exhibit 2. The lessons integrate math, science, history, geography, business, civics, and ethics under the umbrella of free enterprise. The focus is on math, which allows key free enterprise principles to be introduced. In the math classes, the team helped eighth graders understand:

1. What is a business?
2. How is a business managed?
3. How does one keep accurate records?
4. What is the difference between a sole proprietorship, a partnership, and a corporation?
5. Why do businesses have to pay income taxes, and what does the government do with these taxes?
6. Why is it best to do business fairly and honestly?
7. Why are some businesses riskier than others?

The activities included in the program allow students to incorporate mathematics, English, and speech, while the students interact to make decisions. Cases were designed to introduce students to financial statements; percentages, decimals, and ratios; the accounting equation; markups; probability, risk, and reward; time value of money (Einstein's second greatest theory); and the stock market. The most important aspect of the program, however, is that the junior high students each have the opportunity to start their own, real-life businesses. It should be noted that one of the mentees for the spring 1994 semester was awarded third place in the country by the National Federation of Independent Business in its Young Entrepreneur of the Year Award category. The young man made clocks from computer hard drives that had been broken and otherwise would have been destined for the landfill. His product's name? *Hard Times!*

At the end of each semester, one of the area malls hosts a Students in Free Enterprise weekend where all the junior high entrepreneurs get to set up shop and sell their goods and services.

## Why Middle School Math Students?

Currently, junior high students have little or no exposure to business concepts. In order to live happy and productive lives, it is essential that all students learn how to properly manage their money. These students will

**Exhibit 2**

**"Using Math to Make Business Decisions"**

| Lesson 1: | Welcome to Free Enterprise |
|---|---|
| Lesson 2: | Personal Entities vs. Business Entities |
| Lesson 3: | Valuation Rules |
| Lesson 4: | Keeping Track of Personal Net Worth: The Case of Cory's Allowance |
| Lesson 5: | Sole Proprietorship: The Simplest Business Form |
| Lesson 6: | The "Big Two" Financial Statements |
| Lesson 7: | Mary and Tina's Baby-Sitting Business |
| Lesson 8: | Comparing "Annette's Tutoring Services" to "Mary and Tina's Baby-Sitting Business" |
| Lesson 9: | Starting Your Own Business: (1) Questions and (2) Rules and Rewards |
| Lesson 10: | Keeping Good Records -- The Case of Billy's Sports Cards |
| Lesson 11: | Risk and Reward -- The Two-Dice Experiment |
| Lesson 12: | Awarding the SIFE Loans |
| Lesson 13: | The Columbus/Isabella Partnership-Part I |
| Lesson 14: | The Columbus/Isabella Partnership-Part II |
| Lesson 15: | How are Businesses Taxed? |
| Lesson 16: | The Penny Experiment (How Should Your Government Spend Your Tax Money?) |
| Lesson 17: | State and Federal Government Spending |
| Lesson 18: | Good Business Is Good Business: Andrea and the Pop Bottle Boutique |
| Lesson 19: | Einstein's Second Greatest Theory: The Time Value of Money |
| Lesson 20: | Triple Play Publications, Inc. |
| Lesson 21: | The Stock Market-Part I |
| Lesson 22: | The Stock Market-Part II |
| Lesson 23: | Awards Day |

someday be employees or employers, and it is essential that they learn the language of business at an early age.

Prealgebra students (i.e., those without the skills to be in algebra) have been selected because they are most at risk of losing sight that math is a crucial lifelong skill. Furthermore, unlike their peers in algebra, a much higher percentage of prealgebra students are not destined for college and, hence, will be the first ones to enter the workforce. The role model effect cannot be overemphasized. Eighth graders can identify and relate to the older university students more readily than to a teacher or parent. Furthermore, because many of the SIFE students are extremely knowledgeable about computers, they are in a position to teach eighth graders and their teachers. Equipped with the necessary knowledge, skills, training, hardware, and software, these mentors can provide junior high students and teachers with access to an integrated curriculum using new technology. In essence, the teachers can receive inservice training while simultaneously using university mentors to help them reach students who might not otherwise show an interest in math.

At the same time, SIFE mentors planning to become K-12 teachers can obtain valuable preservice training. Furthermore, SIFE students planning careers in business can improve leadership, teamwork, and communication skills.

## Measuring the Project's Effectiveness

Since spring 1994, the lessons have been improved with input from SIFE students, K-12 teachers, business owners, parents, and former eighth graders based on an extensive outcomes assessment program. The first major revision occurred during summer 1994. Changes included making the lessons more interactive, including more in-class, small-group exercises, teaming university students in groups of two or more when delivering the lessons, providing additional inservice training for both the university mentors and junior high teachers, and reducing the number of lessons from 28 to 23. Also, the team worked much more closely with its business advisory board (each SIFE team recruits board members from the local business community who have a strong interest in free enterprise).

As noted, these revisions were the result of our outcomes assessment work. A 10-question, multiple-choice business literacy exam was administered to the eighth grade students on a pre- and posttest basis at the beginning and end of the spring 1994 semester. The questions varied from simple recall to moderate analysis to complex analysis. Students scored *significantly* better on seven of the 10 questions.[1] These questions tested them on (1) their knowledge of assets, liabilities, and equity; (2) their understanding of the primary purpose of a balance sheet; (3) their ability to discuss the effect on a company's financial statements if the wrong amount of income taxes was paid; (4) their understanding of why a business plan is important; (5) their ability to discern the difference between an expense and an owner's withdrawal; (6) how a bank's financial statements are affected when a business owner takes money out of a checking account; and (7) their understanding of the difference between a balance sheet, an income statement, and a statement of cash flow.

In addition to the empirical test described above, numerous samples of authentic assessment material have been analyzed (e.g., completed business plans, completed financial statements, ethics essays, and products produced by the "miniature" businesses). Completed essays by the SIFE students provide a glimpse into how they view the program, while simultaneously providing the reflection component of service-learning. Exhibit 3 contains excerpts from three essays.

One of the most objective ways to measure the effectiveness of a SIFE team is through the regional and international competitions held each spring. The fact that *competitions* are held each year motivated me to start a SIFE team because competition provides external measures of effectiveness. Teams are judged by a panel of business leaders based on the five criteria described in Exhibit 4. The top two teams from each "league" (a league consists of between four and eight teams) at a regional competition advance to the national competition. Winning teams not only earn plaques and trophies; they also win prize money contributed by the businesses that support SIFE's mission.

# Benefits to Stakeholders

There are many benefits from service-learning. This section briefly describes benefits accruing to faculty, participating university students, and the community as they relate to my experience as faculty adviser for a SIFE team.

## Benefits for Faculty

Why would an accounting faculty member, or any business faculty member, want students to participate in service-learning projects? There are several intrinsic and extrinsic benefits. Intrinsically, the SIFE team's success has been extremely gratifying to me. By observing students work together to carry out projects that are directly linked to course objectives, I have seen how their knowledge of subject matter has improved. I have also seen students' skills develop by helping them with their written reports to judges; guiding them as they prepare their oral presentations; traveling with them as they make presentations at conferences and competitions; and offering

## Exhibit 3

## Excerpts From Three "Reflection" Essays

"Soon after joining SIFE, I realized that my reasons for remaining in it went far beyond extra credit. SIFE is a unique organization on campus. You can actually see hands-on involvement in the community by the college students. Mentoring in the classroom and working with other members of the team was a pleasure this semester. The times I went to Chico Junior High were experiences all in themselves. It was foreign to me at first, to be the one standing in front of the classroom. I am so used to being the student and not the teacher."

"Working as a mentor was a very enjoyable and enlightening experience. Never before had I been required to teach in a class setting. The whole thing was very exciting and a little bit scary. After preparing for my first day out in the field I thought I was ready. I sure found out how important it is to teach in groups. After my nerves had calmed halfway through the lesson I really started to enjoy it.

"Not only were we teaching the students about free enterprise, but I was surprised at how much I learned myself. Teaching this subject made me remember and understand what an old man once said to me. He said, 'The best way to master a subject is to teach it.'"

"My original motive for volunteering for the SIFE mentor program was not noble and altruistic. I wanted extra credit and it seemed like it would be simple, since I had a lot of experience counseling junior high kids. In retrospect, the program has been challenging, frustrating, humiliating, and a lot of other things but it was anything but easy. Would I do it again? In a heartbeat.

"I would do it because all my life I have wanted to make a difference, to be a leader. This program has made that possible. I have been able to experience real numbers, real school, real students, real satisfaction, and real frustration. Mentoring has taught me patience, the importance of measuring what you say before you say it, and most importantly, how to listen. I look for the faces where the eyes tell me this young person wants to know what I have to say in spite of the lack of respect my fellow mentors and I occasionally get from many of her peers. And I mentor to her, just her. When I do that, others in the class know I am serious and they begin to pay attention. I feel as though I can only reach a few of them in this short time, but maybe one or more of them will be stimulated by math and accounting and end up wanting to go on to college, and perhaps even to major in business."

**Exhibit 4**

## Judging Criteria

1. How creative, innovative, and effective were the students in teaching others an understanding of how market economies and businesses operate and helping them use this knowledge to better themselves, their community, and their country? (40 points)

2. Did the students quantify the results of their educational programs, and did they ensure the continuation of their successful SIFE programs in the future? (20 points)

3. How successful were the students in utilizing their resources, which included but were not limited to: (1) their Business Advisory Board (BAB), (2) college students and faculty from nonbusiness disciplines, and (3) the mass media available (taking into consideration the size and location of their community)? (20 points)

4. How effectively did the students document their activities in their written annual reports sent in advance to the judges? (10 points)

5. How effectively did the students document their activities in their competition presentation to the judges? (10 points)

---

These criteria have been taken directly from page 14 of the *SIFE 1996/1997 Information Handbook.*

advice as they author grant proposals to support their projects. But most important, by being *their* mentor as they, in turn, mentor younger students — that is what service-learning has done to reenergize my academic career.

There are also numerous extrinsic rewards. For example, I have (1) learned an enormous amount about various software tools and techniques from some of my more computer-savvy students; (2) been recognized inside and outside the university for my duties related to SIFE; (3) received an annual $1,000 stipend as a Samuel M. Walton Fellow; (4) met some of America's business leaders, many of whom serve as judges at the competitions; (5) authored articles in magazines and journals; and (6) obtained grant funds to pursue service-learning projects for business students.

## Benefits for University Students

There are numerous benefits for the students who participate in service-learning projects related to SIFE.

• Richer *faculty-student interaction,* because the faculty adviser and students often work together as colleagues.

• *Teamwork skills* are improved, because all projects involve at least two students working together to achieve a goal that is specific, achievable, and measurable.

• Opportunities to gain the *leadership* experience of establishing free enterprise community outreach programs; having students conceive, implement, and assess their projects allows them to practice leadership skills that normally cannot be taught in a traditional classroom environment.

• Additional practice at improving *oral presentation skills,* especially for those students who teach at the middle schools and make presentations to local, regional, and national education and business leaders.

• Additional practice at improving *writing skills,* especially for those students who author, edit, and publish the team's newsletters and annual reports; also, students who have authored grant proposals from their student government to disseminate their best projects have improved their writing skills.

• A better understanding of how their *student government* works, by serving on various committees that decide how student fees are collected and distributed.

• Learning more about *accounting* and *community service* (this has been reflected in their end-of-semester essays).

## Benefits for the Community

There are two primary community groups that benefit from the projects completed by the CSU–Chico SIFE team — those who are directly involved in K-12 education and those who will be hiring high school students upon graduation. Cindy Cox, an eighth grade math teacher at Bidwell Junior High in Chico, has participated in the SIFE program for two semesters and has seen positive results in her students. "This program is a great liaison with the university," she has said. "And the kids find it exciting and enjoyable. They actively learn math outside of school, which is one of the primary goals of our state framework in teaching mathematics." Cox was one of three teachers involved with the SIFE program during fall 1995.

Debra Cowan, who participated in the program in spring 1995 and fall 1996, added, "I've seen kids completing homework who don't normally complete homework. Because of the experiential, hands-on nature of the program, the kids really want to get involved, and when they get involved, they learn."

One of the program's greatest advocates is Robert J. Barbot, superintendent of the Chico Unified School District. Barbot sees the importance of bringing the business community into the classroom, but he also sees the importance of bringing the classroom into the business community and the community at large:

> This type of program provides students with meaningful and necessary knowledge of the American enterprise system. The hands-on actual experience is invaluable for our students. And it's made all the more valuable by the multilevel assistance and cooperation among the teachers in the classroom, students from the university, and the university faculty who have expertise in this area.

The SIFE team has made strong efforts to enlist the active involvement and support of the business community. One of the business owners involved is Clifford Neill, an investment broker who is also the chair of the Chamber of Commerce's Education Committee. In his opinion, "The math project delivered by the university mentors, with us helping out, is one way to provide a key link in bringing the business community closer to K-12 and the university."

## Service-Learning: Starting a SIFE Team

An accounting faculty member can begin incorporating service projects into his or her courses starting next semester. Almost all campuses have community service organizations like CAVE, where students can participate in myriad different projects. But faculty members who want students to become involved in projects that are directly linked to the accounting curriculum should read this volume closely and select one or two approaches that best match their interests and course objectives. To implement service-learning effectively, I believe students should be offered a bonus in a course they are currently taking, or they should be offered independent study cred-it. At CSU–Chico, after introductory students have completed the SIFE ser-vice-learning component, they are invited to sign up for a three-unit, credit/noncredit course called Service-Learning in the Community.[2] In this way, students can continue to earn compensation in the form of "academic cur-rency," and they also become known as "veteran" SIFE mentors.

If an accounting faculty member would like to consider adopting the CSU–Chico middle school project, he or she is encouraged to organize a group of students on campus and form a SIFE team. Currently, about 25 per-cent of all U.S. community colleges and universities with business programs have active teams; therefore, there are well over 500 business faculty who share a common goal. Unfortunately, there are only about 15 accounting faculty who serve as fellows.

It is best to begin planning a SIFE team late in the spring semester. To start a team, the following steps should be completed:

1. Request an application from SIFE's home office (The Jack Shew-maker Center, 1959 E. Kerr, Springfield, MO 65803, ph 800/235-9595, *SIFETeams@aol.com*) to become a Samuel M. Walton Free Enterprise Fellow.

2. Visit one of the 12 regional competitions and observe SIFE teams as they compete. Competitions are split into two divisions: a two-year division and a four-year division. It is a good idea to bring a few entrepreneurial stu-dents with you to this competition.

3. Select a veteran team at the competition nearest your campus and ask the Walton Fellow whether he or she would adopt your team as part of SIFE's Adopt-a-Rookie program; the veteran team must actively assist and mentor the rookie team. (CSU–Chico adopted five rookie teams in 1995-96; in 1996-97, it adopted nine rookie teams.)

4. Begin recruiting students.

5. Attend the fall Leadership Conference, along with several of your stu-dents. These conferences are held at 20 cities nationwide in September; the interaction with other faculty and shared learning is beneficial to all participants.

## Conclusion

One national network of business faculty interested in service-learning exists through the SIFE organization, and there currently are more than 500 business faculty who share a common goal: to integrate service-learning into undergraduate business curricula to give students a more valuable edu-cation. However, most communication is between individual faculty and the home office in Missouri; communication among faculty is limited. One rea-son for this, undoubtedly, is because many small community colleges and four-year schools are still not on the Internet, or faculty may not yet feel comfortable using email. However, this problem is becoming less of an issue as more educational institutions realize that Internet access is a requirement in today's Information Age.

What is currently lacking is a network that brings these business faculty together to exchange project ideas, to point out pitfalls, to discuss assessment issues, and to suggest ways of disseminating the most successful service-learning projects. Therefore, I have become the list owner of a "listproc mailing list," sometimes referred to as "listserv." This provides interested faculty with a vehicle for two-way interactive communication.

## SIFESERV

The name of the new listserv is SIFESERV, and its objective is to bring business education in touch with service-learning. The goal of SIFESERV is to provide an extensive, world-wide database of information and increase the opportunities for greater interaction via email. To subscribe to SIFESERV, send an email message to:

*listproc@galaxy.csuchico.edu*

with the following message in the body of the email:

subscribe SIFESERV-L yourfirstname yourlastname

Who should subscribe to SIFESERV? Anyone who has an interest in having business students complete service-learning projects that add value to their own business education and benefit the community. This includes faculty, students, business advisers/donors, K-14 teachers and administrators, parents, community leaders, and elected officials. All business students are students in free enterprise, and having them serve their communities by teaching the principles of free enterprise can add greatly to their undergraduate learning experience.

### A New Vehicle

An editorial in *Accounting Horizons* described the management philosophy of Edward de Bono that distinguishes between vertical and lateral thinking (Burton and Sack 1991). Vertical thinkers try to improve the current state of affairs by "making one's hole a better place," while lateral thinkers go outside the existing hole and create a new hole. The authors asserted that "it is vital for the future growth of the profession as well as in the broad interests of society to see a great expansion of lateral thinking in the accounting world" (118). An example was used to illustrate this:

> If customers who took the long coach ride from London to Edinburgh around 1800 were asked how service could be improved, they would likely mention the need for fresh horses, better springs on the coach, and improved inns along the way. Few, if any, would have suggested inserting

*the passengers in a metal tube and flinging them through the air at 500 mph in the direction of Scotland. Indeed, were a coach company to offer such a service, it is unlikely that there would be a long line waiting to board. But innovation plays a key societal role, and if we do not have someone working on new holes, we are not likely to see progress. (1-2)*

Service-learning can become the vehicle by which calls for accounting reform can be heeded. While the vertical thinkers are trying to improve existing stovepipes, lateral thinkers can envision a new mode of education. Arguments should not be centered around the horse of academic content pulling the cart of community service, or vice versa. It is time to leave the horse and cart behind and buckle up in a new space capsule called service-learning. As faculty, we can take a role in designing service-learning projects that are inclusive, entrepreneurial, and flexible. If one believes that students can benefit from such projects, then one should consider strongly integrating service-learning projects into one's courses.

## Notes

1. The McNemar test was used, which is a test of distributions by categories of two related samples. This test is appropriate when the researcher wants to analyze category changes by individuals following some event (Tull and Hawkins 1990).

2. The syllabus is available on request, or by downloading the file from the SIFE team's homepage at *http://www.csuchico.edu/sife*. The homepage also includes a detailed description of many of the SIFE team's other projects, in addition to the middle school project described in this article.

## References

Accounting Education Change Commission. (Fall 1990). "Objectives of Education for Accountants." Position Statement No. 1. *Issues in Accounting Education* 5(2): 307-312.

————. (June 1992). "The First Course in Accounting." Position Statement No. 2.

American Accounting Association, Committee on the Future Structure, Content, and Scope of Accounting Education (The Bedford Committee). (Spring 1986). "Future Accounting Education: Preparing for the Expanded Profession." *Issues in Accounting Education:* 168-195.

Andersen, A., and Arthur Young, Coopers & Lybrand, Deloitte Haskins & Sells, Ernst & Whinney, Peat Marwick Main & Co., Price Waterhouse, and Touche Ross. (April 1989). "Perspectives on Education: Capabilities for Success in the Accounting Profession." White Paper. Chicago, IL.

Astin, A.W. (1993). *What Matters in College? Four Critical Years Revisited.* San Francisco: Jossey-Bass.

Burton, J., and R. Sack. (June 1991). "Time for Some Lateral Thinking." *Accounting Horizons:* 118-122.

Lynton, E. (1993). "New Concepts of Professional Expertise: Liberal Learning as Part of Career-Oriented Education." Working Paper No. 4. Boston: New England Resource Center for Higher Education.

Tull, D.S., and D.I. Hawkins. (1990). *Marketing Research Measurement and Method.* 5th ed. New York: Macmillan.

Wingspread Group on Higher Education. (1993). *An American Imperative: Higher Expectations for Higher Education.* Racine, WI: The Johnson Foundation.

Zlotkowski, E. (January/February 1996a). "Linking Service-Learning and the Academy: A New Voice at the Table?" *Change* 28(1): 20-27.

———— . (January 1996b). "Opportunity for All: Linking Service-Learning and Business Education." *Journal of Business Ethics* (5): 5-19.

# Expanding the Boundaries of Accounting Education Through Service-Learning

by Lynn M. Pringle

## Growing Impetus for Integration of Service-Learning With Accounting Education

Porter and McKibbin (1988) report that business schools need "to concern themselves with the education of the whole student . . . [by exposing students] to a wider range of issues and ideas than is true of the typical business school graduate today" (316). Williams (1993), while chairman of the Accounting Education Change Commission, echoed this notion, stressing that accounting curricula should assist students in becoming "productive and thoughtful citizens through gaining a broad understanding of social, political, and economic forces" (80). It is questionable whether students will achieve such educational breadth if their learning experiences consist of a series of discrete and unrelated courses taught in a passive lecture-discussion format. Accounting education must undergo a paradigm shift whereby the traditional, dominant fact-delivery system is replaced by a rich, value-laden, and interactive process, whereby fact absorption and memorization are replaced with the "boundary-less" education that personal experience can provide. Barr and Tagg (1995) refer to this as a shift from providing instruction to providing learning; more specifically, as a shift from an instruction paradigm to a learning paradigm that "frames learning holistically, recognizing that the chief agent in the process is the learner . . . [i.e., students who] must be active discoverers and constructors of their own knowledge" (21). As Palmer (1987) has argued, we have been teaching students about a world that is divorced from their personal lives instead of inviting students "to intersect their autobiographies with the life story of the world" (22). One possible means by which this intersection can be accomplished is by incorporating service-learning into the accounting curriculum.

Kendall's reference work on service-learning (1990) defines the latter as an educational approach "that emphasize[s] the accomplishment of tasks [that] meet human needs in combination with conscious educational growth. . . . [It] combine[s] needed tasks in the community with intentional learning goals and with conscious reflection and critical analysis" (20). Inherent in this definition is the planning of projects so that they contribute to learning as the service is being performed. In other words, it is important to link technical skills learned in the classroom with community needs. The definition also emphasizes the importance of guided reflection that allows students to question the accuracy of their preconceived notions about marginalized members of society. As Kolenko et al. (1996) note:

> The danger of the experiential learning approach is that behavioral and moral principles will not be drawn out from the practical application: the experience. This becomes doing without learning. It is not enough to just experience, to just do, or to just act. Learning by doing must be performed in combination with critical reflection on experience. (135)

By critically reflecting on their experiences, students develop new ways of thinking about society's disadvantaged.

## The Institutional Framework at Santa Clara University

In their article about the history of Campus Compact and its Project on Integrating Service With Academic Study, Morton and Troppe (1996) outline strategies for institutionalizing service-learning. They note that much of the "actual work focuses on integrating service with the curriculum, because we recognize that the curriculum is the core institutional structure around which most campuses are organized" (25). Bringle and Hatcher (1996) concur, noting that "the work of an office of service-learning must focus on interesting faculty in service-learning and providing them with support to add a service-learning component to a course" (227-228). At Santa Clara University, integration of service-learning projects into the curriculum is facilitated by the Eastside Project, which was founded in 1985. The goals of the Eastside Project, according to its *Handbook of Information* (1995), are threefold:

- *to bring the life experiences of diverse peoples into the consciousness of the University community;*
- *to create situations in which faculty, staff, students, and alumni/ae can interact with the community, especially with the poor and underserved;*
- *to integrate and supplement theory with practice in the University's curriculum so that concern for justice is at the heart of the university's educational effort and not at its periphery. (4)*

In accomplishing these goals, the project assists faculty by placing students in community programs where they spend at least two hours a week in direct, interactive contact with impoverished and marginalized people. Since its inception, the project has grown to the extent that each quarter approximately 400 students, 40 academic courses, and 30 social service agencies are involved.

In addition to providing a student placement program, the Eastside Project invites interested faculty to its annual Summer Faculty Workshop. A week is spent visiting community agencies, writing reflection papers, discussing developmental learning models, listening to students and faculty discuss their Eastside Project experiences, and brainstorming in large and small groups about strategies for implementing experiential education in courses currently being taught by the participants. It was during these brainstorming sessions with College of Arts and Sciences faculty that the idea of integrating service-learning and accounting education ceased to seem in any way incongruous. As a result, during the fall term of the 1993-94 academic year, I became the first faculty member in the School of Business and Administration to incorporate the Eastside Project into the curriculum. My Intermediate Accounting I students were assigned to one of four placements: a center for homeless families, a center providing preschool and after-school care for children whose parents are enrolled in job training or school, a shelter for mentally ill homeless men and women, and a program providing educational services to unemployed teenage mothers. Each student spent at least two hours per week at his or her assigned placement, and was required to keep a journal and to write a reflection paper at the end of the term.

## Kolb's Developmental Learning Model

At Eastside's Summer Faculty Workshop, the experiential learning model of David Kolb (1984) was introduced. In critiquing nine service-learning projects within schools of business, Kolenko et al. (1996) describe Kolb's model as "one of the most widely accepted approaches to understanding action-based individual learning" (135). The model is a four-stage process consisting of concrete experience (e.g., discussing potential topics of a money management workshop with residents at a homeless shelter), reflective observation (e.g., writing in a journal as to how to operationalize the workshop at the specific shelter), abstract conceptualization (e.g., developing a model for the workshop, including goals, content, and time frame), and active experimentation (i.e., conducting the workshop at the shelter, which leads to new concrete experiences as the cycle is repeated).

Svinicki and Dixon (1987), in describing Kolb's model, note "that it may be appropriate to take into account the fundamental differences in the nature of the discipline being taught" (144). For example, Kolb (1976) suggests that business is based in concrete experience (experiencing) and active experimentation (applying). Let's look more closely at the personal money management workshop that my students conducted at the shelter for the homeless mentally ill. During the first week, the students interviewed residents regarding workshop content, drafted a confidentiality agreement, and developed a math pretest to get a feel for the residents' skill levels. Future sessions were devoted to basic remedial math (e.g., fractions and percentages were explained in the context of purchasing merchandise on sale), basic banking skills (e.g., residents were encouraged to open bank accounts so as to avoid sizable check-cashing fees and were taught how to use ATM cards), and personal budget development (e.g., one resident was pleased to learn that he could buy 10 additional packs of cigarettes per month and save $8 if he bought packs by the carton instead of individually). The residents were provided with monthly budget forms to track expenses and were also told how much in wages they could earn before their monthly Supplemental Security Income (SSI) checks would be reduced. The final session wrapped up the workshop and included a math posttest. Improvements in performance prompted one student to reflect that the residents "were not people with mental disabilities, but rather suffered from mental illness."

The money management workshop is similar to community service programs at other institutions and involves coordination of course learning objectives (e.g., an understanding of banking and budgeting) with available service opportunities. As reflected in their journals, however, many students still view themselves as "volunteers." Hirsch (1996) notes that

> There is a distinction to be made between activities that fall under the rubric of good citizenship — philanthropic work, volunteering, committee work on campus and in one's discipline — and those that draw upon the special expertise of a college or university — courses that use service to enhance and deepen theoretical frameworks, or action research that yields practice-based knowledge. (7)

In a similar vein, Tony Scholander, S.J., former experiential learning coordinator for the Eastside Project, states in the *Handbook of Information* (1995) that the student "must wrestle with questions that are not necessarily within the purview of the volunteer. Rigorous analysis and investigation into what causes and supports homelessness . . . and a whole host of other social ills that affect our society are the appropriate domain of the student" (16). Although voluntarism is generous and important, involvement in the Eastside Project is more than community service; it is also an intellectual enterprise.

## Nolan's Developmental Learning Model

The Eastside Project's Summer Faculty Workshop also discusses a second, more important level of service-learning that takes place as students develop personal, one-to-one relationships with men and women who are living at the margins of society. As noted in students' journals and reflection papers and from personal observation, these direct interactions often trigger a chain of events where roles are reversed; i.e., students find that those they have come to "help" have become their guides to a more accurate, deeper, and broader understanding of human experience. This learning process has been studied by Albert Nolan, a white South African Dominican priest who has devoted his life to grass-roots training in the fight against apartheid. As a result of his observations, Nolan framed a four-stage developmental model of growth that takes place within those who work with the poor.

The first stage is characterized by compassion, which leads to relief work and acts of charity. For example, a mother at the center for homeless families told one of my students that she was going to the Salvation Army to get some toys for her children's Christmas presents. My student, being very moved, wrote in her journal that "before, I would only donate clothing but never toys because they had memories. But now whenever I think about Anne and her children, I realize that giving my stuffed animals away is nothing." This personal exposure to Anne triggered a very powerful sense of compassion in my student, but Nolan points out that this is only the first stage and that it is very important to go on, to realize that relief work and charitable giving deal only with the symptoms rather than with the causes of poverty, homelessness, etc.

The next stage of this process begins when students focus on the causes of poverty, homelessness, etc. They discover that these social ills are a direct result of political and economic structures. For example, at the program for unemployed teenage mothers, my students realized the inefficacy of our nation's welfare structure after preparing current (on welfare) and future (postwelfare) budgets with the program participants. One student observed that "a sad reality of the welfare system is that it pays more per month than a minimum wage job. . . . Thus, it is hard to encourage the girls to work when their standard of living will go down by doing so." At this stage of the process, many students get indignant or angry when they see that governmental and economic structures can lead to suffering. For some students, this leads to paralysis; others, however, may be motivated to work for social change by getting involved in politics or civic affairs, by performing research projects in other classes, etc.

The third stage of the learning process can be characterized as "humility"; i.e., students realize that the problems they encounter are too great for them to resolve, that they cannot save the poor and the homeless. So how are the problems of poverty and homelessness going to be resolved? Gradually, some students will discover that they are not really needed, that the poor and the homeless must and will save themselves. In fact, it is the students who learn from the disenfranchised, from their experience, wisdom, and values. One student, reflecting on his experiences at the center for homeless families, noted that "the people there have honestly taught me more than I ever imagined possible. The realities I have been exposed to over the last few weeks have affected my emotions like few things around the university can." This student's thoughts parallel Nolan's, who stated that the poor "know better than I what is needed and they, and only they, can in fact save me. I need something that only they can give me. It is not that I have things that only I can give them" (3). In other words, the poor can teach us that material superfluity is not what makes life meaningful; rather, it is our approach to life and our values that can fill our hearts with peace and serenity.

The final stage of Nolan's model is the solidarity that occurs when we no longer think in terms of *we* and *they*. One student "figured that these families [at the center for homeless families] were there because they had no other place to go and that most of them really didn't want to help themselves and were just using the system. After talking to some of them, [he] realized that they are no different than [he is], except they had no permanent home." Nolan points out that we all have faults and weaknesses; they just differ as a result of our social backgrounds, conditions, and roles. In spite of these differences, all of us are inextricably bound together; all of us have chosen to be on the same side against oppression.

Nolan states that the four stages of his model are not rigid in that you have to go through one stage after another. The third and fourth stages are quite complex, and it may take considerable development to reach them. Students, however, generally attain stages one and two, and stage two (recognizing poverty as a structural problem) provides a rich matrix for class discussions, reflections, and research projects.

## Implementation of a Service-Learning Component in Intermediate Accounting I

I incorporate the service-learning component into Intermediate Accounting rather than into Principles of Accounting for several reasons. Intermediate students, who are juniors, have had another year to mature. Generally, they are more self-confident and less likely to be intimidated when discussing financial matters with an adult at a homeless shelter. Intermediate students are also more comfortable with the technical material, such as bank reconciliations and cash flow analysis. The concepts that they learned in Principles of Accounting are reinforced and strengthened in Intermediate Accounting. Finally, most of the Intermediate Accounting students have declared accounting as their major; therefore, they may be more serious about the discipline than Principles of Accounting students.

Prior to the beginning of an academic term, I meet with the placement coordinator for the Eastside Project, and we discuss which agencies are most suited for linking technical accounting skills with community needs. We target agencies that serve adults who can benefit from a workshop covering banking, budgeting, and other money management skills. The placement coordinator, who acts as liaison between the faculty and the agencies, contacts the targeted agencies to determine whether they are interested in the workshop. I am notified of interested agencies, whereupon I set up a site visit with agency staff to discuss student and agency responsibilities. Most important, a staff person who will provide the opportunity for student interaction with the individuals served must be identified. It is also important that the agency schedule the workshop at a regular time on its weekly calendar of events so as to foster attendance.

When I distribute my Intermediate Accounting I syllabus to approximately 25 students during the first class session, they are somewhat surprised to see a section entitled "Eastside Project Placement." Most of them have heard of the project, and some have participated, but primarily through communication, psychology, religious studies, or education courses. In the syllabus, I refer to a portion of the university's Statement of Purpose and also to two of the university goals based on that statement: namely, to "create a learning environment that integrates rigorous inquiry, creative imagination, reflective engagement with society, and a commitment to fashioning a more humane and just world" and to "promote throughout the University a culture of service that fosters the development of personal responsibility." I emphasize that we will strive toward these goals by participating in the Eastside Project. I also point out to the students that mandatory participation in the project will provide them with an opportunity to apply technical concepts learned in class to practical, real-world settings. It is apparent, however, that many students are questioning the relation between the project and the purpose of an accounting education. I usually say something akin to what Collins (1996) tells his MBA students at the University of Wisconsin–Madison: "Relax, this is just the first day of class, it'll make more sense as the semester evolves. But in a nutshell, for capitalism to be a viable economic system it must reduce poverty, and to reduce poverty businesspeople must meet and serve those who live in poverty" (81). I also allude to Williams's "one right answer" syndrome:

> Many students study accounting because of their misperception that accounting is orderly, structured, and precise and [that] problems are solved as easily on the job as those in the classroom. This misperception is reinforced by traditional accounting curriculums that focus on assigned problems designed to arrive at only one acceptable answer. In the real

*world, however, many situations may have more than one defensible solution. Accountants are constantly called on to apply judgment, address ethical dilemmas, and deal with "messy" or incomplete data. Problems in practice, unlike typical accounting textbook problems, often are unstructured and require making assumptions and estimates. (1993: 78)*

The syllabus also provides a list and brief description of the placement opportunities that students will choose from. Most of the placements require a two-hour weekly commitment of the student's time for eight weeks. In addition, I give the students general instructions regarding a personal journal they will be required to keep for recording their observations and reactions about Eastside placement settings and the people they encounter in those settings: What were your preconceptions? What did you see and do? What did you learn from or about the homeless? The journal can be either handwritten or typed, and is collected twice during the quarter. This encourages students to keep their journals current and provides me with an informal check on participation. Interim readings of the journals also point out problems that the students may be having at the placements. At the end of the quarter, a typed, two-page summary reflection paper is due. These papers are an important link between theory and practice, and allow students to look critically and analytically at problem solving. Ten percent of a student's grade is based on participation in the Eastside Project. Students who have fulfilled their commitment (attendance at the placements is noted when reading the journals) generally receive the full 10 percent.

To reinforce the project, the placement coordinator visits class during the first week to inform students about the program and the types of placements, and to field questions. Common-sense items are discussed; e.g., students should go to the homeless shelters in groups as a safety precaution and should not dress in an upscale or preppy manner. In addition, I ask several accounting seniors who have previously participated in the project to address the class. They are very effective in ameliorating the junior students' fears that they do not know enough to assist adults in financial matters. (It's not that students can't balance their own checkbooks or prepare a monthly budget; many of them just don't bother.) Finally, I read a few excerpts from student journals that extol their service-learning experiences. By this time, any lingering resistance to the project has largely abated. And because there is an overload of material in Intermediate Accounting, I assure the students that very little class time will be spent on the service-learning component in the forthcoming weeks.

For each of the four placements, I accompany the students on their first visit to reduce their anxieties about entering unfamiliar surroundings. During this visit, the agency provides an orientation, which includes a tour of the facility and an introduction to the staff. Time permitting, we meet with the residents of the shelters to discuss the money management workshop. After introducing ourselves, we ask the residents what topics they would like to cover. It is very important to make them a part of the process, to get them to open up as to what their needs are. Based on this feedback, the students plan the structure of the workshop. Because personal financial matters are being discussed, I ask the students to draft a confidentiality agreement that is signed by the director of the agency, the student, and the resident. Surprisingly, the residents have been extremely open and forthcoming with financial documents such as bank statements, Supplemental Security Income check stubs, etc. There has not appeared to be any trust problem whatsoever.

Collins (1996), in discussing his society/business ethics class projects at the University of Wisconsin–Madison, notes that he himself did not visit any homeless shelters due to lack of time and because he had prior experience working with low-income people. He realized that this was a mistake after some students had unpleasant experiences, whereupon he visited certain shelters "to experience what my students were experiencing" (82). I agree that this is important and attempt to visit each placement at least twice during the quarter. My students (as well as agency staff) see that I have a vested interest in the success of the project, that it is not just another assignment. As Kenworthy (1996) observes: "If the faculty member is not committed . . . , the students and agencies with whom we work will not be supported to the fullest extent possible, defeating our overall purpose as educators" (131). Visitations also provide an opportunity to obtain direct feedback from students and agency staff as to what is and what is not working. Problems that are addressed early in the term will make the project more successful. Finally, observation of students at the placements aids me in grading the subjective Eastside Project component of the student's final course grade.

## Project Outcomes

Hogner (1996), in discussing the most significant outcome of the service-learning projects at Florida International University, notes that "many students do, indeed, get 'it,' i.e., that the service activity has its greatest impact on students and not on the community" (41). This notion echoes the third stage of Nolan's developmental learning model, referred to earlier as "humility"; i.e., the level of development where students realize that it is the poor who are their teachers. It is the impoverished and marginalized who suffer from our social, political, and economic structures who are best able to educate our students as to the demands that must be met for justice to be realized in our world.

In addition to increasing students' awareness and sensitization to issues of social justice and inequity, service-learning helps to answer the clarion call by educational reformers in the accounting arena. Williams (1993), former chairman of the Accounting Education Change Commission and a past president of the American Accounting Association, in arguing for more general rather than technical education, states that:

> Because future accountants must develop the capacity for inquiry, abstract logical thinking, and critical analysis, the new curriculums should develop students' speaking and listening skills, historical consciousness, international and multicultural knowledge, appreciation of science, and the study of values and their role in decision making, including the ability to resolve ethical dilemmas. (77)

Wyer (1993), a director in the national office of Coopers & Lybrand, also writes about a changing accounting education agenda that is "providing more active learning experiences, improving communications and teamwork skills, and exercising a broader range of cognitive abilities" (14).

Students, by participating in the money management workshop, improved many of these skills. Preparing budgets with the homeless required critical analysis of their financial straits and engendered logical thinking. For example, my students, in developing budget forms, showed the difference between income and expenses as "savings," not the traditional "net income." Although this is perhaps a subtle difference, my students recognized that "savings" and "net income" connote different meanings to the homeless. "Income" implies extra spending money, whereas "savings" implies hope — what is needed to get off the streets.

The money management workshop also improved speaking and listening skills as the students developed personal, one-to-one relationships with the residents. Writing skills were enhanced by the journal and reflection paper requirement. Structuring the general workshop sessions built teamwork skills. Multicultural sensitivity was fostered as students stepped beyond their confined campus life into a world not limited by race, culture, or class origin. (Students were shocked to meet a Stanford MBA at the homeless shelter. They were equally shocked when homeless people at the shelter assumed they too were homeless — an experience that must have affected their thinking about diversity. Perhaps this experience helped them to approach Nolan's fourth stage of learning, i.e., the solidarity that begins when we no longer think in terms of "we" and "they.")

Students also exercised "a broader range of cognitive abilities" (borrowing from the above quotation from Wyer). They became aware of multiple perspectives and developed their ability to think relativistically rather than dualistically. Hursh and Borzak (1979) refer to this cognitive shifting across two or more perspectives as "decentering" (70). Students abandon black/white ways of thinking and become aware that reality is complex and multifaceted. Consider the following journal excerpt by one student, who noted that welfare mothers

> . . . *exist in somewhat of a "catch-22" situation. Now the government provides them with a modest income, medical care, child-care needs, meals, transportation, and more. They are being strongly encouraged, if not pushed, into providing for themselves. This, however, requires a great commitment from them. Once they obtain gainful employment, they will no longer receive the "perks" mentioned above. This forces them to strive for a job [that] gives them a high salary so that their life-style can continue and they can provide for their children. This, however, is difficult for them to attain, since they have such limited education.*

This student had clearly developed an awareness of the complexity of our nation's welfare system, a multifarious problem that continues to be hotly debated. "To the extent that [this student and others] learned to manage the multiple perspectives in problem-solving efforts, i.e., to decenter, they learned an important skill [that] traditional, unidisciplinary classrooms seldom convey" (Hursh and Borzak 1979: 74).

Wyer (1993) also writes about providing more *active* learning experiences in accounting education. As developers and presenters of the money management workshop, students learned to take initiative and to be productive, to be authoritative and in control, and to be more autonomous and independent; i.e., they became more *active* rather than passive, receptive, and submissive to authority. As Barr and Tagg (1995) would express it, they became "active discoverers and constructors of their own knowledge" (21).

Not only did my students benefit in many ways from their Eastside Project experiences; marginalized and disenfranchised members of the community benefited as well. They found in my students friends, fellow human beings who took an interest in them, who cared about them. On a more specific level, many learned to open bank accounts, into which Supplemental Security Income (SSI) checks were deposited directly. Prior to having their own accounts, shelter residents would cash their checks at a check-cashing service, grocery store, or liquor store that took a percentage of their benefits. The students also taught residents how to use ATM cards and how to track expenses on their budget forms. The students explained to them that they could earn a certain level of wages without having their SSI benefits reduced. As a result, several homeless residents got janitorial jobs at the nearby San Jose Arena. Did the Eastside Project save any of the poor? No. To paraphrase Nolan, only the poor can save themselves. But perhaps the project and the efforts of my students, in some small measure, encouraged and empowered them in their long personal struggle to overcome oppression.

Finally, the university, business college, and accounting department benefited from favorable publicity about the Eastside Project. My Intermediate Accounting I class was described in a *San Francisco Chronicle* article entitled "The Coolest College Classes in Town." Articles about this class also appeared in the campus newspaper and in a newsletter sent to accounting alumni. I have, in addition, generated positive public relations by making presentations about the project at regional and national accounting conferences and by speaking at a campus forum on community-based learning and at the Eastside Project's Summer Faculty Workshop. Lastly, a linkage between the business school and the College of Arts and Sciences has been established; specifically, Spanish students have interpreted at workshops that primarily serve the Hispanic community.

## Obstacles and Constraints

Collins (1996) has grouped obstacles to service-learning as follows: student complaints, grading, professorial time commitments, organizing student/ resident interactions, low workshop turnouts, and legal liabilities. In addition to these categories, there exist broad barriers such as lack of institutional support, lack of a campus culture that rewards service-learning pioneers in promotion and tenure decisions, turnover of agency staff that leads to reinventing the wheel, etc. I am going to take a narrower focus and discuss the major obstacles that my Intermediate Accounting I students encountered.

Workshop turnout was not a problem as much as was consistency of resident participation from week to week. At one of the homeless shelters, a staff person would announce over the loudspeaker system that the money management workshop was about to begin and all those in the building must proceed to the lab room and sign in. Agency staff even went door to door and herded the residents to the lab. Residents could avoid the workshop simply by being out of the building. Attendance, however, was not a problem. The problem was the new faces encountered each week. My students adapted by replacing their structured workshop format (e.g., basic banking skills in weeks two and three and personal budget development in weeks three and four) with a format focusing almost entirely on the development of one-on-one relationships. Although consistency then became less of a problem, students reflected disappointment, frustration, discouragement, and even hurt in their journals when the person they were working with (learning from) did not show up. This often happened on the first of each month after benefit checks were received.

Perhaps the greatest obstacle that my students (and I myself) encountered was lack of involvement and support by agency staff. This led to a lack of communication that occasionally resulted in a duplication of effort. At the program for unemployed teenage mothers working to complete their GED, the women complained to my students that they had already prepared budgets. Once again, my students adapted by having the program participants prepare projected or postwelfare budgets, which were compared with their "on-welfare" budgets. The women soon grasped the concept of opportunity cost, that having your nails done meant buying fewer diapers.

Problems such as those at the homeless shelter and at the teen parent program are always going to exist. If nothing else, they help students become more flexible and adaptable learners. However, attempts should be made to ameliorate these problems. The Bentley Service-Learning Project (Kenworthy 1996) uses a student and agency contract that defines project content and duration. Bentley also has in excess of 20 service-learning community scholarship students who serve as site coordinators and liaisons for all projects. Kenworthy notes that these measures have helped communication enormously. Not all colleges and universities have these resources; however, a student/agency contract is rather costless, and a student at each placement could be asked to volunteer as site coordinator and liaison. Since incorporating service-learning into my classes, I've realized that we do not ask enough of our students. This is evidenced by students' asking me whether they can continue the project after the end of the quarter. Perhaps an even greater testament to the success of the project is that I've had students from another instructor's Intermediate Accounting sections ask whether they could participate. Finding a student to act as a site coordinator and liaison at each project placement should not be a difficult proposition.

## Conclusion

Kolb (1984) argues that "learning is the process whereby knowledge is created through the transformation of experience" (38). Service-learning projects provide experience: They open new pathways to knowledge as students expand the walls of the classroom and make connections with a wider range of people, places, and problems. Students are able to confront their negative stereotypes and develop a sense of citizenship and social responsibility. As Kolenko et al. (1996) state, "Outside of the 'safe' zone in traditional business school programs, the student is called upon to construct new concepts of reality and make adjustments to ineffective personal concepts and models of the past. It is here where the real potential for personal learning arises" (135). In a similar vein, Zlotkowski (1996) notes that "for many traditional students, the opportunity to work in a truly diverse environment, to risk stepping outside their psychological comfort zones, may represent the single best chance they have to learn to appreciate — and value — cultural differences" (9-10).

Citizenship is a goal traditionally associated with a liberal education. To once again quote Zlotkowski:

*Unless business students are given in the course of their regular assignments an opportunity to internalize not just arguments but also faces and places, personal stories, and encounters that elicit "a sense of moral obligation and personal responsibility . . . , " it is unlikely that they will bring to the rarefied air of corporate America an ethical impulse capable of asserting itself. (1996: 11)*

In sum, I encourage my accounting colleagues to consider service-learning in their accounting curriculum. By linking theory with service-learning projects, students gain a more personal understanding of the material presented in class and hone critical-thinking, communication, teamwork, problem-solving, and a host of other skills. And just as many of our liberal arts colleagues have done, we can broaden our academic endeavors in an effort to redeem and liberate the human community from suffering and oppression. As William J. Wood, S.J., former director of the Eastside Project, has stated, we "must do this precisely *as a university,* not as a social service agency, not as a church, and not as a political party, but as an institution of higher education, dedicated to excellence in teaching and research."

## References

Barr, Robert B., and John Tagg. (November/December 1995). "From Teaching to Learning: A New Paradigm for Undergraduate Education." *Change* 27(6): 12-25.

Bringle, Robert G., and Julie A. Hatcher. (March/April 1996). "Implementing Service Learning in Higher Education." *Journal of Higher Education* 67(2): 221-239.

Collins, Denis. (1996). "Serving the Homeless and Low-Income Communities Through Business & Society/Business Ethics Class Projects: The University of Wisconsin–Madison Plan." *Journal of Business Ethics* 15(1): 67-85.

Eastside Project. (November 14, 1995). *Handbook of Information.* Rev. ed. Santa Clara, CA: Santa Clara University.

Hirsch, Deborah. (May 1996). "An Agenda for Involving Faculty in Service." *AAHE Bulletin* 48(9): 7-9.

Hogner, Robert H. (1996). "Speaking in Poetry: Community Service–Based Business Education." *Journal of Business Ethics* 15(1): 33-43.

Hursh, Barbara A., and Lenore Borzak. (1979). "Toward Cognitive Development Through Field Studies." *Journal of Higher Education* 50(1): 63-78.

Kendall, Jane C. (1990). "Combining Service and Learning: An Introduction." In *Combining Service and Learning: A Resource Book for Community and Public Service*, edited by Jane C. Kendall and Associates, pp. 1-33. Raleigh, NC: National Society for Internships and Experiential Education.

Kenworthy, Amy L. (1996). "Linking Business Education, Campus Culture, and Community: The Bentley Service-Learning Project." *Journal of Business Ethics* 15(1): 121-131.

Kolb, David. (1976). "Management and Learning Processes." *California Management Review* 18(3): 21-31.

———. (1984). *Experiential Learning: Experience as the Source of Learning and Development.* Englewood Cliffs, NJ: Prentice-Hall.

Kolenko, Thomas A., Gayle Porter, Walt Wheatley, and Marvelle Colby. (1996). "A Critique of Service Learning Projects in Management Education: Pedagogical Foundations, Barriers, and Guidelines." *Journal of Business Ethics* 15(1): 133-142.

Morton, Keith, and Marie Troppe. (1996). "From the Margin to the Mainstream: Campus Compact's Project on Integrating Service With Academic Study." *Journal of Business Ethics* 15(1): 21-32.

Nolan, Albert. (June 29, 1984). "Spiritual Growth and the Option for the Poor." Presentation at the Annual General Meeting of the Catholic Institute for International Relations, London, England.

Palmer, Parker J. (September/October 1987). "Community, Conflict, and Ways of Knowing." *Change* 19(5): 20-25.

Porter, Lyman W., and Lawrence E. McKibbin. (1988). *Management Education and Development: Drift or Thrust Into the 21st Century?* New York: McGraw-Hill.

Svinicki, Marilla D., and Nancy M. Dixon. (Fall 1987). "The Kolb Model Modified for Classroom Activities." *College Teaching* 35(4): 141-146.

Williams, Doyle Z. (August 1993). "Reforming Accounting Education." *Journal of Accountancy:* 76-82.

Wyer, Jean C. (January/February 1993). "Change Where You Might Least Expect It: Accounting Education." *Change* 25(1): 12-17.

Zlotkowski, Edward. (January 1996). "Opportunity for All: Linking Service-Learning and Business Education." *Journal of Business Ethics* 15(1): 5-19.

# Service-Learning in Accounting:
# A Role for VITA Tax Programs

by Janice Carr

The changes occurring in accounting education frequently focus on developing and improving instructional methods. Active learning methodologies are supplementing and replacing the traditional lecture mode of learning. The Accounting Education Change Commission (AECC) addressed this issue in its Position Statement No. 1:

> The overriding objective of accounting programs should be to teach students to learn on their own. . . .
>
> Students must be active participants in the learning process, not passive recipients of information. They should identify and solve unstructured problems that require use of multiple information sources. Learning by doing should be emphasized. Working in groups should be encouraged. . . .
>
> Instructional methods and materials need to change as the environment changes. . . .
>
> Teaching methods that expand and reinforce basic communication, intellectual, and interpersonal skills should be used. (1990: 3-4)

Many new and innovative teaching methodologies have been developed as a result of the AECC's work, yet most accomplish only one or two of its recommendations. One program that is successful in incorporating nearly all of the AECC's recommendations is the Internal Revenue Service's Volunteer Income Tax Assistance (VITA) program. VITA has the added advantages of employing the concept of service-learning, simulating a real-world accounting job, and being easy to implement because it is an established program.

VITA is an effective teaching methodology because it utilizes two learning techniques that effect the highest retention of knowledge: learning by doing (as recommended by the AECC) and teaching others (National Training Laboratory, cited in Forgeng 1995: 2). Students "learn by doing" tax returns for eligible members of the community. At the same time, students learn by teaching these taxpayers to prepare their own tax returns, which is one of the IRS's objectives for VITA.

## Program Description: One Approach

The VITA program is offered as a stand-alone course at California Polytechnic State University, San Luis Obispo, where students must complete a senior project requirement during their senior year. The university encourages faculty to identify projects that provide a "hands-on, learn-by-doing" experience. Accounting students are allowed to choose the VITA tax program to fulfill this requirement. Since an introductory tax course is required of all accounting majors, students enrolling in the VITA course have completed the only prerequisite of our program.

Cal Poly's VITA program is a two–quarter unit course and is obviously offered only during the winter quarter. The students are required to attend a three-hour class once per week during January to learn tax law changes that have occurred since their introductory tax course, tax issues unique to our community, how the program operates, and the specific requirements for successfully completing the course. During February and March, they are in the community preparing tax returns. The program ends the last week of the quarter (see Exhibit 1).

Each student is required to work at one of two community site locations for four hours per week. Students are further required to perform a minimum of eight hours of marketing activities throughout the quarter, since the program's marketing campaign is organized and conducted entirely by the students.

A tax faculty member is responsible for several administrative functions during the quarter. These include interacting with the IRS and the state tax agency, filing various initial documents and ordering tax forms, coordinating the training classes in January, arranging for local volunteer reviewers, and evaluating the students. Although the faculty member may work at a community site as a reviewer, he/she never interacts with the taxpayers: Students are completely responsible for this interaction.

One aspect of using VITA as a service-learning course that is more difficult than in the traditional classroom environment is assessing students' performance and level of learning. Students in the Cal Poly VITA program receive a letter grade for the course. They are required to satisfactorily complete take-home federal and state tax return exams. This portion of the evaluation is fairly objective. The evaluation of the remainder of the VITA activities is more subjective. This includes the quality of their work at the community sites, their attitudes throughout the quarter, and two written assignments (a journal and a reflection paper) due at the end of the program. It is important, therefore, to establish specific standards and guidelines at the beginning of the program that will be used in the evaluation process during the tax return preparation and marketing activities (see the Course Outline at the end of this chapter). At this time, the taxpayers and reviewers are not part of our program's evaluation process, although such input could be incorporated.

**Exhibit 1**

**VITA Activities Time Line**

| Jan | Start of Program | Training Session ▼ ▼ ▼ ▼ ▼ ▼ | Marketing Campaign ▼ ▼ |
| Feb | | Tax Return Assistance ▼ ▼ ▼ ▼ ▼ | ▼ ▼ ▼ ▼ ▼ ▼ |
| Mar or Apr* | End of Program | | |

---

* The program can end in March for quarter system schools or April for semester system schools. The remainder of a semester can be used for discussion of the learning that occurred or for surveying the community for feedback on quality of service, adequate knowledge of program, etc.

There are many university-run VITA programs in existence throughout the United States, each with a unique set of characteristics. Cal Poly's program is only one approach. Different approaches to service-learning using VITA are presented in other chapters in this volume.

## Learning Opportunities With VITA: An Overview

The outstanding educational value of including VITA in accounting programs is that it provides learning opportunities far beyond improving tax knowledge. Students learn skills that are essential for any career in accounting. All accounting students benefit, even those who are not specifically interested in a career in taxation. Students who have participated in this program repeatedly identify three major benefits gained from the experience: (1) how much they have learned by applying their knowledge to real-world situations, (2) increased self-confidence, and (3) the reward of using the knowledge acquired in their coursework to help people in the community (see Exhibit 2).

This form of learning is successful because it operates in a realistic and meaningful environment. VITA offers what no traditional classroom environment can — working with real-life customers who need the students' skills and knowledge, and need them now, not sometime in the future. Using real-world experiences is not unique to service-learning courses. Internships provide many of the same learning benefits but, unfortunately, are usually available only to the top students. Service-learning courses, including VITA, have the capability of serving a large number of accounting students, especially those who need this type of experience the most.[1]

VITA also forces each student to take responsibility for his/her own learning. There is little or no lecturing by faculty to convey the information needed to complete the assignment. Instead, each taxpayer brings a new set of facts, issues, and unstructured problems, which the student must sort through and identify. If the student lacks sufficient knowledge to solve a problem, he or she must search for a solution on his/her own. Although the student may ultimately ask the faculty supervisor or volunteer professional reviewer for help,[2] the student is the one solving the problem.

The skills and competencies that can be learned or enhanced through VITA include the following: (1) *technical skills,* which involve reviewing and improving basic tax knowledge, learning new tax concepts, and developing issue-identification, research, and problem-solving skills; (2) *communication skills,* which involve speaking, writing, and listening skills; (3) *interpersonal skills,* which involve group and leadership skills; and (4) *personal capacities,* which involve self-confidence, ethical awareness, and community service awareness. Although recognized as part of the general business knowledge

# Exhibit 2

## Student Reflections on Learning in VITA*

Technical Skills:

"The best thing I learned was to look up all my questions and do my best job before taking it to the reviewer."

"VITA helps with your ability to apply technical skills under pressure."

"I feel almost as if I am a teacher, sharing what I know."

"The intensity was far beyond working on any vigorous textbook problem. Textbooks usually provide all the relevant information to solve the problem, followed by a definite solution. Since a solution manual was not available, I learned how and where to find answers."

Communication Skills:

"In my last job (a 'Big 6's internship), I had trouble communicating with the client. VITA was different, I realized the people were in need of my help."

"We fished for the necessary information from people [who] may have no idea as to why we wanted to know some very personal information."

"Learning and incorporating interviewing skills such as verbal communication, nonverbal communication, and symbolic communication made my job easier."

"A definite lesson learned was that verbal communication and social skills are invaluable in the service industry."

Interpersonal Skills:

"I got a glimpse of what it is like to interact with a client, as opposed to solving problems on an exam."

"This project is one that proves the need for a change in education to close the gap between simply understanding accounting information and understanding the importance of human interaction skills needed to be flexible in varying situations."

"Partners need to compliment each other -- work together to portray an image of competence."

"Being a coordinator, I learned how to take charge in the correct manner -- I mean in a way to get people to help you."

Personal Capacities:

"I built up my own self-confidence throughout all of these processes as it forced me to take a more active role, rather than the passive one that I sometimes take in the classroom setting."

"I feel lucky to have participated in such a worthwhile and successful program and maybe someday I can help with the VITA program again."

"Though the U.S. is known as a 'melting pot,' the VITA experience highlights the fact that this is not the case. Many of our clients did not speak English, and they were not crippled by the fact that they don't share the exact same culture that I do."

"The notion of community, and what it means to help for the sake of bettering it, was a lesson I learned."

"In Introductory Tax, many are satisfied with a C or a B; but in VITA, I felt obligated to produce A-quality work. Because of this course, my self-esteem and drive to do better in all of my other courses [have] improved tremendously."

"First and foremost, the skill I learned from VITA was confidence."

---

* Excerpted from reflection papers submitted by students participating in our VITA program. Their reflection papers are based on the students' learning experiences and must be submitted at the end of the program.

needed by accounting students, *marketing skills* are not usually identified as one of the essential accounting competencies. Marketing skills are, however, necessary for a successful career in accounting and can be easily included in a VITA course.

# Specific Learning Opportunities in VITA

## Technical Skills

**Improving basic tax knowledge.** Accounting students participating in VITA are required to have completed an introductory tax course covering basic federal income tax regulations. Some students have also completed one or two advanced tax courses. As a result of this background knowledge, the training normally required by the IRS can be reduced. In lieu of covering basic tax laws, special topics unique to the needs of the community can be introduced or reviewed at the beginning of the semester or quarter before work in the community begins (see Exhibit 1).

Although some of the technical learning occurs during the training period, the real reinforcement and expansion of tax knowledge take place while working with the taxpayers. Every tax return involves another opportunity for technical practice and growth. Even the most basic tax returns include exceptions to the tax laws the students learned in their tax courses.

**Learning new tax material.** Students also have many opportunities to increase their tax knowledge. Many introductory tax courses do not have sufficient time to cover state income tax law. Since the IRS coordinates VITA in conjunction with state tax agencies, basic tax law for the state in question is covered in the training session. Students are then ready to prepare state tax returns for the taxpayers as well. Frequently, state tax laws of other states are also learned, because many taxpayers have moved from another state or were students with summer jobs in another state. These situations require VITA students to learn about the issues of double taxation and state tax credits, identifying when income is taxed by states, and allocating income and deductions between states. These experiences allow students to gain knowledge in an important area of tax law that they would otherwise not see before working in practice.

Another area where students can increase their tax competencies is in international taxation — an area that will also increase their global awareness. Although the VITA program is limited to assisting with basic tax law, many programs operate in communities where there are foreign taxpayers who qualify for assistance (e.g., low-income foreign students, and resident and nonresident alien community members). These people are frequently required to file federal and state income tax returns. VITA exposes accounting students to some basic foreign tax issues, such as foreign tax credits, U.S.

taxation of foreign income, the interaction of U.S. and foreign regulation, and the impact of tax treaty rules. Even this basic coverage demonstrates to students how international issues affect all aspects of the U.S. economy — even low-income taxpayers.

**Issue-identification, research, and problem-solving skills.** A significant aspect of learning and improving technical skills involves identifying issues, searching for authoritative guidance, and using that guidance to solve problems. These skills are often difficult for students to acquire and practice in a traditional classroom environment. Textbook problems are rarely broad enough to effectively develop issue-identification skills, because they cover only one or two issues. Also, textbook problems are grouped by topic coverage, with all the information systematically provided for students (see Exhibit 2). In VITA, students learn to spot issues from information provided by the taxpayer, usually in an unstructured and often incomplete manner. At first, students identify only the simple issues, while professional reviewers help them detect the more complex problems. After repeated interaction with various taxpayers, however, students begin to identify the complex issues themselves. If students are working in pairs, they often learn from their partner how to spot issues and how to determine the best approach for solving problems.

Once issues have been identified, the student is then required to research the issue using the various tax materials available at each VITA site. This provides excellent practice in learning to search primary references. In traditional classroom learning, students refer almost exclusively to their textbooks for solutions. Students learn in VITA that researching in a real-world environment requires the use of more extensive and authoritative materials than textbooks (see Exhibit 2).

Another realistic factor pertaining to issue-identification, research, and problem-solving skills is the element of time pressure. The taxpayer is sitting in front of the student throughout the tax return preparation process. The students are very conscious of the need to identify the issues, conduct necessary research, and solve the problem in a short period of time, while ensuring accurate and quality work.

## Communication Skills

**Speaking, listening, and interviewing skills.** VITA simulates a workplace environment where employees communicate with individuals on different levels. Students continually practice and refine their speaking skills by explaining issues to the taxpayers, the professional volunteer reviewers, and other VITA students. Students in our program have mentioned the initial difficulty they have in finding an appropriate approach to take with each taxpayer. They gradually learn from each experience and make changes with the next client. When they go to a reviewer with questions or to review a completed tax return, the students are required to shift to a different level of vocabulary, tone, and expertise. Constantly communicating at various levels is difficult to reproduce in a classroom environment and is one of the greatest benefits of VITA identified by students.

Coupled with speaking skills is the often overlooked skill of listening. Working with taxpayers, students learn to pay attention and listen carefully to what the client is saying (and, sometimes, not saying). It takes only one time for students to have to ask a taxpayer to repeat an important fact they missed or heard incorrectly for them to quickly realize the importance of listening.

Interviewing (or questioning) is another special skill needed by all accountants. Knowing what questions to ask and how to ask them is essential in every facet of the profession, not just in the field of taxation. In VITA, students learn *what* questions to ask after identifying and researching the issues. *How* to ask is something they learn through trial and error and by observing techniques used by other students and the professional reviewers.

In our program, bilingual students are identified for assisting non-English-speaking taxpayers. This improves these students' language skills and gives them a sense of pride in providing a unique and valuable service. It also demonstrates to students with no foreign language skills how important such skills are in our diverse society.

**Writing skills.** Our VITA program provides two opportunities for students to practice writing skills. The first requires them to keep a daily journal of their experiences. This is collected at the end of the program, and, surprisingly, most students actually write something after each work session. This exercise forces them to think about the day's activities and to express their thoughts in written form.

The second assignment is a two-page reflection paper that also is collected at the end of the program. This assignment requires students to contemplate everything they learned from the VITA program. In making this assignment, we stress the importance of focusing on overall knowledge gained rather than simply tax knowledge. This paper is part of their overall evaluation and is graded for writing ability as well as content. Although the assignment is modest, it does require students to organize and clearly communicate their thoughts in a concise manner. It also allows them an opportunity to do a self-assessment of the skills they developed throughout the program.

A weakness with the submission date of our written assignments is that it prohibits useful feedback to help students improve their writing skills. An alternative arrangement would require students to submit a draft of their reflections for evaluation midway through the program. A revised paper would then be due at the end of the program. This would give students an opportunity to improve their writing skills.

## Interpersonal Skills

**Group work.** As with communication skills, students are constantly practicing their interpersonal skills in the VITA program. At the beginning of the program, they work in groups to coordinate and conduct the marketing activities and to help with various administrative tasks. If the program is designed to have students work with a partner to prepare tax returns, they learn how to adapt to another individual's work habits. And because the students are working with taxpayers at the same time, they have to learn to adapt quickly. This is another area students often refer to in their reflection papers: learning to adjust to sometimes difficult partners and to work out conflicts without the taxpayer's being aware of the situation (see Exhibit 2).

Students can be assigned different partners each time they work, which enables them to learn to adapt to a variety of personalities. An alternative approach is to have students remain with the same partner throughout the program. This allows students to develop team skills in a "long-term" professional relationship. This alternative makes it easier to match students with greater technical ability with students who need closer supervision. Either approach creates a real-world situation and provides a valuable learning experience.

**Client interaction.** During the program, students are continually working with clients, either preparing tax returns or rotating as a greeter who performs a cursory interview to ascertain whether the client is eligible for VITA. Students learn that providing quality service to a client requires a good attitude, understanding, and, often, assertiveness. In some cases, it also involves delivering unpleasant news to the taxpayer.

In most VITA programs, students are able to interact with culturally and intellectually diverse people. This broadens students' perspectives and allows them to accept and appreciate differences in others. Working with ever-changing clients further enables students to practice and improve such interpersonal skills as patience, empathy, and sensitivity.

**Working with supervisors.** Students work closely with the professional reviewers throughout the program. Discussing issues and responding to reviewers' questions creates a real-world supervisor-staff relationship. Since there are different professional reviewers each week, students learn to constantly adapt to new supervisory techniques. Students comment on how much they learn from the exposure to a variety of reviewers. They also find that working with these professionals is less intimidating than they initially expected, allowing them to develop greater confidence interacting with supervisors.

**Supervising others/leadership skills.** Another kind of interpersonal skill enhanced through VITA is the ability to supervise others. Students function as marketing group coordinators who supervise the group's activities and who have the responsibility of motivating group members to complete their tasks. These coordinators also evaluate and report on each group member's performance.

Additionally, each VITA session has two student supervisors who are responsible for the day's activities. These students arrive at the session early to prepare the site, oversee the other students, monitor student greeters, ascertain that taxpayers are being properly assisted, and handle closing the site for the day. These activities force students to develop a sense of responsibility while also practicing their leadership skills.

## Personal Capacities

Some of the learning opportunities available with a VITA program are not necessarily skills, but involve personal values and self-image. It is rewarding to watch students develop and mature personally and professionally during the program.

**Self-confidence.** One of the personal benefits for students is the positive effect the experience has on their self-confidence. They are often surprised to learn that their skills are valued by the community and that they really do have the knowledge and ability to assist others with complex problems. Although confidence is not a skill, it is certainly an important quality that prospective employers look for when hiring. VITA provides students with the real-life experiences that are usually necessary for building self-confidence. A frequent comment in students' reflection papers is how the program has increased their confidence in their abilities (see Exhibit 2).

**Ethical awareness.** VITA promotes an awareness of ethical issues. Students are reminded during the training session that because the tax returns are not to be signed by the student preparers, the IRS prohibits them from accepting any form of compensation from taxpayers. During training, students listen to this restriction but do not actually relate to it until they experience a situation themselves. They are surprised when a taxpayer attempts to give them money or some other token of appreciation. Students are aware that accepting anything is prohibited, and either take the item to the faculty supervisor if the taxpayer will not take it back or convince the taxpayer that the offering is appreciated but cannot be accepted. Although the item or amount is usually small, students are aware of the conflict between saying no to the taxpayer and violating their signed agreement not to accept compensation.

Ethical awareness is also developed when students realize they cannot ignore facts simply at the taxpayer's request. The students are continually reminded that if the taxpayer's information lacks economic reality, it is the student's job to ask the sometimes difficult questions needed to correct the situation. They are also frequently reminded that an accurate tax return is their responsibility, not the reviewers'. Students learn to identify situations when a taxpayer must be informed that his/her tax return cannot be prepared by the student due to questionable circumstances.

**Community service.** Service-learning courses, such as VITA, offer students the opportunity to grow personally through an awareness of social responsibility and the importance of giving back to society. Students develop a better understanding of how other segments of society live and the challenges these individuals face. This is also a segment of society students will not often encounter in their professional careers. Through the experience of VITA, students realize that accounting services are needed at all levels of society. As a result, many students plan to volunteer for VITA as reviewers in the future, after they are certified (see Exhibit 2).

### Marketing Skills

Although VITA is a course for accounting students, marketing skills and client development play a major role in an accountant's career. Whether the student enters public or private accounting, he/she will need to know how to successfully market his/her services.

As indicated earlier, all students in our program are required to participate in coordinating and conducting the marketing campaign (see Exhibit 1). Students work in groups designing flyers and posters, and go into the community to reach individuals who may need the program's services. These activities continue throughout the program to ensure there will be enough work for the students. Students are informed of the potential consequences of not adequately marketing the services offered by VITA. Some students initially find it difficult to "sell" their services to others. However, most of these students eventually learn to develop the techniques and demeanor necessary to perform these activities successfully.

## Summary

VITA is one of the few courses that offer so many different learning opportunities to accounting students. Nearly all of the skills listed in the AECC's composite profile of capabilities needed by accounting graduates are developed or enhanced through VITA (AECC 1990). Students really do learn to learn in VITA. Yet they are not consciously aware of the learning taking place until they finish the program and reflect on the overall experience. Many students say it was the most useful and meaningful course in their college career.

Given VITA's enormous potential for facilitating learning, every accounting program should consider implementing such a service-learning course in its curriculum. Once such a course is operating, additional possibilities can be developed for enhancing and improving learning (see Exhibit 3).

## Notes

1. Some university-run VITA programs require a minimum grade in the introductory tax course for students to participate. There are several reasons for this requirement. One is to keep the number of students at a manageable size. Another reason is to reduce the risk to taxpayers. Our program has successfully handled more than 100 students each tax season with one faculty supervisor and one student assistant. Risk can be minimized by pairing students who performed below average in their tax course with better students. This arrangement provides learning opportunities for both students. The issue of risk is also addressed through the quality control review by volunteer CPAs and enrolled agents required by the IRS.

2. An IRS requirement for VITA is that all returns prepared by volunteers are subject to a quality control review by local volunteer IRS agents, CPAs, or enrolled agents. Our program solicits the help of two or three professional volunteers for each day of VITA tax preparation.

## References

Accounting Education Change Commission. (September 1990). "Objectives of Education for Accountants." Position Statement No. 1. *Issues in Accounting Education* 5(2): 307-312.

Forgeng, Maureen. (Fall 1995). "Service Scholars: Exploring Service-Learning as a Teaching Methodology at Cal Poly." In *Student Life and Activities*. San Luis Obispo, CA: California Polytechnic State University.

**Exhibit 3**

## Program Design Ideas to
## Increase Learning Opportunities

1. Have students work in groups to coordinate and conduct marketing tasks.

2. Have students work in pairs; rotating throughout program or remaining with same partner.

3. Have students supervise work sites.

4. Have students research issues at the work site, while preparing the returns.

5. Require written assignments: daily journal, reflection paper, etc.

6. Allow students to handle slightly more complex tax returns (but only when level of risk to taxpayer is minimal).

7. Identify opportunities for utilizing language skills of bilingual students.

**CALIFORNIA POLYTECHNIC STATE UNIVERSITY**
**San Luis Obispo, College of Business**

# Actg 462 - VITA
# Winter 1996

## COURSE OUTLINE

1.  ## OVERVIEW

The IRS's Volunteer Income Tax Assistance program (VITA) has been in existence for many years as a means of assisting lower income taxpayers with answers to their tax questions and assistance in preparing their income tax returns. This is the fifth year that CAL POLY has participated in the program.

The program is expected to provide the following benefits to participating students:

a.  Provides a review of the basic tax rules learned in Accounting 304, as well as supplementing that learning with various technical aspects of tax preparation and compliance.

b.  Provides instruction and practice in the preparation of California income tax returns

c.  Increases your communication skills through experience of interviewing clients and keeping a journal of your experiences.

d.  Provides exposure to a broad cross-section of the population. Students will gain knowledge about the general population's understanding of the tax laws and the problems they face in complying with its provisions.

The program is also a service to the community. This may be our client's first one-on-one encounter with CAL POLY students - try to represent your university well!

2.  ## CLASS REQUIREMENTS

a.  Students must receive a passing grade on a federal tax returns test to be completed (individually!) by **beginning of class** on **Wednesday, January 24th**. Also, receive a passing grade on a California tax returns test **due by class** on **Wednesday, January 31th**.
    Note: If you fail the federal test, you may take the "Retest," but the maximum grade possible in the course will be a B. A fail on the second grading will cause you to be disqualified from the VITA program and this class. If you fail the California test, you will be given a second chance to pass the California returns before it will affect your grade.

b.  Students must perform 8 hrs. of publicity activities.

c.  Help with bringing in clients by preparing the returns for at least 6 people you have personally contacted about VITA. Two of these 6 people (or their information) must be brought in during the first two weeks of the program.

1

d.  Work at least 28 hours in the VITA centers during the quarter (i.e. 4 hours per week).

e.  Maintain an activity time log that confirms your activities and 6 taxpayers.

f.  Keep a folder with your time log, a record of your coordinating or publicity activities and a daily journal of your experiences at the VITA sites. Based on the journal, you will submit a typewritten reflection paper on your experiences (2-4 typewritten pages) no later than Friday, March 8th (outside room 03-403). This log and reflection paper are meant to be not just a summary of the number of people you assisted (we have to keep separate records on that) but **comments and thoughts on new things learned, problems encountered, things you would do differently in retrospect, mistakes you realized you may have made, insights about people's knowledge of, respect for the tax laws & the IRS, etc.**

g.  You will also be required to spend approximately 4 hours learning and using tax preparation and tax research software. A tax return problem will be given out as soon as the 1995 tax preparation software is received and installed. You can complete this assignment at times convenient to you. The completed returns will be due in the box outside room 03-403 **by March 8th.**

3.  <u>DETERMINATION OF GRADE</u>

| | |
|---|---|
| IRS & Calif tests | 12 |
| Publicity & 6 clients | 10 |
| Tax preparation, **including your <u>attitude</u>** | |
| **& <u>quality of your work</u>** | 60 |
| Computer packages | 3 |
| Log & Reflection paper | 15 |

4.  <u>HOURS WORKED</u>

You will be given credit for hours worked at the sites, doing publicity, coordinating activities, learning & doing computer aided research and preparation, etc. Because of these varied possibilities it is your responsibility to keep track of your hours worked and have them verified after each activity by an authorized person (Dr. Carr or a person she designates). You are responsible for fulfilling all your commitments. Last, but **not** least, you are going to have FUN. I guarantee it!

2

# Tax Assistance Program Provides Service-Learning at Notre Dame and St. Mary's College

by Ken Milani

A win-win-win situation is a rarity. However, the Tax Assistance Program (TAP), a service-learning effort conducted at the University of Notre Dame and St. Mary's College (Indiana) since 1972, is such a situation. Low-income taxpayers are the primary beneficiaries of the Tax Assistance Program, since they receive free income tax preparation service. Students also benefit from the program, since it provides them with practical experience. A third group, involved faculty members, is able to determine the effectiveness of teaching activities while working together with students on an interesting and challenging project.

## Overview

A scripture reading, a song, and a statement of purpose combine to provide an overview of the Tax Assistance Program. The scripture passage is from Titus 3:14: "Have our people learn to give their time in doing good works, to provide for real needs." The song is a rap lyric written by a participant in the Tax Assistance Program as part of a reflection paper that is required of all participating students. The lyrics of the song read as follows:

> *Real-world stuff is a relevant fling*
> *Do the Tax Assistance thing!!!*
>
> *You help people living on a string*
> *Do the Tax Assistance thing!!!*
>
> *After helping folks, you feel like a king*
> *Do the Tax Assistance thing!!!*
>
> *It's a community effort with a lot of zing*
> *Do the Tax Assistance thing!!!*

The stated purpose of the Tax Assistance Program is "to provide free income tax return preparation service to low-income individuals on a regularly scheduled basis at locations that are convenient."

Students involved in the Tax Assistance Program are enrolled at the University of Notre Dame and St. Mary's College. Certified public accountants from national, regional, and local firms also volunteer their time, along with faculty from Notre Dame and St. Mary's. Many are contacted in November and December, when they are asked to commit to at least one 3-hour session during February, March, or April. Others (i.e., those working for regional and national firms in the South Bend area) are recruited in January. A faculty member handles the initial commitment and recruitment activities, while a student administrator is responsible for later contacts. Participating CPAs serve as technical advisers and are available to answer questions, provide advice, and prepare tax returns. Usually, they work alongside the student participants at a Tax Assistance Program site. Since the low-income criterion used by the program actually represents the median income for the South Bend area, interested taxpayers are rarely denied access to assistance.

## History

As was indicated above, the Tax Assistance Program has been in operation since the early 1970s. At the outset, the primary goal of the program was to help Indiana taxpayers file for a special state credit. Since the starting point of the Indiana tax return was and continues to be federal adjusted gross income, it was determined very quickly that the federal tax return should be done first and then the Indiana return. After the special state credit was dropped, the program began to focus more centrally on the federal return and became more of an academic effort. Formal classes were scheduled, academic credit (one hour, graded using a satisfactory-unsatisfactory scale) was provided, and the program came to be viewed as an important part of the educational preparation of students seeking to enter public accounting in general and tax practice in particular. The Tax Assistance Program is one of several service-learning opportunities offered at Notre Dame and St. Mary's. However, it is the only service-learning course offered by the College of Business Administration.

## Training

Since its inception, students involved in the Tax Assistance Program have all completed a one-semester federal income tax class at either Notre Dame or St. Mary's. Prior to beginning the actual preparation of tax returns, the students receive an additional 10 to 12 hours of training. These sessions occur during the first four weeks of the semester. Homework assignments play an important role, and a reflection paper (described later) is part of the Tax

Assistance Program experience. (Note: It is a long-standing Notre Dame tradition to provide academic credit for service-learning activities. Thus, when the Tax Assistance Program sought this status, approval was readily granted.) The training emphasizes situations students are most likely to encounter when preparing tax returns for low-income individuals (e.g., earned income credit, child-care credit, credit for the elderly or disabled, tax treatment of welfare benefits, claiming a dependent). During the training sessions, students are given a variety of factual scenarios. Oftentimes, the information with which they are provided is incomplete, so the students have to ask questions of the instructor in order to clarify a situation, obtain more information, and determine the proper treatment of a given factor. For example:

• *Clarification* — Information about spending for the care of children is provided. The students must seek clarification about the ages of the children being cared for and why the care is being provided.

• *More information* — Information about life insurance proceeds is provided. In order to determine the proper treatment of the proceeds, the students must ask for additional information about the person who died and the taxpayer's relationship to the deceased.

• *Proper treatment* — Medical expense information is included in a set of data. The students must ask about the nature of the expense (e.g., is the item prescribed by a physician?).

Since the Tax Assistance Program also prepares state tax returns, some time is devoted to the Indiana tax forms. Again, there are exercises that focus on special tax treatments allowed by Indiana law (e.g., renter's deduction, military pay deduction, special credit for spending money to insulate one's home).

## Administrative Matters

There are usually 60 to 70 students enrolled in the Tax Assistance Program. Most of them are involved in tax return preparation. However, four or five students are responsible for the administrative details of the program, such as supplies, public relations, contact with the CPAs who volunteer their time, and coordination of the efforts of other support services. The administrative experience is also part of the service-learning activity, since the students who staff the positions become aware of the problems and possibilities involved when dealing with a large group of people. A description of the administrative positions would include:

• *Chairperson* has overall responsibility for Tax Assistance Program operations.

• *Supplies director* handles the ordering, replenishment, and distribution of supplies to TAP personnel. The supplies director is also responsible for other materials needed (e.g., stamps, envelopes).

• *Public relations director* is responsible for the publicity that describes the services available to the community. Newspaper, radio, and television outlets are contacted concerning the activities of TAP.

• *External contact director* is responsible for contacting the various locations where the TAP activities are carried out. The external contact director also coordinates the efforts of the CPAs involved in TAP.

Some of the individuals holding administrative positions receive two credit hours for their participation due to their expanded responsibilities.

## Operations

After the training sessions described above, the students are assigned to a specific location, where they prepare returns. Each student works at his/her specific location approximately eight to 10 times, and spends between 25 and 40 hours preparing returns. In a typical year, Tax Assistance Program personnel (working in two-person teams) will assist 900 to 1,100 taxpayers, and file between 1,500 and 2,000 tax returns.

The team approach employed by the program serves as its primary means of quality control, although the participating CPAs also serve this function. Quality assurance is always an issue, but the normal error rate is fewer than five returns per year. Many of the errors are due to missing tax-payer information — a problem later discovered by the Internal Revenue Service. Should a problem occur after the return has been filed, the Tax Assistance Program faculty coordinator handles it. The usual time frame for the Tax Assistance Program course — offered only in spring semester — is four weeks for training and organizing, and 10 weeks for preparing tax returns.

## Reflection Paper

At the conclusion of the course, the students write a reflection paper. In the paper, the students respond to the following topics: (1) what I liked most about the Tax Assistance Program; (2) what I liked least about the Tax Assistance Program; and (3) what I learned from my participation in the Tax Assistance Program. A recent set of reflection papers included the responses shown at the end of this chapter.

# Conclusion

The Tax Assistance Program served 10 different locations in 1997. In addition, Tax Assistance Program volunteers visited taxpayers who were unable to come to any of the locations (e.g., elderly, disabled). This latter group of students — referred to as the SWAT (Students Working at Taxes) group — visits personal residences, work sites, hospitals, and other facilities (e.g., nursing homes, sheltered workshops) to prepare tax returns. Currently, all returns are prepared manually. However, in the near future, electronic filing and preparation using software will be implemented at pilot sites.

Several positives emerge from the Tax Assistance Program. As an instructor, one begins to understand how the coach of an athletic team feels. One has selected the Tax Assistance Program participants and has trained them. Now, the students are ready to encounter "real-world stuff." At times, one will provide advice, answers, and affirming comments. But eventually one will watch from one's spot on the sidelines as the students struggle, search, sweat, and succeed. Obviously, taxpayers have their tax returns prepared at no charge. Students, on the other hand, are utilizing their professional skills in a community service while gaining invaluable experience. Several former participants in the Tax Assistance Program have continued their involvement through similar programs following graduation. At least four of the former participants have started their own programs in cities where they work.

# Sample Student Responses

## What I Liked Most About the Tax Assistance Program

"Probably the thing that I enjoy most about the Tax Assistance Program is the opportunity it gives me to be of service to the South Bend community. Service to others is a major part of life on campus, and because of things like late-afternoon classes, dorm commitments, and work schedules, I have often felt like I did not have enough time in my schedule to participate in some form of service on a regular basis. The Tax Assistance Program offers me this opportunity, since it is only a few hours a week, and it only lasts for the middle portion of the semester, not conflicting with finals."

"One of the most rewarding things about TAP is the knowledge that the service you provide means so much to the clients. Often they are very thankful, which makes all the participants feel like their help is much needed and desired."

"I enjoyed the chance to apply some of the accounting I have learned and get some hands-on experience working with people and obtaining the appropriate information from them."

## What I Liked Least About the Tax Assistance Program

"I was miserable during my first day at our site. I felt completely inept, and not having a CPA to back me up made me very nervous. On one of the first returns I filled out, I forgot to attach a very important schedule and did not realize it until it was almost too late. This shook my confidence."

"We also had a large, somewhat impatient crowd that was expecting much more experience and efficiency than we were able to provide. When we had been there well past our allotted time and were forced to turn away some who had been waiting, we had some pretty angry customers."

## What I Learned From My Participation in the Tax Assistance Program

"I learned how to do a federal and Indiana state return. That was basic. The knowledge about the tax code was valuable, but secondary. I was glad that I learned about the earned income credit, and how to do a 1040NR."

"I really learned how much people appreciate Notre Dame in the South Bend community. They seemed so grateful, and it made me feel bad in a way. Notre Dame students tend to give South Bend and its residents a bad rap, and it is undeserved. These people really did like us, and were grateful for what we did."

"I learned that I have an interest in tax. I want to try it next year. I also want to participate in a program of this nature in the Cleveland area next spring. I really learned how much I enjoy helping other people, and that was a lesson I am glad that I got."

"I learned how blessed and lucky I was. Many of these people made less money all year than I made last summer. I realized that I do not have a right to complain about things like not having money to go out on a Friday night, when these people struggle to survive. Being in college and having a job next year, I guess that I tend to forget what I have. That was the most valuable lesson to me."

# Volunteer Income Tax Assistance and the Use of Technology

by Nathan Oestreich, Carol Venable, and Martha Doran

The IRS's Volunteer Income Tax Assistance (VITA) program is an example of service-learning in action. With the IRS's emphasis on electronic filing of tax returns and the explosion in computer preparation of tax returns, VITA offers an opportunity to combine service-learning with the efficiency of recent technological advances.

This essay investigates opportunities for using technology to train accounting students to efficiently and accurately prepare returns while simultaneously providing meaningful feedback to the students themselves. Such feedback is provided not only during the actual preparation process but also later in the form of reviews and reports. These reports are similar to outcomes assessments or performance evaluations, and can be used to facilitate reflection on various aspects of the community service experience. Structured reflection provides the basis to meet the combined goals of academic, civic, moral, and career learning.

Since extensive coverage is given in this volume to service-learning in the accounting curriculum in general and in VITA programs in particular, the following sections will not duplicate the range of observations and conclusions offered elsewhere. Instead, it will seek to address how technology can enhance the service experience.

## Background

The VITA program reaches far beyond the college campus to public libraries, community centers, churches, and military bases, just to mention a few off-campus sites. VITA and the IRS companion program Tax Counseling for the Elderly exist to provide service, without a fee, to taxpayers who do not feel comfortable preparing their taxes and who cannot afford to pay for assistance.

In her own essay in this volume, D.V. Rama provides an overview of service-learning in accounting education that explains that not all community service is service-learning. For there to be effective service-learning, there must be action followed by reflection, involving judgments related to the services provided and an appraisal of the services and the processes. She also points out that service-learning provides an opportunity to "enhance the quantity and quality of experiential learning" [see p. 6] and a framework for lifelong learning.

A few essays later, Janice Carr points out that VITA "utilizes two learning techniques that effect the highest retention of knowledge: learning by doing . . . and teaching others" [see p. 101]. She discusses numerous service-learning opportunities in VITA, including improving technical skills, communication skills, interpersonal skills, certain personal capacities, and marketing skills. In the process, students "learn to learn."

Nearly all of the skills identified by Carr are impacted by the use of technology. Most significant among these are technical skills, because the computer ensures accuracy of output after data input, feedback, and interaction, and the student thus has immediate information for the client. The present article speaks to the role of technology in the tax filing and consulting process, with specific reference to San Diego State University's (SDSU's) VITA site.

## SDSU's VITA Site

San Diego State University is an urban, mostly commuter campus with a population of more than 30,000. Most students work to support themselves, many working full-time and attending the university on a part-time basis. As a result, there is a substantial night program.

The School of Accountancy has cosponsored a VITA site with the IRS and California's Franchise Tax Board (FTB) for more than a decade. Income tax return assistance and tax counseling are provided on campus, primarily for fellow students; however, assistance is also provided for staff and campus neighbors.

Historically, participating students were asked to work approximately two hours per week from mid-February until April 15. Most work was completed at a table in the student center. Generally speaking, simple returns were involved, with a few clients having itemized deductions, small businesses, or rental properties. Many returns, although simple, involved dependents and the earned income credit.

Simple returns were completed by the client, with assistance from the student participant. When more complex issues were involved, advice was sought from other students, graduate tax students, or faculty members. Students were provided the option of registering for one semester-unit of an accounting elective on a credit/no-credit basis.

Two defining changes have occurred recently at the SDSU VITA site: the decision to file returns electronically and the use of Internet newsgroups to share information. These changes and access to a new collaborative technology classroom are expanding the services VITA is able to provide as well as enhancing the learning experiences and skills of student workers.

As network technology has become more prevalent on campuses and as teaching has shifted toward more interactive and group learning (Shneiderman et al. 1995), faculty have sought richer designs for their classrooms to enhance the learning experience (Shapiro, Roskos, and Cartwright 1995). Faculty also have sought ways to include new job skills applicable in a group-oriented workplace, including communication and group effectiveness — skills not typically included in the traditional classroom format (Davis and Miller 1996). A combination of these developments within the VITA program has expanded student opportunities on our campus.

## Electronic Filing

The IRS has several initiatives intended to increase electronic transmission of tax information. Two of importance to individual taxpayers are *Telefile,* by which taxpayers with very simple returns can transmit their tax information from a touch-tone phone, and *electronic filing.* Virtually any individual income tax return can be transmitted electronically. Of course, the key advantage here is that most returns are prepared electronically anyway, and transmitting the information from machine to machine reduces IRS processing time and costs.

During the mid-1990s, the IRS developed a plan to increase electronic filing from volunteer sites. In the process, it contracted with Universal Tax Systems (UTS) of Rome, Georgia, and adopted its Tax Wise individual tax preparation software. This software is provided to volunteer sites at no cost.

SDSU's VITA site began electronic filing during the 1996 filing season (1995 returns). Initially, tax returns were submitted to the IRS on disk and were transmitted by IRS personnel to the service center. More recently, electronic files have been submitted to UTS, which batch transmits the files to IRS. In either case, errors such as erroneous identification numbers, name changes, and similar problems are identified immediately, and the return is rejected until the problem is resolved.

In 1996, only 75 returns, including 39 federal returns, were successfully filed from the SDSU site. During that year, only the federal returns were submitted electronically, with the state returns being filed on paper. In 1997, approximately 610 total returns, including 310 federal returns, were filed. Both the federal and the state returns were filed electronically. Of course, returns for earlier years and amended returns were filed on paper, as were state returns for states other than California.

This rapid expansion of services can be attributed to the popularity of electronic filing. Few clients object to the electronic submission, and many solicit it so they can get their refunds sooner.

### Internet Newsgroups

For more than five years, SDSU accounting students have been expected to communicate with their instructors and classmates using electronic mail and electronic conferencing. Although other computer conferencing vehicles were used previously, currently Netscape newsgroups are used. A newsgroup is set up for VITA, and announcements such as training times and work schedules are posted. This does little to foster learning, but the newsgroup is also used for student questions. When a problem is encountered, a question can be posted on the newsgroup. Either another student, a graduate tax student, or a faculty member can answer the question. More often than not, the question is answered by a student, and the site coordinator can monitor responses for accuracy. As a result, all volunteers benefit from the query and the answer.

# Training

Participating students must learn site procedures and use of the software. But they must also understand the technical tax knowledge needed to advise clients and assist with tax preparation. This should amount to little more than a review of prior coursework, but because student backgrounds vary, some participants have had more thorough training than others.

Use of software facilitates the process of technical review. As students learn and practice software procedures, their exercises reinforce their knowledge of the technical material. Selecting exercises especially relevant to work at a VITA site is important.

Training typically takes place in SDSU's collaborative technology classroom. In this classroom, up to seven students can work at each of six computer stations. We prefer to schedule groups of four to encourage interaction and dialogue on the cases presented. Students are given various tax return problems for which they must determine relevant facts, input data, and complete computerized returns. The groups work together, answering one another's questions. Only when uncertainties still exist is the instructor consulted. Feedback is instantaneous, since the return is recalculated each time data are entered. Students immediately see the effect of a particular item on the total tax liability, thus providing them with a better understanding of the effect of various factors.

Another advantage of this arrangement is its capacity to raise "what if" questions. Once the tax is calculated, one can ask what would happen if a particular input were changed. Such a move allows the trainees to observe the marginal impact of various changes.

For those who cannot attend scheduled training sessions, the exercises can be completed in a computer laboratory. Here, group interaction is missing, but immediate feedback is still available.

## Feedback and Interaction

The feedback and interaction that have been described under "Training" are also present throughout the tax return preparation process. A student can spend his/her time checking for input accuracy and alternatives, since calculation and transfer errors (i.e., transferring information from one form to another) do not occur with use of the software. Also, since feedback is instantaneous, alternative scenarios can be tested at no additional cost.

Whenever possible, the collaborative learning technology classroom is used for tax preparation. Since clients and student workers (usually more than one per client) are together at the computers, they can interact as the returns are actually being input. Clients can be interviewed by students on a real-time basis and can get immediate feedback, as can students. All can see the impact of various items and the results of alternative scenarios. These can be useful in explaining particular items. Both clients and student workers can gain confidence in the course of this proceeding.

## Efficiency and Accuracy

The system's potential to increase accuracy and avoid transfer errors has already been mentioned. When students prepare returns manually, those returns must be checked by other students. Sometimes this check is unreliable. In addition, such duplication engages students' time in mechanical activities instead of more difficult decision-making tasks. Since the software helps students avoid many common errors, more time can be spent checking for input errors and errors of omission, and handling additional clients.

Indeed, electronic filing provides still another check. Since all electronic returns are submitted from a single machine, a graduate student or faculty member has an opportunity to add a cursory review before the electronic file is submitted. Other possible errors can be caught during filing by the IRS.

## Site Management

The VITA process really represents an accounting practice scenario. A valuable service is provided to a client by a specialist (a preprofessional). The only missing element is the fee. Given this fact, the SDSU VITA site is increasingly being run as much like a tax practice as possible. During the fall 1997 semester, graduate students in a tax practice seminar were required to organize and plan the 1998 filing season. They prepared written procedures, developed a system of accounting, and designed reports. These procedures dealt with regulation of time and performance, and with tracking returns and information. Even fictitious billings were to be prepared.

This process allowed not only for performance monitoring but also for continuous improvement. As a result, future clients and students should benefit from the program even more than past participants.

## Educational Value

Student responsibilities in the SDSU VITA program are clear: Learn the technical information and the computer software, review the technical material, and perform the required client-related operations. Together, these steps result in community service. However, as D.V. Rama has noted in her chapter, community service, while an integral part of service-learning, is not identical with it. Service-learning must also include a learning strategy that links the service performed to educational goals. By simulating a tax practice in both design and development, the community service provided at the VITA site becomes a strategic part of the accounting curriculum.

In addition, the SDSU VITA site requires the simultaneous use of technology, teamwork, and communication skills. Students trained in teams at a single computer site, where they also meet taxpayers, experience an integration of skills in a real-world setting. This arrangement helps them develop powers of judgment faster than do students participating in traditional class discussions. As Abercrombie, a British medical researcher, discovered, students who learn diagnostic skills in a collaborative format can acquire sound practical judgment faster than those learning via a more traditional approach (cited in Bruffee 1992).

Still another important aspect of service-learning discussed by Rama in her opening chapter is the process of reflective observation, as described by David Kolb in his theory of experiential learning (Kolb 1984). Tax practice at the SDSU VITA site offers many opportunities for reflective observation, including:

• Reflection during training, when feedback is instantly available, and the student receives confirmation of his/her technical understanding.

• Reflection regarding the resulting practice. This is especially true when the taxpayer and the student(s) review and evaluate results together. The taxpayer has a direct financial interest in these results; the student is available to explain and evaluate. Both are aware of the valuable service that has been provided.

• Reflection upon the preparation of reports. These performance reports make it possible to evaluate the total impact and efficiency of the "practice" as a whole and for each volunteer individually.

Such opportunities can, of course, also accommodate the various kinds of nontechnical reflection that Rama discusses. Indeed, if properly designed and effectively used, technological systems can represent a tool that significantly enhances the learning environment. When this tool is combined with some of the other dimensions of service-learning described in this volume, accounting students can experience an unusually rich opportunity to become lifelong learners.

## References

Bruffee, K.A. (1992). "Collaborative Learning and the 'Conversation With Mankind.'" In *Collaborative Learning: A Sourcebook for Higher Education,* edited by A. Goodsell, M. Maher, and V. Tinto, pp. 22-33. University Park, PA: National Center on Postsecondary Teaching, Learning, and Assessment.

Davis, B.D., and T.R. Miller. (1996). "Job Preparation for the 21st Century: A Group Project Learning Model to Teach Basic Workplace Skills." *Journal of Education for Business* 72(2): 69-73.

Kolb, D.A. (1984). *Experiential Learning: Experience as the Source of Learning and Development.* Englewood Cliffs, NJ: Prentice-Hall.

Shapiro W.L., K. Roskos, and G.P. Cartwright. (November/December 1995). "Technology-Enhanced Learning Environments." Technology. *Change* 27(6): 67-69.

Shneiderman B., M. Alavi, K. Norman, and E. Borkowski. (November 1995). "Windows of Opportunity in Electronic Classrooms." *Communications of the ACM* 38(11): 19-24.

# Service-Learning Project in the Accounting Information Systems Course:
## Implementation Without the Benefit of Hindsight

by Alfred R. Michenzi

## Objectives

Loyola College in Maryland has a long tradition in the involvement of the undergraduate students in service activities. Several courses in the humanities, sciences, and social sciences incorporate the concept of volunteer service as part of the course requirements. The Department of Accounting provided no opportunities for students to participate in any accounting course sponsoring service-learning activities. The Accounting Information Systems (AIS) course offered an opportunity to start a service-learning project. The AIS students would participate in a meaningful academic activity by providing consulting service to not-for-profit agencies and assist in the solution of their business and accounting problems. From these encounters with not-for-profit agencies, the students may engage themselves in the concept and activity of service to others, along with the integration of their academic skill in problem solving. This service to others might blossom into future involvement in community service once the students graduate and launch their careers.

## Motivation

In fall 1994, three visiting members of the Bentley College faculty presented the concept of service-learning projects and their benefits from a pedagogic standpoint. The Bentley faculty stressed the value of the service-learning project. They stated it would provide a community-based project for the students to use their academic skills in a meaningful way to serve the community. Also, they stressed the value of the reflective journal entries that each student records as part of the service-learning project. These entries form an integral part of the service-learning experience. The entries provide the students with an opportunity to examine their personal feelings and help the students grow in appreciation of the not-for-profit's impact on the community.

At this time, I searched for a new direction for group projects that are meaningful and an integral part of the AIS course materials. Service-learning projects offered the potential for the AIS course to serve as a capstone course where accounting practice and theory might meet. On Loyola's campus, the Center for Values and Service provided support for faculty who wish to develop and carry out a service-learning project in courses. The Center for Values and Service personnel gave assurances that they would assist me with the various aspects of the service-learning activities that were unfamiliar to me. My key concern related to the reflective journal entries that constitute a critical element of the service-learning experience.

In November 1994, the Center for Values and Service provided me a list of eight not-for-profit agencies in the Baltimore region. These agencies indicated that they could use the assistance of business school students to solve business-related problems.

The Bentley College faculty who presented service-learning to our faculty said that they used a variety of approaches to involving students in group projects that offer service-learning experiences. A group project concept has been an integral part of the AIS course since I began teaching it at Loyola College. Giving the students the opportunity to act as consultants on projects dealing with real-world problems offered the best possible scenario for students to interact with each other and outsiders, and to apply their academic knowledge to help others. This, I felt, would benefit the students, for it added to their skills and would (1) promote and encourage creative thinking; (2) promote the understanding of how organizations work; (3) promote the integration of academic experiences with real-world issues and problems; and (4) improve the students' communication skills. These service-learning projects would draw upon all the accounting, business, and liberal arts courses that the students encountered throughout their academic careers. The students would integrate their academic and project experiences to improve their skills.

## Process

Since the AIS course is offered in the spring term, I began in early November to contact the not-for-profit agencies identified by the Center for Values and Service. I called each agency and set up appointments to discuss the possibilities of doing a service-learning project with them. At these appointments, my agenda consist of several items. The first item concerned the possibility of having student groups do meaningful projects at the agencies. I discussed with the agencies' administrators the possible problems that they believed the students could address, the time-period constraints for the projects, the availability of the administrator or the staff to interact with the students, and the value of the project to both the students and the organization. My second agenda item was to sell the concept of service-learning to the agencies' administrators. These individuals had not worked with students in this way before, so they were not eager to commit their agencies, since they had little concept of the time commitment and usefulness of the result. My final agenda item was to define a project for the students to address. The constraints were that the project must be within the scope of the students' knowledge and manageable within the period of one semester.

In the end, I identified seven project topics at three different agencies. The remaining five agencies decided not to participate in the project. Then, I contacted the three agency administrators to confirm the project topics, and they all agreed to participate. I prepared a one-sentence description of the problem that I later gave to the groups for their project topic. The next task consisted of the development of a project requirements and evaluation package (see the outline of project requirements *below*). The project requirements and evaluation package gave the student groups the required project milestones, due dates, and reports required. For grading purposes, I assigned 100 points to each of the four milestones. *System profile,* the first milestone, required the team to describe the problem in detail, list the goals and objectives of the system, identify the capabilities of the system, and write a contract between the student group and the agency administrator. *Project management,* the second milestone, required the student groups to list the tasks needed to complete the project, prepare time and cost budgets, and write a letter to the agency administrator detailing the second milestone's information along with the expected solution to the project's problem. *Design of inputs and outputs,* the third milestone, required the students to plan and implement the solution. *Implementation and review,* the final milestone, summarized the results of the project, prepared a client satisfaction questionnaire, and described the results of the questionnaire; each student team member evaluated the other members of the group as to their contribution to the project's success. This student team member evaluation was incorporated into each student's individual grade. For each project milestone, each student had to prepare three reflective journal entries. These entries could be field notes or a personal reflection on their experience as a member of a service-learning team.

## Implementation

During the second week of class of the spring semester, I assigned students to groups based on their response to several questions that related to their grade point average and their experiences, both positive and negative, concerning working in a group. I used this information and assembled groups that contained an even mix of grade point averages and group experience levels. I created seven groups of approximately six students and assigned projects to each group.

# PROJECT MILESTONES - DESCRIPTION

**Milestone #1**                                                          [POINT VALUE 100]
System Profile -- description of the current system, its purpose, its users, its capabilities
    REQUIREMENTS:
        1. Describe the current system and the problem.
        2. List the measurable goals and objective of the new system.
        3. Identify the direct and indirect users of the system, and their interest in the new system.
        4. Prepare a contract between the group and the client and have it signed by all interested parties.


**Milestone #2**                                                          [POINT VALUE 100]
Project Management -- description of the approach the group will take in achieving its proposed solution
    REQUIREMENTS:
        1. Using the System Development Life Cycle list the tasks required to complete the project.
        2. Create a GANTT chart for the project and a project budget detailing cost to implement the solution.
        3. Prepare a project letter to the client contact person describing the project, the budget, implementation timing and the expected solution.


**Milestone #3**                                                          [POINT VALUE 100]
Design of Inputs and Outputs of the System
    REQUIREMENTS:
        1. List the tasks completed and training of client personnel required.
        2. Describe the input and output documents of the system.
        3. Prepare data and document flow diagrams for all transactions and reports of the related to the system.


**Milestone #4**                                                          [POINT VALUE 100]
Implementation and Review
    REQUIREMENTS:
        1. Prepare a client satisfaction questionnaire and report on the results.
        2. Summarize the previous milestones and prepare a report to your client.
        3. Give a project team evaluation of the success of the project.
        4. Each team member must evaluate all other team members' contribution to the project. (Peer Evaluation)

Throughout the course, I allocated approximately 30 minutes per week for in-class meeting times. This allowed the students to meet and avoid the scheduling difficulties that often accompany group work. The students' first task was to make contact with the agency. I required that this be done immediately, since this would be the only way that the students could complete Milestone #1's requirements. The groups met with their respective client agencies, and I discovered that the projects I assigned were not always the projects that the students and agencies agreed upon. The groups negotiated with the agencies to identify a problem that they could handle based upon their level of expertise and the time constraints of the students. For one group, I had to help in the negotiation of the project scope and reassure the students that the project, while not dealing directly with accounting information systems, was acceptable for the course.

The table on the next page contains a listing of the projects I assigned to the student groups. It also shows the final projects contracted between the students and the agencies. The projects I assigned gave the students a focus but did not result in an exact description of the final project contracted by the students.

The first milestone reports and journal entries were reviewed. The reports and journal entries showed immediately the differences between the originally assigned projects and those contracted by the groups. (See the table for details of the differences between the initial project and the final student-developed projects.) The reflective journal entries showed confusion and misgivings about the project and the students' ability to meet the requirements of the course. I did not expect this type of problem to occur, but I fully expected some modification of the projects. The journal entries gave me an opportunity to gain a sense of the class's success and frustration with the service-learning project. I used this information to speak to the class about the value of the project work and the value of flexibility in taking on tasks. Also, I had to modify my grading and the requirements for subsequent milestones, since one group's project did not conform to the model originally envisioned at the start of the course. This modification relaxed the students, and they accepted that their project would not follow the model identified in the outline. Further, I reassured them that I would not penalize their group grade for this deviation.

In March 1995, a social worker and a staff member from the Center for Values and Service addressed the class. Each had experience in service-learning. They explained in detail how the agencies are often overworked, understaffed, and underfunded. As a result, the agencies often look for individuals to volunteer their time to help in providing service to the agency. This explained to the students why they found themselves looked upon as volunteers and not as consultants. The social worker explained that the

## Service-Learning Group Initial Project Topics
## & Final Project Completed

| Initial Topic | Final Project Completed |
|---|---|
| Financial Information & Budgeting -- need to match revenues and expenses and identify sources of funding. | Identified and evaluated various accounting software packages that the agency could use in improving its accounting activities. |
| Develop an Inventory System for Physical Therapy and Occupational Therapy Supplies. | Developed two spreadsheets, one tracked year-to-date usage of inventory and the other tracked the status of inventory orders, showing date requested, date ordered, quantity ordered, and date received. |
| Hospital Gift Shop -- develop an updated system for recording daily transactions and a system for efficient restocking of items sold to satisfy customer demands. | Developed and distributed a survey instrument that was given to hospital staff, patients, and visitors. The results of the survey were that the shop needed to lengthen the hours of operations, especially on weekends, improve the reading materials on hand, improve the selection of prepackaged snack food, and increase the quantity of toiletries on hand. |
| Develop a process to identify hospital assets to be transferred to a new facility and tag these items for transfer. | Using the hospital's current procedures for identification of assets, the group tagged approximately one-half of the assets and made recommendations for asset identification in the new facility. |
| Develop and establish a Peer Lending Bank for low-income women entrepreneurs and develop policies and procedures for its operation. | Developed a spreadsheet that keeps track of the deposits of the members of the lending bank, loans, interest computation, and other financial information that the members would need to run the bank. |
| Develop a system of bookkeeping for low-income women entrepreneurs, assist in the preparation of loan applications, and assist in teaching accounting procedures. | Tutored the entrepreneurs in the areas of accounting and marketing. |
| Assist and teach low-income women entrepreneurs in the preparation of business plans. | Tutored the entrepreneurs in the development and preparation of their business plans. |

agencies considered the business function a necessary evil that the agencies would prefer not to do. Consequently, the business functions received little attention unless there was a funding crisis. The Center for Values and Service staff member discussed the importance of reflective journals and gave the students ideas for content of these journals. This session of the class proved extremely useful to the students. I also realized that I should have had this discussion earlier in the semester, for it sensitized the students to the nature of agencies' concerns and the personal developmental value of reflective journals.

Each milestone was graded based on the requirements shown in the outline. As noted earlier, one project did not conform to the original expectation. It turned into a clerical project that required the students to inventory the fixed assets of the hospital, their client. This project required no system development or implementation, since the client had already defined the work requirements of the student group. This project required a liberal interpretation of the project requirements. All other projects came close to conforming to the original expectations. The reflective journal entries helped me identify groups that experienced confusion and conflict with their clients. The entries gave me the opportunity to encourage all groups to continue dialoguing with their clients to conclude their projects. The results of the project and the evaluation of the reflective journal entries led me to believe that most students experienced the reality of limited success in changing approaches and implementing solutions to long-term problems. These experiences run contrary to their academic experiences, which have a definite structure and where results correlate directly with the effort they exert in achieving a grade in the course.

Each student group prepared a satisfaction questionnaire for its client. I did not require any specific set of questions, so each group developed its own questionnaire. The overall responses showed a very favorable level of satisfaction with the students' effort and results obtained. One group received a below-average rating, since it did not communicate frequently with the client and the spreadsheet program prepared for the client was not compatible with the version of software the client owned.

## Conclusion

At the end of the project and before the final college-sponsored course evaluation, I administered a short service-learning project survey evaluation questionnaire. The general outcome of the survey supported the concept of service-learning. The students realized that they were the first group of Loyola undergraduate accounting students ever required to participate in the service-learning activity, and they accepted some of the uncertainty that accompanied the concept. The evaluation gave me insight into the positive and negative feelings the students had regarding the not-for-profit agencies. For example, one student expressed the feeling that "I don't want to be forced to do good works," while another student wrote, "I don't like hospitals, they scare me." One student learned that you can offer help but an individual may not want to accept it from you. Other students thought the project would benefit them in their future careers, since they dealt with an unstructured problem and learned to work together for a solution that conformed to constraints placed on them by the agencies.

The reflective journal entries showed a maturation of the students from uncertainty to a sense of focus on the problems the project presented and the possibilities of assisting the agency in delivery of its service to its clients. Without the reflective journal entries, I would not have known of the uncertainties that the students faced. I discussed these in class in a general way to allow the entire class to benefit from the experience. Further, I believe that by sharing this information with all the students, it let them know that their feelings were similar to those of most of their classmates. Therefore, they experienced some relief associated with the uncertainty of service-learning.

Examples of reflective journal entries appear at the end of this chapter. These entries represent a range of feeling. The feelings range from apprehension, to maturation, to complaining, to satisfaction with a job well done. Not all student journal entries were informative, and several students produced entries that showed little thought or effort. I read all of the entries and gave all students the same grade, penalizing no one for poor effort.

Several lessons learned include the importance of having a social worker or a member of the Center for Values and Service address the class early in the semester. This will help students in thinking about the benefits of the service-learning and the value of the reflective journal entries. Expect the unexpected. Therefore, when the student groups meet with their assigned clients, they must realize that the project assigned may not be the one they will work on. The assigned project is a guide or discussion topic. Also, assure the students that their grades are under their control, not the control of their client or the value of the assigned project. Further, I had to accept that service-learning is not a simple activity that will result in complete success for all participants. Some clients and students benefited more than others from this activity.

In the final evaluation, I believe that the students received valuable experience that deals with the concept of consulting. This required the students to bring together many of the skills learned in all their courses, both business and liberal arts courses, to define a problem, negotiate a project that they could analyze, solve and implement it in a semester, communicate with and motivate their peers and their client, and, finally, organize a report describing their efforts. This exposure to a real-world problem, with all of its uncertainty, benefited the students and added to their maturity. It also exposed the students to the business aspects of delivering social services to others. Further, the students observed individuals whose goals and measures of success were not clearly defined by a job title, position, and financial reward. This experience should broaden their vision of the world in which they will participate.

# Reflective Journal -- Fieldwork Notes

## Milestone #1

Student 1

"Tomorrow morning I will go down to the women entrepreneur site for the first time and meet with the administrator. I have not spoken with her yet and have no idea of what to expect of her. Kim [a student group member] set up the meeting with her and has been the only [one] in our group to have personal contact with her. If I knew something about her or her background, I might have some idea what to expect of this project. I don't know her level of education, her background, where she is from (if she is a Baltimore native), or what exactly her role in the organization is. Given the fact that she works for a nonprofit organization, I would assume she is very service oriented and expect her to be very helpful, rather than stuffy. However, I realize this is a very sheltered opinion.

"Aside from my curiosities about the administrator, I am interested in seeing the neighborhood it is located in. You can learn a lot about something by its surroundings. I hope we are able to meet with other individuals who work there and some of the women who apply for loans. The Loyola community is so exclusive that I am fascinated to meet people who are culturally diverse. You not only learn a lot about them and the whole [community] but also about yourself. I do not consider myself prejudice[d] or snobby, but I do have preconceived notions of various classes of people. I grew up in a very fortunate environment and have involved myself in service work to try and expand my viewpoint. The majority of my encounters have been very beneficial learning experiences and I expect the same of this one.

"I am slightly concerned about my group as a whole. It consists of three residents and three commuters. All three commuters work rather lengthy hours and do not seem flexible about meeting times. Two of them are unable to join us on our first visit to the women entrepreneurs. Everyone seems eager to get involved, but finding coordinating times may be difficult."

Student 2

"My thoughts prior to heading for the meeting are ones of nervousness and excitement. Just from talking with Allison last week, I feel much more comfortable about the project. I do wonder, however, if the other members of the group feel as though I am trying to 'take over.' It seems as if Mike and I are much more excited about this project than some of the others. I realize it is a busy time, but I hope that we can provide some help.

"I arrived at the agency, which is located three offices away from a client of ours, at 10:50 a.m. I thought that the rest of the group might already be there, so I went inside. They had not yet arrived.

"I first met Allison, who was sitting at her desk, and introduced myself, shaking hands. She is younger than I had expected, but very pleasant. She then in turn introduced me to Tim, the executive director. He seemed genuinely friendly this time, unlike the impression I got from the initial phone conversation.

"I took a seat by Allison's desk and we talked in general while waiting for the others to arrive. She then took me to a conference room where we will be meeting; she had a few things to take care of.

"The rest of the group arrived. They got lost; there was misunderstanding in the directions given. We sat and talked among ourselves because Allison is still detained with a phone call.

"Allison enters and our meeting begins. I seem to be asking most of the questions and we all are taking notes. Mike jumps in with a few questions and then some of the others follow with their own. Allison is very comfortable, putting her feet up in the chair she is sitting in. She leaves the room several times with some questions to ask Tim, to get us copies of the most recent financial statements, etc.

"Allison handles us very well and is very informative as to what they are hoping we can accomplish. She is ready to 'work' with us in all matters. She says that anything we can do would be of great help because they are so understaffed to handle this situation at the present time. (They need to match their revenues with the expenses on an event-by-event basis.)

"Allison then leaves the room to allow us to discuss some things among ourselves. We decide on an approach to take in tackling this problem and also discuss how to handle Milestone #1. Mike and Kendra are going to take requirement #1, Marta is taking #2, Jenn #3, Sharon #4, and I am going to handle the contract, typing and meshing the paper together.

"We also decide that we need to do some research into some software packages available to meet their needs. We need to find a word processing program to link to their database in order to generate receipts for contributions. Also there is a need for the computer to 'kick' out a member that has not donated within a specified time period.

"The big thing we need to resolve is the issue of matching revenues and expenses. We are going to research some software and hopefully present them with some ideas soon.

"We then take a very brief look at the office. Allison, Janet, and Tim each have computers at their desks. They also have access to each other's terminals. The computers are not the same and do not have the same programs on them. Tim showed us the newest computer addition; it had been donated. It was larger, faster, and had more programs.

"We then thanked them for the opportunity to help and left the office.

"My afterthoughts of this meeting are great! It seems that we are going to be doing exactly what was stated, but in more detail. I think that this can and will be a rewarding experience. I just hope that everyone else feels as I do."

### Student 3

"OK. It's Saturday afternoon and I'm sitting here wondering what to expect from this semester. Actually, I'm thinking about the community service project for AIS. Honestly, I'm not looking forward to the work. I'm worried that this project will take up a lot of time. Sorry, I know that this is not the kind of thought Dr. Michenzi would want to hear, but I can't help it. I understand what he wants us to learn from this experience, but still, does having to understand what it is like working in groups to solve an actual problem faced in the real world have to take up so much time? Honestly, I'm having mixed feelings because part of me is feeling very lazy (it's called 'senioritus' and I'm suffering from an acute case of it) and on the other hand, having some exposure to consulting sounds interesting (if it weren't for the work involved).

"Luckily, I feel comfortable with the group. So far the group seems OK, although I don't know Angie or Sharon very well. I think we will all get along and each do our share. I must admit that working with Mike should be fun with his dry sense of humor. Angie's boss agrees with us. He thinks this project will be a lot of work. OK, I'll try to be positive. Who knows? It may be a lot of fun.

"I'm glad we were assigned to this diabetes agency. I think that because we have this particular charity organization that part of me doesn't mind doing this project. Diabetes runs in my father's family. Both my grandmother and aunt have the disease, although I don't know the type of diabetes that they have.

"Considering that Angie has talked to the organization and said that there are only three employees, I'm assuming the project can't be that hard. The general topic sounds relatively simple (Financial Information and Budgeting). At least if it is going to be time-consuming, it can be easy.

"Why are we doing this again? It seems that all my professors this semester have some kind of fixation with group projects. I have three projects this semester. Whatever happened to having an easy semester for your senior year?

"OK, OK. So this Wednesday we're going in to meet all three employees. So it takes time out from my already busy schedule, it's only one day. So I can't roll out of my bed for Spanish class and now have to actually get up early and get dressed. I can handle it. (By the way, I like to complain and whine a lot.) It really doesn't matter."

## Milestone #4

### Student 4
"My most surprising (to me) personal reflections deal with my feelings toward helping an organization, rather than directly assisting the people that the particular nonprofit agency serves. I had expressed, in an earlier journal entry, my dismay at designing an inventory system which would better track certain items in order that the patient be properly billed, whereas the items were previously free to the patient.

"I came to terms with this, as a result of the guest speaker presentation, during which nonprofit survival was discussed. I now view the notion of tracking and charging patients for these products as necessary in order to ensure the availability of these supplies for future patients.

"Still, the service-learning project with the hospital did not embody the spirit of volunteering. I came away feeling a void. Perhaps this is for selfish reasons. I think I need to know that my efforts are appreciated. This is seen immediately when one helps another directly. This was not seen at all with this hospital."

### Student 5
"On Wednesday, I am going for my last tutoring session at women entrepreneurs. I am looking forward to this not only because this will be the last time I will have to drive to downtown Baltimore in rush-hour traffic, but because I really know what to expect and I believe that I can handle any questions that the students might have about their business plan. This is not meant to sound arrogant, but I have confidence in the area that I can give assistance.

"The women entrepreneur students appreciate all of the help we give them, even though they have some bad feelings about me being a man. It takes them a little while to get past this, but usually they respond when they realize that I can offer them help. This can be attributed to the 'all-women' organization.

"I do wish that I would be asked about another area besides accounting. This does go against the project definition, but it would be nice to know if I had the abilities to teach in other areas besides my major. I did give some assistance in Marketing, but Marketing is basic knowledge. I would love to have a student ask me about another area of their business plan.

"I am excited that this project is coming to an end, but I do wonder what will become of the students. I cannot help [but] ask myself if our instruction was useful to the organization and the students?"

Student 6
"As far as my overall feelings about the project are concerned, I am going to make these as positive as I can. I know that you have heard every negative aspect of the service-learning project, and I am sure that you are quite tired of hearing that side. I know that I benefited enormously from the experience, and I was very glad to find out that the women entrepreneurs students felt that they also benefited. I think that the Loyola students who said that they didn't gain anything from it did not put anything into it, so they got what would be expected — nothing.

"I enjoyed helping the women entrepreneurs students because they were so enthusiastic about their businesses, and they sincerely wanted to learn and understand. Honestly, I believe that I had a little more to offer than most of the Loyola students because I have been deeply involved with my parents' small business since I was very young. I helped with their bookkeeping since I was in high school, and my parents were always talking about the business and listening to ideas from me and my sister. Their restaurant business went bankrupt, so I learned a lot of things that you shouldn't do in a small business. Now my parents still have the restaurant business, and they also have a smaller business with low overhead and just the two of them working. So, basically, I have been emerged in small businesses since I was about 7 years old. It was wonderful to be able to use some of this practical knowledge to help these women.

"My feelings toward this project have changed significantly since the beginning of the semester. I truly dreaded this project because I had to tutor, which I don't like, and I had to deal with people on a one-on-one basis, which I don't particularly enjoy, and I had to work in a group with Loyola accounting students, which I was definitely not looking forward to. I can't say that the group work situation improved, but I am much more positive about the other two aspects.

"I think that the projects should be continued in future classes, but I think the milestone work was too much. A possible way to reduce that would be to have the milestones as short essay questions rather than individual, detailed requirements for each milestone. I think the milestones are definitely necessary to keep the groups focused, but they really didn't need to be so formal.

"I wish we could have chosen the people in our groups — I know that isn't the way it works in real life, but it would be easier in the classroom setting where we still have our normal assignment due also. It would have relieved a lot of the stress that I associated with the project.

"I guess that's all that I wanted to say — in the end, it was a good group project. It got us out into the real world rather than having us stuck in the library doing research. I wish some people would be a little more open-minded though. It is going to hurt them when they get out there — batting of eyelashes and whining does not a problem solve!!"

Student 7
"During class on this day we were informed by Dr. Michenzi of the project that our group is to undertake. The organization that we will be affiliated with will be

the women entrepreneurs. This project, according to Dr. Michenzi, entailed our group to assist in preparation of business plans and prepare a system for teaching this skill to the women.

"This project will be a service-learning project. We will be required to keep individual journals that will document our thoughts and feeling. Along with these journals we will be required to keep detailed field notes regarding the events that transpired while our group is on premise with our appointed agency.

"My initial thoughts upon receiving all of this information was that this project will be a class unto itself. I did not have a clue as to how to prepare a business plan. I have never created one. What I felt was initial panic.

"My group met on this day and we discussed how we plan to proceed on the project. Debbie volunteered to call our contact person, Amanda, and set up an appointment. She would then inform us of the date and time.

"I think all of us were experiencing the same degree of confusion and anxiety. We did not know what was expected of us, therefore there was nothing we could discuss. On that note we ended our group meeting."

Student 8

"Our project increasingly got better as we went along during the semester. The first day was trying. They had a series of objectives that simply were not feasible for our group to complete. We compromised, but I did not have a warm feeling about offering my time for the Hospital.

"However, since the initial meeting and contract formation, relations became less tension-filled. Personally, I recognized that the hospital needed someone to perform this tedious work for them, and they viewed us as a resource that could be used. I felt we accomplished a lot during all of our visits.

"Finally, I feel we left them with some valuable recommendations that I hope they would seriously consider implementing. They were very appreciative at our last visit. In the beginning of the project, I did not feel quite as appreciated as now I do. I wish them the best in their transfer to the new hospital. I learned that everyone needs to be flexible in their expectations of a group project such as this to allow for productivity.

"Working with my group has been very smooth. Everyone has been very dependable in terms of visiting the hospital and meeting to write the group Milestones. No one person in the group has anointed themselves king. Rather, it has been a very successful group effort."

# Reaching Our Goals Together in Service-Learning: A Multi-Semester Accounting Information Systems Course Implementation

by Margarita Maria Lenk

The strategic alliance model (Lenk 1997) was developed in response to Ehrlich's (1995) challenge to the faculty in professional disciplines to become more active in service-learning. The key features of this model are its long-run nature, its linked goals of research and service-learning, and its ability to accommodate different service-learning activities across semesters. The model, developed from four consecutive semesters of experience in an upper-level undergraduate accounting information systems course, has four stages: an inquiry stage, a modeling stage, an analysis stage, and a dissemination stage.

Students in the inquiry stage visit nonprofit organizations and identify research issues. Classroom discussions compare observations with existing accounting and organizational theories, prioritize issues, and determine the scope of subsequent in-depth research to be performed. An educational research-outreach grant proposal is sent to a relevant external organization (a decision is made as to whether the local chapter, the state office, or the national office should be contacted).

During the modeling stage, students conduct the research, often in the form of in-depth field studies, structured interviews, etc. Research methods are highlighted at this point, especially issues of consistency of measure, objectivity, and documentation skills. Students in the analysis stage interpret the results of the research. The students develop theoretical conclusions and/or propose practical solutions as warranted. The rigor of this analysis will vary depending upon the students' backgrounds or the placement of the service-learning course in the curriculum (i.e., statistics, tax, and law).

Students in the dissemination stage distribute the research results to nonprofit organizations in the form of continuing education or extension services. A key strength of this model is that this stage may be indefinitely repeated in future semesters for as long as there are interested nonprofit

An essay related to this article was published in the *Michigan Journal of Community Service–Learning* (Fall 1997). The author is grateful to the editor of *MJCSL* for permission to utilize materials from that essay.

organizations. Moreover, this stage is the easiest to implement if a professor is new to the service-learning pedagogy.

Benefits abound for all of the parties involved in the strategic alliance. Accounting students get hands-on, real-world experiences that reinforce their coursework and provide them with a sense of social responsibility in terms of the power of and the need for their accounting knowledge in non-profit organizations. Nonprofit organizations benefit by receiving free consulting services and tailored continuing education that would otherwise be financially impossible. Academics and professional organizations are able to provide outreach and perform research that would otherwise be cost-prohibitive.

This sequential four-stage process transforms the students' learning experiences from "deductive" academic experiences to "holistic, synergistic" experiences that balance academic and service-learning goals (Howard 1993). Moreover, the active and unstructured nature of the students' involvement fulfills the Accounting Education Change Commission (AECC) recommendations that students be exposed to business and accounting knowledge in environments that exercise intellectual, interpersonal, communication, and personal integrity skills (1990a, 1990b).

## Implementation of the First Stage: Inquiry

The strategic alliance model was originally developed in an upper-level accounting information systems course. Specifically, internal controls in nonprofit organizations was chosen as a focus for three reasons: (1) the newness of the Committee of Sponsoring Organizations (COSO 1991) and SAS No. 78 (AICPA 1996); (2) a rising number of reported embezzlement and fraud incidences in nonprofit organizations; and (3) a desire to have the students learn firsthand about the cost of internal controls. The participating nonprofit organizations were solicited through communications on our community's computer network, personal telephone calls, newspaper advertisements, and mass invitational mailings. Because this implementation occurred at a state university, religious organizations were assigned only to student teams that specifically requested them. Teams of two students were assigned to each nonprofit organization. Students who desired to work alone were allowed to do so.

The service-learning projects accounted for 25 percent of the students' final course grades and required each student:
- to volunteer at least 10 hours at a local nonprofit organization
- to obtain a copy of and read the organization's charter and bylaws
- to interview employees, volunteers, and the treasurer
- to attend at least two board of directors' meetings

• to keep a weekly journal (a typed copy of which was due at the end of each week: whom did they talk to about what when; what did they learn; and how did they feel about their experiences)

• to write a professional report of the internal control strengths/weaknesses of their organization; and to orally present their findings to the organization's board of directors.

In addition, each student completed a confidential self/peer evaluation form and participated in an exit interview with the professor after the project grades had been assigned and sealed, but before they were distributed. This process was designed to increase honesty in the students' self-reporting, as it occurred after the grade was assigned. In the self/peer evaluation, each student described the strengths and weaknesses that he/she had brought to the team, the strengths and weaknesses of his/her partner, what he/she would have done differently (given the opportunity), and what personal skill areas still needed improvement. The exit interview asked broad questions: How did the experience change your feelings about yourself, your career, your community, and society in general? How do nonprofits differ from for-profit organizations? Did you find the experience worthwhile? This experience supports the students' subsequent job interviews, where many of these same questions are asked (e.g., describe a leadership experience, a team experience, a performance evaluation experience, etc.).

A primary decision for a faculty member sponsoring such an opportunity is whether the project is process-oriented or product-oriented, a decision that affects both the focus of classroom discussions and project grading. The unit being described focused upon the process of service-learning, and significant classroom time was dedicated to the discussion of action choices, observations, feelings, and problems throughout the semester, and how those experiences related to textbook materials and career goals. Another decision the faculty member must make is whether the service-learning will involve a single project or multiple projects. In this particular implementation, the faculty member chose a single-project approach: Each of the student teams worked on the same internal control system. Single projects are significantly more efficient with respect to faculty administrative and grading efforts. Multiple projects, on the other hand, allow for more tailored need-filling work in a diverse set of nonprofit organizations, and usually involve higher student commitment thanks to the students' opportunity for personal involvement in the project definition. These benefits must be evaluated against the additional costs associated with a significant increase in project management efforts by the faculty member, especially in terms of keeping the projects equitable across groups.

Tangible outcomes of the service-learning process include multilayered classroom discussions, journals, internal control reports and presentations, exit interviews, and improved examination scores. Intangible results include, but are not limited to:

- perceptions of the similarities and differences between for-profit and nonprofit organizations
- first-time considerations regarding careers/volunteering in nonprofit organizations
- realizations of the time involved in internal control assessment and evaluation
- an enhanced sense of personal responsibility for the nonprofit sector
- increases in self-confidence with regard to accounting knowledge and the efficacy of that knowledge.

## Implementation of the Second Stage: Modeling

The modeling stage occurred the following semester. The service-learning project requirements were similar to the prior semester's requirements, but two new components were added. First, students reviewed the results of the first semester's inquiries and decided to design an internal control survey for nonprofit organizations that would test the applicability of the COSO (1991) internal control framework to nonprofit organizations, as well as provide much descriptive data about smaller nonprofit organizations. The students tested and revised their survey during interviews with assigned local nonprofit organizations. They also wrote a grant proposal to the Colorado Society of Certified Public Accountants to be considered by the society's educational grant program. The proposal described the research to be performed and requested funds to cover the printing, mailing, and return postage needed by the survey. The grant was awarded with enough funds to mail more than 500 surveys to nonprofit organizations across the state of Colorado.

Second, the students were required to resolve at least one of the internal control weaknesses that they found in their nonprofit organization. The projects ranged from documenting jobs/procedures, counting inventory or fixed assets, and creating forms, to building spreadsheets and databases, helping with fundraising efforts, and reviewing endowment and grant compliance restrictions.

The addition of this project requirement allowed for many practical classroom discussions about project management, and proper spreadsheet and database design and documentation — discussions that the students found very beneficial for their future careers.

## Implementation of the Third Stage: Analysis

During the analysis stage, the service-learning requirements were modified to omit the unit on resolving internal control weaknesses and to incorporate analysis of the prior semester's research results. Slightly more than 250 surveys were returned, representing a response rate of approximately 50 percent. Student teams were provided with the survey data and were required to complete a research summary document. An interesting aside is that this analysis stage may be utilized whenever research data are available (the faculty's own research, a colleague's research, a professional organization's data, etc.).

The classroom discussions during this stage were significantly different from the prior stages or in traditional lecture courses. Each student's participation provided the professor with rich data concerning that student's ability to attend to cues, process and edit them, relate them to underlying theory, determine personal conclusions, and defend those conclusions. These discussions created opportunities to collect individual observations that would allow each student to receive detailed feedback at the end of the semester.

In this semester, the students concluded that many nonprofit organizations experience communication breakdowns and significant loss of knowledge from the high turnover of employees, volunteers, and board members. The students felt that many miscommunications could be avoided and information secured if clear procedure manuals existed for each of an agency's operational positions. In addition, they recommended exit interviews when turnover occurred in order to minimize subsequent learning curve costs. The students' conclusions were combined into a booklet that summarized many free or low-cost solutions to common internal control problems faced by smaller nonprofit organizations.

## Implementation of the Fourth Stage: Dissemination

The focus of the dissemination semester was to communicate the conclusions and recommendations of the internal control research to interested nonprofit organizations. Instead of data analysis, this semester's students were required to make complete internal control presentations to the boards of directors and principal staff of their nonprofit organizations. The new task required the students to create a presentation graphics slide show that could be utilized in the future for internal control training seminars for nonprofit organizations. All of the other course requirements with regard to service-learning continued, and again, the project constituted 25 percent of the course grade.

Further participation by the professional association was solicited. A second research/outreach grant proposal was written that offered to investigate the differences in internal controls between (1) nonprofit organizations that received a copy of the booklet in the mail and (2) nonprofit organizations that participated in the service-learning activities and received a detailed internal control presentation by the students. Such a comparison would effectively measure the demand for future outreach investments. The grant proposal requested funds to cover the booklet's printing, presentation-related costs (e.g., backup overhead slides), and postage costs, both for the mailing of the booklet and for the mailing of a subsequent survey to both of the participating nonprofit organization groups.

Once again, the Colorado Society of Certified Public Accountants supported the proposed research and a number of other related outreach activities. To date, more than 50 nonprofit organizations have participated in the program. The Colorado society has agreed to publish and provide the handbook free of charge to any interested nonprofit organization in the state for the indefinite future. The booklet is also available to any interested accounting professors in the state. An excerpt from this booklet is provided *opposite*. These channels for information dissemination demonstrate the kind of widespread community outreach that is possible with the use of the strategic alliance model. Furthermore, the university's student accounting club has offered to provide the internal control presentation to any interested organizations in the future, freeing the professor for new strategic alliances before the demand for dissemination has been satiated.

In many ways, this fourth, dissemination stage is the most efficient for the faculty member's time, the most adaptable in terms of accounting course application (outreach education may be performed on almost limitless accounting topics), and the most popular in the students' opinion. Students found this stage more concrete, structured, and defined for them, consistent with how they prefer to view the world of accounting and accounting course assignments.

## Grading Issues

Grading choices for service-learning projects are multiple and should reflect the participating faculty member's grading philosophy. Some key decisions are whether the grade is primarily a product grade or a process grade, how much of the grade will be provided by the input of the participating nonprofit organization, and how much will be provided by the students (e.g., their teamwork experience). In many cases, the nature of the service-learning work at issue helps determine the appropriate grading choice. For example, some faculty feel that completion of the service hours, the journals, and

# Internal Control for Smaller Nonprofit Organizations

Internal Control (IC) is the process that an organization uses to become confident that all its resources are appropriately and efficiently utilized to achieve stated goals. A 1996/97 survey of over 300 nonprofit organizations in Colorado indicated that the internal control in these organizations could be easily increased through awareness of the elements that determine and affect internal control.

The following components have been identified as critical to internal control in smaller nonprofit organizations:

1  Accurate knowledge of the internal and external operational environment.

2  Identification and understanding of the internal and external operational risks to the organization.

3  Management of the culture, policies, and procedures of the organization.

4  Strategic use of the system of organization' information and communication systems.

5  Monitoring and maintaining the above four steps for changes.

The three goals of internal control are effective and efficient operations, reliable financial records, and legal/regulatory compliance.

*-- Adapted from COSO's Internal Control Framework (1991) and SAS No. 78 (AICPA 1996).*

\* \* \*

The following internal control features lead to strong internal control:

1  A pervasive attitude of integrity, respect, commitment, information sharing and continuous process improvement throughout plans, actions and evaluations.

2  Clearly documented organizational mission, goals, plans and job descriptions.

3  Active board and management involvement throughout the organization.

4  Competent operational and administrative staff and volunteers.

5  Current and complete documentation of plans, activities, and outcomes.

6  Documentation of all fund raising plans, contacts and activities, successful and not.

7  Special control policies over cash receipts and cash disbursements due to the high vulnerability of cash.

8  Formal budgeting processes for capital, operations, cash flows, followed by documented reviews of actual results to plans.

9  Clear documentation and pervasive knowledge of any contract restrictions/obligations.

10  Clear documentation and pervasive knowledge of deadlines, especially for compliance tasks, such as payroll or grant-related documentation.

11  Whenever possible, utilization of external payroll, compilation, audit, and tax services.

12  Communication is essential in a nonprofit organization. When communication is emphasized, high efficiency and effectiveness of operations, security of cash and other assets, and high levels of public trust are realized. When communication is lacking, excessive errors, high costs, low goal attainments and poor morale may result.

*-- Adapted from* Internal Control for Smaller Nonprofit Organizations, *CSCPA (1997)*

the required board meetings are best graded on a "yes it was done" or "no it wasn't" basis, while interviewing skills, database or spreadsheet format, presentation, or report-writing skills may lend themselves to more rigorous evaluation.

In the implementation semester, the nonprofit organizations were contacted at two points: after the students had made their initial contact and after the project was completed. The initial contact helped to identify the student teams that were experiencing difficulty with the project as well as answer many questions the nonprofit organization had developed concerning the scope or purpose of the project. Inclusion of the students' participation in the classroom discussions as a graded part of the project helped to ensure their contributions.

## Conclusions

The strategic alliance model has numerous benefits to the participating students, nonprofit organizations, faculty, university, and professional society. The projects allow the students (1) to integrate accounting information systems theory, real-world observations, and the scientific process; (2) to practice teamwork and communication skills; (3) to acquire an awareness of how much their accounting knowledge is needed by the nonprofit members of their community and to develop a working sense of social responsibility; and (4) to develop many new community contacts — useful for future searches and professional society information exchange.

The projects also provide many tangible and intangible benefits to the participating nonprofit organizations. The organizations are motivated to critically evaluate all of their operational methods. Many of those involved in this implementation indicated a renewed sense of enthusiasm sparked by the students' energy and efforts. At the same time, the participating professional society and the university are better able to provide outreach to the community, while the sponsoring faculty member has access to field research he/she can utilize for both publication and instructional objectives. In short, the strategic alliance is a win-win-win proposition for all of the parties involved.

### References

Accounting Education Change Commission. (1990a). "AECC Urges Priority for Teaching in Higher Education." Issues Statement No. 1. Torrance, CA: AECC.

——— . (1990b). "Objectives of Education for Accountants." Position Statement No. 1. Torrance, CA: AECC.

American Institute of Certified Public Accountants. (1996). "SAS No. 78: Consideration of the Internal Control Structure in a Financial Statement Audit. An Amendment to SAS No. 55." New York: AICPA.

Committee of Sponsoring Organizations. (1991). "Internal Control: Integrated Framework." Washington, DC: U.S. Congress, National Commission on Fraudulent Financial Reporting.

Ehrlich, T. (March 1995). "Taking Service Seriously." *AAHE Bulletin* 47(7): 8-10.

Howard, J. (December 2, 1993). "Service-Learning Pedagogy." Presentation at the Lee Honors College, Western Michigan University.

Lenk, M. (Fall 1997). "Discipline-Specific Knowledge in Service-Learning: A Strategic Alliance Amongst Universities, Professional Associations, and Nonprofit Organizations." *Michigan Journal of Community Service–Learning* 4: 104-108.

# Service-Learning in a Capstone Course

by James W. Woolley

## Service-Learning in Action

The University of Utah's School of Accounting recently revised its undergraduate curriculum. The changes included adding two senior-level "accounting integration" classes. The courses were designed to integrate various subjects —financial, tax, managerial, systems, and auditing — into a more cohesive paradigm. Ethical and social issues associated with the accounting profession were included in the "integration" concept. One approach chosen to help bring all the issues together involved designing service projects for both nonprofit service organizations and struggling profit-making enterprises. This paper concentrates on some of the nonprofit experiences associated with the class.

The School of Accounting receives calls from organizations having difficulty with some aspect of their information system. The calls are usually the result of conversations the organization's director has had with either members of the board of directors or donors uncomfortable with the information they receive. Such organizations offer an opportunity for students to blend their educational experiences into a real-life experience.

The experience gained with nonprofits may be more valuable than with profit-making enterprises. The administrators of the organizations needing assistance have backgrounds that do not easily lend themselves to good business practice. They are usually concerned with providing service to individuals in need and prefer to avoid the more mundane issues of taxes, accounting reports, and budgets. The inevitable results are systems and reports that are either incomplete or inadequate.

The projects are designed to help both students and assisted organizations better understand the latter's information needs, provide systems that will meet those information needs, enable the managers to better run their organizations, and improve communication practices between managers and their constituents. More than 20 projects have been completed involving more than 100 students and several hundred hours of service-learning experience. Four of the projects, of varying degrees of difficulty, are outlined in the following section.

# Case Studies

## Local Chapter of National Council

A phone call from the national office of an organization dealing with Hispanic issues indicated that the local chapter was in need of major and immediate assistance. Required tax returns had not been filed. There were no financial reports that would allow the preparation of the tax returns. Financial and other operating information was not available for budgeting or decision making. Finding and organizing the records necessary to reconstruct three years of financial history would be a problem. The records were in disarray, missing, and incomplete. Additionally, the local chapter had recently hired a new director charged with the responsibility of putting on a statewide conference while at the same time learning her new job. The well-meaning and college-educated director had little experience with financial information, financial statement preparation, budgets, or the budgeting processes.

The director was aware that her new assignment required extensive fundraising. In addition, she would be responsible for operating the chapter in an effective and efficient manner. She needed a system that would enable her to meet all of the organization's diverse goals.

During class discussions, it was determined that the critical issues facing the organization were three in number: (1) meeting the tax deadlines facing the local chapter and avoiding loss of the organization's tax-exempt status; (2) designing a new accounting and information system compatible with the skill levels of the personnel involved; and (3) selecting and implementing a database system that would allow the organization to maintain an active record of its donors and potential donors.

Two groups of five students were assigned to deal with the basic accounting problems. The first group was to be responsible for reconstructing financial statements for the preceding three years. It was also responsible for defining basic accounting information needs of the organization. The second group was assigned the design and implementation of an information system commensurate with the skills of the administrators. A third group of five students was responsible for recommending and, if time allowed, implementing a donor database system.

Group one determined it first needed to understand the basic tax requirements. Two individuals were assigned the necessary research associated with defining the tax requirements for tax-exempt organizations. The three remaining members of the group were assigned the responsibility of determining whether there were adequate records to reconstruct the financial statements for the previous three years.

The students researching the tax requirements encountered little difficulty in defining the tax requirements. They obtained the necessary forms and familiarized themselves with the relevant sections of the code. Their efforts were completed prior to the time accounting data became available.

The students trying to obtain information and documentation for preparing the financial statements faced a greater challenge. Checkbook stubs, bank statements, and disorganized boxes of documents that were purported to contain all the information necessary to complete the statements were found in various locations. Students were aware that they were under an ethical obligation to prepare statements that accurately reflected the financial results of the organization. There was little leeway for error.

After working an average of 45 hours per individual over a seven-week period, the students completed financial statements for the three-year period. Additionally, tax returns were also prepared that allowed the organization to meet its federal tax-reporting obligation. The tax-exempt status was saved. While researching the financial statement information, the students also defined basic accounting information needs that could be integrated into the information system proposed by the second group.

The second group of students began its work by carefully defining and outlining the information needs of the director, board of directors, and national offices. The information requirements included all items necessary for financial reporting, but the students' major effort was directed toward building a system that would improve budgeting systems, operating information, and computer hardware and software requirements.

The third group of students designed a donor database system. Because the organization is small and staff members have limited experience dealing with systems, each of the student groups decided that the systems must be simple. They also determined that any software recommended must be off the shelf. All software decisions were made assuming the software must be unusually user-friendly.

The members of the second and third groups each logged nearly 45 hours in meeting time, systems design, and computer and software evaluation before presenting their reports and outlining the steps necessary to successfully implement their recommendations. One student volunteered to help in the implementation of the project on her own time after the class was completed.

## Homeless Assistance

The service-learning project for an organization specializing in assisting homeless individuals was started as a result of inquiries from local members of the board of directors. The board was having difficulty in obtaining timely financial information. Repeated requests for data were met with less than enthusiastic responses. Initial offers of help were not met with enthusiasm. In fact, the director was very reluctant to have others involved in "his operation." Encouragement from a local CPA member of the board was needed before the project was started. The six-person student group began its project in a semihostile environment.

As the students worked on the project, they discovered both strengths and weaknesses. The accounting staff consisted of a supervisor and two assistants. The supervisor had inadequate experience but was enthusiastic about the work. The assistants had specific responsibilities and were hardworking, dedicated individuals. The assistants were open-minded and willing to take suggestions when offered, but they lacked the experience necessary to implement the suggestions.

The major problem encountered related to the accountant's lack of knowledge. The lack of knowledge created a variety of problems. The organization had insufficient documentation, inappropriate cash deposit procedures, missing entries and incomplete information, incorrect payroll checks, and weak cash reimbursement procedures, which resulted in incorrect amounts being disbursed and recorded. Control procedures were simply missing.

In addition to inexperience, other problems surfaced. Staff members would simply "plug" numbers when they wouldn't balance. Turnover was high, leading to inconsistency and a lack of timeliness. Suggestions from the students were met with suspicion from the local manager. The manager felt threatened by the proposals of the students. (The manager resigned near the end of the students' project.)

As a result of its research and evaluation, the student group proposed a number of changes. Some of its recommendations were simple, short-term control procedures, and others would require more time to implement. Among the recommendations were the following:

• design and implement a plan for training accounting employees
• cross-train the employees in key areas to reduce dependency on one individual
• initiate same-day recording of deposits and other critical items in the ledgers (daily deposits were encouraged)
• segregate duties of accounting employees to minimize chances of both errors and misappropriation of funds.

The project was not limited to recommendations. The students' other accomplishments included correction of payroll errors and completion of bank reconciliations. Bank statements had not been reconciled for a 10-month period. The reconciliations provided the administration with a correct starting point for cash in financial reporting and budgeting activities.

In their required written report, the students concluded with the following comment: "We have enjoyed our experience with this organization. It gave us valuable hands-on training with accounting systems by allowing us to apply our accounting curriculum experience."

The six students working on this project maintained time logs for the project. They reported spending 40 to 50 hours each over a seven-week period. The total reported hours were 265.

## Housing for Families With Hospitalized Family Members

An organization opened a home for families with hospitalized family members in Salt Lake during 1988. A major expansion was added in 1994. Since opening, more than 6,500 families from 30 states and nine foreign countries have used the facility. The house is like a small motel, with 29 regular rooms and one apartment set aside for bone marrow patients. There is a common living area with kitchens, laundry, and playrooms. In addition to providing a convenient temporary living facility near five major hospitals, the program has been designed to provide emotional support for families. The cost of operating the facility is approximately $250,000 annually.

Families desiring to take advantage of the facility must live more than 50 miles away. A family may not stay longer than 30 days. Families are charged a nominal $10 per night.

The student group became involved when a newly named director became concerned about the adequacy of her information system and the availability of information for a variety of purposes. Insurance requirements and missing capital items such as TVs and stereos were among the problems. Conversations with the director resulted in a work program designed to accomplish the following:

- complete a physical inventory of all assets and supplies
- prepare schedules of accrued salaries and payroll taxes for 1995
- evaluate Niteclerk, a hotel software package, for possible use at the facility.

The physical inventory project was successfully completed. The project included the design and preparation of schedules and forms necessary to complete the count. The form designed included items such as code numbers, locations, descriptions, and applicable serial numbers. Special emphasis was given to items with value exceeding $500. Since the organization is required to undergo an independent audit, it was considered particularly important to minimize the auditor's efforts. All significant assets were properly tagged and prepared for audit.

The inventory was the first in the history of the organization. For the first time, accurate information was available for insurance purposes. Additionally, it became easier to trace items that had been misplaced as people transferred in and out of the facility. An accurate valuation of the various physical assets was also completed.

A group of students from a previous quarter had already recommended that a more accurate record of payroll taxes and related liabilities be maintained. Using Quattro Pro for the project, the current students researched and re-created employee data from both W-2 forms and fragmented quarterly payroll reports. The spreadsheets that were prepared enabled organization personnel to respond to federal and state agencies requiring corrected payroll information.

The evaluation of the Niteclerk software and its applicability was perhaps the most important long-term part of the student project. At the time of the review, all activities relating to registration and occupancy were being performed manually. The procedures were time-consuming and often produced incomplete and inaccurate data.

The students began their Niteclerk evaluation by interviewing key personnel to determine and prioritize their information needs. With the information prioritized, phone calls were made to the software company. Specific questions concerning the adaptability of Niteclerk for this organization were at issue. The general conclusion was that Niteclerk would be usable but that many aspects of the software package were not necessary and some were overly sophisticated. Changes had to be made. Since Niteclerk was designed for profit-making enterprises, some things had to be added and others deleted. For example, since the facility is operated by a tax-exempt organization, information relating to some taxes needed to be eliminated. All references to credit cards also needed to be dropped. On the other hand, it was necessary to add capability that could identify a social worker or a hospital, along with information concerning each patient. Required patient information included name, birth date, sex, and diagnosis.

The students working with facility personnel and the software company completed all the necessary steps required for installation. Once installed, all registrations and reservations will be on the computer, revenue and occupancy reports will be prepared, and operating statistics will be available for management use.

The project was not without difficulties. Students learned that everyone (including themselves) was on a tight schedule, making it difficult to coordinate meetings and activities. Adjustments to Niteclerk delayed the software until late in the quarter. This caused delays in implementing the system and provided a major inconvenience for students as they neared the end of the quarter. Late discovery of the capital expenditure policy (board approval before purchase) for both software and hardware introduced the students to the approval process and the necessity of adhering to it.

Nonproject activities, such as helping raise money for new computers and other equipment, provided each student with new insights into "cash flow" realities. Most of the group assisted at a yard sale and also donated items for the sale.

The quarter ended before all the elements of the management information system could be put in place. The students compiled a list of recommended activities and equipment required to complete the project. Among their recommendations for a more complete information system were:

1. *Standardize software packages.* A variety of software applications were in place, but lack of compatibility caused delays and confusion when more than one individual needed the same information.

2. *Network the systems.* The facility does not have a networked system. Networking would provide the administrators better and more reliable access to needed information.

3. *Upgrade all computers.* They now have a number of mismatched computers. Standardization with either an IBM or Mac platform would enhance the ability of administrators to effectively network. Effective systems also require newer and faster computers.

The concluding section of the students' report outlined specific steps administrators should take to implement the course of action outlined above. The students suggested that another student group could help in implementing the remaining systems. They also suggested that the organization digest the new applications before starting new projects. The students on this project reported spending 280 total hours over a seven-week period.

## Youth Activities Organization

The organization is a significant force in meeting the needs of many disadvantaged students in the Greater Salt Lake area. Two of the organization's facilities are situated near two schools having a high percentage of at-risk students. In the evenings, the organization's facilities serve as transitional areas until the parents return home from work. Organization administrators are eager to make this time as productive as possible. One way of making this time productive is to assist students with their homework. In an effort to make homework assistance more effective, two projects were designed. The first would involve networking the computers at the various facilities so administrators could maintain better control. The second would involve tying the schools' Parent-Link programs to the organization's network. The first project also included improved administrative and programmatic information.

The networking project involved basic systems analysis, systems design, hardware and software evaluation, and implementation. A detailed report was prepared that summarized user needs, specific system requirements, alternative networking options with detailed lists of strengths and weaknesses, and a recommended networking option. A detailed plan outlining the specific steps required for networking was prepared and presented to organization administrators. The steps included recommendations for the hardware and software needed for networking. Finally, a detailed implementation plan for the network itself was also prepared. The report concluded with an appendix detailing technical specifications for the recommended system. The five students working on this project each contributed more than 50 hours of time to the project. The total time spent on the project exceeded 300 hours.

The second project involved tying Parent-Link capabilities of the schools to the organization's existing and planned systems. Parent-Link systems are designed to allow parents the chance to call at any time in the evening and determine the assignments their children should be completing in a given class. Helping the youth organization become a part of the system involved complex analysis and required that the students become involved with a variety of technical issues.

The primary systems issue related to integrating the schools' systems, which have multiple communication and software systems, into the hodgepodge of computer and communications systems at the youth organization. The solution to many of the technical problems included a recommendation for an advanced networking system for the organization's facilities.

Although all of the recommended changes had not been implemented at the end of the quarter, the organization has been successful in encouraging school personnel to keep their homework assignments current, thus allowing the organization to be more effective with students. The project objective, allowing children to complete their homework before their parents return home in the evening, has been partially achieved. Approximately 250 student-hours were involved in this project.

## Reflections

In two quarters of actively integrating service-learning into the accounting curriculum, a variety of responses and emotions have arisen. Time has been a major concern for both students and recipients. Students working in groups encountered coordination problems because of diverse work and school schedules. More than 90 percent of the students exceeded 50 hours over a five-to-seven-week period. In a few cases, students would spend nearly 100 hours on the assignment. The education process has not been limited to students. Conversations with individuals within the organizations indicate that real problems have been solved. The instructor has also gained new understanding from the projects. Outlined below are some of the implications for the groups involved.

## Students

The primary knowledge recipients are the students. Conversations with them and a review of diaries, time logs, and other sources indicate they feel they have benefited by:

- gaining an understanding of attitudes and motivations of individuals working for not-for-profit organizations;
- understanding that the technical skill levels within an organization are not necessarily correlated with commitment to the cause;
- recognizing that administrators can become very interested in preserving the status quo even when they are committed to a good cause;
- discovering that "their education" can become a valuable resource in helping organizations improve their operations;
- realizing that the "basics" play a significant role in improving the operations of organizations;
- having a change of pace with a new focus on the education process;
- interacting with individuals and groups they would otherwise miss;
- developing a closer relationship with their classroom peers;
- scheduling their time so they can be an effective provider of services to those in need of help.

## Community Partners

The organizations involved in the process were as varied as were their needs. The individuals had different reactions to the student assistance. Some were reluctant, others were ecstatic, and a few tolerated the inconvenience. In the end, all of them indicated that their organization had benefited from the project. Specific areas of concern were identified:

- Successful projects required a major time commitment from administrators. This has created conflicts for some administrators. Staff workers within organizations appeared to be frustrated by the new assignments while maintaining current workloads.
- Most organizations discovered they needed to upgrade their training if they were going to use the systems designed by the students. Some organizations recognized that their existing employees could not handle the new requirements. This resulted in some unpleasant employee terminations and job shifting.
- Some administrators were introduced to "computers" for the first time. This introduction has created problems and discomfort for some of these new users.

## The Instructor

How would it work? Would the students take hold of their projects? Would the time requirements be too great? Would the projects be beyond the capabilities of the students? Are there enough projects available? These were the questions the instructor asked as classes began. At this point, the answers indicate a long-term educational opportunity for accounting students. Conclusions and implications for the future include:

• Service-learning works. The projects are not uniformly exciting, and the students are not equally motivated, but a significant contribution to community organizations can be made in a 10-week quarter. The workload for students does not seem excessive. The amount of time required of students appears about equal to normal classroom activity.

• Most students are eager for an opportunity to apply the education they have received. Application after theory and concept seemed to have invigorated many students as they were ending their academic career. Most, but not all, were ready to make a time commitment because of their enthusiasm for the projects.

• Students devoted the time necessary to do both an effective and efficient job.

• Service organizations are generally staffed with individuals having little business or "systems" experience; as a result, the experience level of the students is sufficient to complete projects successfully.

• Organizations rendering social services usually operate on tight budgets. The lack of budget is reflected in the lack of accounting systems and controls. Service project assignments are readily available to those who are willing to find them. Accounting and systems projects for service-learning classes should be available for the indefinite future. The various projects would not have been completed without the students, because most of the organizations cannot afford outside consultants.

• Expanding the areas of activity is a distinct possibility. Many of the organizations receive funding from sources that require an annual audit. Many of the audits are performed on an at-no-cost basis by CPA firms. Working in conjunction with firms, students will have an opportunity to perform an actual audit. Additionally, compliance and operational audits are another way in which the project base can be enhanced. One small firm has even suggested a "fraud audit" would be possible.

The projects have been fun, intellectually challenging, time-consuming, and sometimes disconcerting. However, the positives overwhelm the negatives. What can be accomplished in service-learning is limited only by one's imagination. Academic accountants and their students can make major contributions to organizations in need of systems, basic accounting, policy and procedure design, managerial analysis, and audits — financial, operational, and program.

# Teaching Professional Accounting Ethics With Service-Learning

by Susan P. Ravenscroft

Educators often promote service-learning because it provides students with a complex, dynamic, reality-based environment, offering a richness difficult to duplicate in a classroom. A well-designed course project may enable students to understand and see hitherto unperceived connections and relationships, but it cannot offer the embedded context and the motivation afforded by service-learning experiences. Service-learning enriches student learning by the complexity of the assignments and the environment, as well as through the added motivation that actions taken will have real-world consequences (Markus, Howard, and King 1993).

However, there is another and equally important reason to consider service-learning. It provides students with an opportunity to reflect on their civic responsibility, i.e., their obligations as professional accountants to work for the good of their community. The Carnegie Foundation for the Advancement of Teaching has noted that "the quality of the undergraduate experience is to be measured by the willingness of graduates to be socially and civically engaged" (cited in Stanton 1990: 1). Service-learning provides an excellent vehicle for students to explore and define their civic responsibility, and to become aware of their obligation to promote the public good (Boss 1994; Giles and Eyler 1994). It is this aspect of service-learning that is the focus of this essay.

The organization of this essay is as follows. The first section is a discussion of the meaning of accounting professionalism and its relationship to the public good. The second section is a brief review of the objectives of teaching accounting ethics and how those objectives are being measured and met. The third section provides an argument that service-learning is particularly effective for developing students' sense of responsibility to the public. The fourth section is a description of an Iowa State University capstone course in a master's of accounting program, in which service-learning was a major course requirement. Student projects will be described, and student essays will be quoted. The last section includes observations on successes, failures of the class, and pedagogical considerations for other faculty looking into service-learning.

# Professionalism in Accounting

As accountants, we recognize that there are multiple career paths falling under the broad aegis of accounting. However, to the public, the prototypical accountant is the certified public accountant, and that is the role assumed in this discussion. Accounting professionals have a position of privilege and of responsibility, holding the exclusive right to perform the attest function for companies whose equity securities are publicly traded. The accounting profession formulates current accounting requirements for publicly traded and nonprofit organizations, and is basically self-policing in terms of entrance requirements and adherence to professional codes and rules. To moderate and justify that monopoly power, the profession has assumed an obligation expressed in the *Code of Professional Conduct* (AICPA 1991b) to "act in a way that will serve the public interest" (5). This implicit exchange "constitutes a fiduciary relationship; that is, the professional is expected to act on society's behalf and not just on his own" (Camenisch 1988: 19).

However, beyond discussions of adherence to the *Code of Professional Conduct,* little attention is given to defining the public interest and the responsibility of the individual accountant to foster that good. One seldom sees such discussions given in-depth attention in the professional literature. This inattention by professionals increases the need for educators to encourage students to explore these issues as they enter the field of accounting.

# Current Practice in the Teaching of Accounting Ethics

Calls to teach professional ethics to accounting students have been made by several bodies, notably the Treadway Commission, the American Accounting Association (AAA 1986), and the Accounting Education Change Commission (AECC 1990). When surveyed, faculty express agreement with the need to teach ethics, although the extent to which faculty teach ethics is not clear. Milam and McNair (1992) found that while more than 77 percent of surveyed accounting faculty cover ethics in some way, 70 percent feel that more coverage is needed. In a study of business faculty, Solberg, Strong, and McGuire found that 91 percent of faculty who teach ethics have total discretion in deciding the "type, amount, and scope of ethics coverage" (1995: 74). Given the indeterminate nature of the term "ethics," some agreement on the definition of the scope and the goals of teaching ethics is critical.

Loeb provided a list of goals that has been influential in setting the agenda for accounting ethics education. In addition to goals based on improving ethical judgments and the ability to recognize ethical issues, Loeb includes the following: "Develop 'a sense of moral obligation' or responsibility; develop the abilities needed to deal with ethical conflicts or dilemmas; and 'set the stage for' a change in ethical behavior" (1988: 322).

Other commentators have similarly pressed for the development of a sense of responsibility as a goal of ethics education. The AAA said that "the general effort to develop in students a concern for individual needs and for the overall advancement of society must be given more emphasis" (1986: 179). The AECC includes "an awareness of personal and social values" and "sensitivity to social responsibilities" among the capabilities needed in accounting graduates (1990: 311). Fulmer and Cargile say that "it might behoove us as educators to go beyond the teaching of correct attitudes (toward inanimate problems or the activity of 'others') and emphasize more the personal involvement of the individual in ethical issues and actions" (1987: 217). Armstrong says that "as educators we should stress the role of our profession in society" (1990: 189). Piper notes that professionalism needs to be "attached to a purpose, and that purpose to other people in some substantial way, and to larger purposes" beyond self-interest (1993b: 4). Parks observes that even when students have a well-developed sense of personal responsibility, they may not understand the broader societal implications of their profession, which if not addressed, would leave them unable "to provide ethical leadership in public life" (1993: 19). In summary, there are many calls for faculty to expand professional ethics education into the realm of developing a sense of social responsibility and to provide learning experiences that could result in changes in behavior.

Despite this repeatedly expressed need to develop students' sense of responsibility, much of the accounting education literature reports that ethics is taught primarily in terms of recognition of issues and ethical judgment, as assessed by the Defining Issues Test (DIT). The DIT presents subjects with six short cases in a forced-choice format. Responses address the actions people would select from among the alternatives and the reasons for those actions (again among those offered by the test). The test is designed to capture level of moral judgment, but does not measure other elements of moral development (Rest 1986).

There is increasing evidence that ethics education in accounting is not consistently resulting in significant growth in moral judgment, as measured using the DIT (Ponemon 1993). Given the lack of linkage between improved DIT scores and subsequent actions, it is possible that there is less effect on students' behavior (S.A.S. 1996). Ponemon's 1993 study is unusual in that both DIT scores *and* behavior are measured to assess moral development due to ethical training. Ponemon found no improvement either in DIT scores or in students' willingness to anonymously contribute to the cost of course handouts after a semester-long ethics program. Hiltebeitel and Jones (1991) observed some improvement in students' ability to solve ethical dilemmas related to professional issues, but noted that this improvement did not occur in students' responses to dilemmas of a more personal nature. This finding may indicate a lack of internalizing of higher-level values, such that students' actual behavior would be modified. The mixed results on the effects of ethics instruction in accounting summarized in Ponemon indicate that the accounting educators must continue to "develop and implement innovative approaches for integrating ethics into the core accounting curriculum" (1993: 186).

## Using Service-Learning to Teach Ethics

While understanding ethical theory and concepts is helpful in developing more sophisticated moral judgments, analytic ability is not the entire aim of ethical educators. We expect and hope that ethics education will lead to a sense of responsibility, which is reflected in action. Although the literature in accounting is based primarily on teaching ethics via cases and readings, there is a growing movement in other fields to include other pedagogies that are more experiential, especially service-learning, as a way to inculcate a greater sense of social responsibility or citizenship.

Service-learning was devised precisely to instill greater involvement and responsibility. The mission of the Campus Compact, which was created to encourage civic involvement by students, is to "address the larger goal of nurturing citizens with a broad comprehension of — and long-lasting commitment to — the civic responsibilities of individuals and institutions" (Smith 1994: 38). College administrators and directors of campus community service programs believe that civic responsibility, civic participation, and citizenship are the chief outcomes of service-learning (Smith 1994). That such outcomes are significant is clear in a Carnegie Foundation report: "If there is a crisis in education in the United States today, it is less that test scores have declined than it is that we have failed to provide the education for citizenship that is still the most important responsibility of the nation's schools and colleges" (Newman 1985: 31).

That language reflects a need expressed by students. An AICPA survey showed that for many students the goal of serving society is very important to them (AICPA 1991a). Piper observes that many students wish to have ethical issues addressed in an actual context, rather than as deductive exercises completed in a classroom (1993a). Based on research with MBA students, Parks concludes that students express a desire to do good for their society, even though they often simultaneously reveal a rather shallow understanding of community (1993). Students' need to contribute to the greater good and to be part of a larger community (Barber 1994) can serve as the entering point and motivation for the teaching and learning of professional ethics, focusing on responsibility and community.

Several factors lead to the conclusion that teaching ethics could be strengthened by greater use of service-learning, which combines activity, commitment of time and energy, and reflection. First, there is evidence in the general literature on higher education that active learning is superior to passive learning on a variety of outcomes (Bonwell and Eison 1991; Davis and Murrell 1993; Kerr and Smith 1995). Second, involvement in the college community has been shown to influence students' "humanitarian and civic involvement values" (Pascarella, Ethington, and Smart 1988). Third, as noted in the previous section of this paper, the inconsistent results of research in accounting education suggest that traditional teaching methods have had minimal effect on moral judgments and no reliable effect on moral actions. Fourth, alternatives to the paradigm of ethics as deductive conceptual systems are emerging, and with changes in our characterization of ethics, concomitant changes in the teaching of ethics should follow. The latter point will be elaborated upon in the next few paragraphs.

The conception of ethics as a basically deductive conceptual system is being questioned by philosophers. Many business ethics texts, rooted in that conception, begin with a brief exposition of the two major ethical philosophies — utilitarianism and deontology (Derry and Green 1989). While philosophical overview may serve as a helpful beginning, few texts consistently integrate theory and cases in such a manner that theory could be used to illuminate practice and to help students reconcile the two conflicting theories or to decide how and when to apply the theories (Derry and Green 1989). Johnson (1993) argues that such difficulties are inevitable because much of ethical theory is based on a fallacious model with erroneous assumptions about ethical reasoning. Instead of moral judgments' being primarily the application of universal principles deductively applied to specific fact situations, he and a number of other theorists assert that ethics is based strongly on metaphor, requires development of a moral imagination, and demands a creative problem-solving approach to generating alternatives. They argue further that actions are critical to moral development (Johnson 1993; Margolis 1995; Pritchard 1992; Whitbeck 1992).

Relying on cognitive psychology, linguistic analysis of ethical discourse, and anthropology, Johnson (1993) argues that imagination is a primary basis of cognition, including moral reasoning. He urges us to develop a moral imagination based in universal experience and structured by metaphors, with the final goal being more ethical action. People are "beings in process whose identity emerges and is continually transformed in an ongoing process of reflection and action. Our actions express who we are, and they may also transform who we are at the same time" (Johnson 1993: 148).

Similarly, Margolis argues that syllogistic reasoning does not describe how ethical values develop. Instead, "an individual's personal values often become apparent only when action is contemplated, taken, or reflected upon" (1995: 285). By formulating alternatives and acting, we clarify our ethical principles. Whitbeck (1992) too argues that students should take active roles, performing as moral agents rather than as moral judges who evaluate the actions of characters in cases.

Given this evolving conception of ethics and moral reasoning, it is not surprising that educators are beginning to call for alternative, expanded approaches to teaching ethics. Solberg, Strong, and McGuire say that "learning environments extended beyond the walls of the classroom will be required. . . . Alternative modes of education are more likely to be effective in real-life situations than principled reasoning and ethical theory courses" (1995: 75). Barber warns that "without schools that take responsibility for what goes on beyond as well as in the classroom, and work to remove the walls that separate the two worlds, students will continue to bracket off all that they learn from life and keep their lives at arm's length from what they learn" (1994: 92). Kerr and Smith (1995) urge accounting educators to make ethics education more active and to involve more hands-on experiences.

In this context, service-learning provides an alternative model for teaching and reinforcing ethical values of social responsibility. Service-learning links the positive aspects of professionalism and a developing sense of public, or civic, responsibility. It provides "a natural extension of the virtues professionals already exemplify in their everyday professional activities" (Pritchard 1992: 170). Piper notes that "many schools have introduced community outreach programs in recent years in the conviction that community service is an integral responsibility of leadership and that their students should cultivate a habit of service" (1993a: 147).

Service-learning provides students an opportunity to make connections between helping their community and themselves when they help a member of the community. It also allows students to focus on the notion of public good, and to see that "self and community, private interest and public good are necessarily linked" (Barber 1994: 88). Markus, Howard, and King say that students should consider the broader implications of their service, viewing it as a social or political phenomenon rather than strictly the provision of assistance to "vulnerable individuals" (1993: 417). This viewpoint is echoed by Barber, who says we need "active citizens who see in service not the altruism of charity but the responsibility of citizenship on which liberty ultimately depends" (1994: 92). Service-learning can help future professionals begin to "locate and imaginatively develop positive potentials" for public service (Sullivan 1988: 43).

# Description of Capstone Accounting Course Using Service-Learning

This course was offered for the first time in a Master's of Science in Accounting program as a capstone course and was taken primarily by students in their last or penultimate semester. The focus of the course was on professional responsibility; the question "what should accountants do?" was posed and addressed on several levels. Students were asked to write several personal essays about their values. The purpose of these essays was to situate students' thinking in their values, rather than in some externally imposed ethical system, which enabled students to relate what we were doing with service-learning and the other class project. The second aspect of the course was a series of readings on environmental accounting, the purpose of which was to explore the issue of how accountants, as a professional group, could and should respond to the social issue of environmental protection. Students wrote answers to thought questions on the readings and prepared a technical letter to send to an outside agency regarding some aspect of environmental accounting, auditing, or taxation (an excerpt from the syllabus is provided at the end of this chapter).

The third, and most time-consuming, portion of the course was a service-learning project. For the service-learning project, students were linked with clients assigned to them, based on their interests and client needs, by the local community development board. The board had a program of helping low-income people to become entrepreneurs, by offering training, financial service advising, and, in some cases, start-up loans. Students were expected to do a minimum of 50 to 60 hours of service, although progress was measured in achievement of goals rather than in hours spent. Students worked with clients to define goals and then reported to the development board representative and me on their progress.

Students were told at the beginning of the course that they should plan to spend 50 to 60 hours on their project and that if they were assigned a shorter project, they would have more than one client. Students filled out an information sheet and were interviewed to determine what their interests and concerns were. The community agency representative had more clients than the students could work with, so she selected clients whose needs meshed well with the students' interests and abilities. Students were given a brief history of the client and then arranged an initial meeting with the client at which they filled out the questionnaire *below* formulated specifically for this class. This gave students the information needed to prepare a formal plan of work, outlining what the students agreed to do during the semester. At least once each month, students completed standard forms provided by the agency describing the work completed to date. Students dis-

# Questionnaire for Accounting Clients

Client Name: _____

Students' Names: _____

1.  When did you start your business?  Can you tell me more about your products and/or services?

2.  What type of business is it -- sole proprietorship, partnership, or corporation?

3.  How do you keep your books currently?

4.  Do you have a computer to help you with bookkeeping, or would you rather keep your books manually?  Do you have a calculator or adding machine?

5.  Do you use any outside professionals to assist you with accounting or tax preparation?

6.  Are you keeping up with annual and/or quarterly tax form filings?

7.  Do you have separate business and personal checkbooks/bank accounts?  Do you balance your checkbook monthly?

8.  Do you have experience or training in bookkeeping/accounting?  Have you taken any classes relating to this subject?

9.  What concerns do you have about accounting?  What areas would you like help in?
    - ☐ Assessment of current accounting system
    - ☐ Establishment of appropriate new accounting system
    - ☐ Assistance in compiling financial statements
    - ☐ Assistance in preparing cash-flow projections, budget, business plan (circle all that are appropriate)
    - ☐ Suggestions regarding:
        - ☐ ways to increase sales/revenues
        - ☐ ways to decrease costs
    - ☐ Assistance in preparing tax returns

    - ☐ Other: _____

10. Are there other areas of your business that are in critical need of assistance currently? (marketing, personnel, etc.)

11. Do you know about the free workshops on accounting and tax obligations available from the Community Development Corporation and the IRS?

tributed copies to me and to the community agency. The community agency representative reviewed the students' work with them and with me. I was willing to meet with students by appointment to discuss their projects and to meet with their clients, if they felt it was necessary or would be helpful. We also used class time to discuss problems and issues as they arose.

Some projects were extensive, such as computerizing records of a fairly well-established company ($185,000 in annual sales). Others were rather short in duration, and students were then reassigned or given more than one client. Most projects involved preparing financial statements, upgrading accounting systems, preparing tax returns, preparing Form 990s, and in one case designing an inventory cost system. Financial statements were prepared because the clients were required to submit those annually to the community development board. Clients included a tailoring shop, a toner-cartridge recycler, a custom shirt maker, a tea importer, a child-care center, and office and residential cleaning services.

An essential aspect of service-learning is the "opportunity for preparation and reflection. This last element is today incorporated in most definitions of service-learning" (Schine 1995: 34), and is the component that provides the greatest possibilities for a lasting effect. Students were asked to regularly make entries in a service journal. An excellent reference for faculty new to using journals is Goldsmith (1995). I did not require that specific questions be answered, but did provide some suggested questions (see the next page). The service journals were submitted on four different dates through the semester. They were not graded, but I did provide written responses and reminded students that they were to do more than provide a written record of their activities. Some of them were reluctant to reflect on their experiences and preferred to merely list their accomplishments. Another approach to reflecting and journaling that may encourage some students to probe more deeply is through a caucus or computerized group discussion. This provides students a larger readership for their entries, as well as a larger group of respondents. Knowing that a group of people, rather than only the professor, will read the entries will probably change what students write in ways that are not entirely predictable, and could be inhibiting for some students but invigorating for others. Thus, faculty may want to consider using both print and electronic media.

The pedagogical benefits of dynamic, messy, complex experiences for learning about traditional ethical issues can be significant. When a student is presented with an ethically difficult situation involving other people who are relying on that student for professional advice, problems become very salient. Reasoning and theories help, but then they must be manifested in actions (Johnson 1993; Margolis 1995). Johnson describes moral deliberation as "the way in which our imaginative ideals inform our exploration of possi-

# Using Journals for Reflection

Goldsmith (1995) suggests several activities to assist students in writing in their journals. Two of them seem particularly appropriate for graduate students. Touchstone questions are "broad and provocative" and tend to be used more than once throughout the term. Goldsmith also recommends using quotations and asking students to respond to them. Below are some sample questions and quotations:

1. Briefly describe what you did during the past week.

2. What went well? Why?

3. What went badly? Why? How might you avoid a repeat of that experience?

4. Is there help that you need? Do you know where or whom to get it from?

5. Do you see value in providing professional services to members of the community? How do you define your community? Are there other ways you would rather provide service? Or do you feel that public service is not your responsibility? How has this experience helped you to formulate your opinions on these issues?

6. Thomas Piper, the Senior Associate Dean for Education Programs at the Harvard Business School, said one of the goals of Harvard's ethics program is to instill "excitement about a career in business and about the opportunities in such a career to contribute beyond self." What meaning does this statement have for you? For example, how could a career in business allow you to contribute beyond self? Has your academic training encouraged or enabled you to reflect on those opportunities?

7. The Carnegie Foundation has said:
   > If there is a crisis in education in the United States today, it is less that test scores have declined than it is that we have failed to provide the education for citizenship that is still the most important responsibility of the nation's schools and colleges.

   What is your reaction to this quote? What has this program done to educate you for citizenship?

8. Do you generally learn better by reading or by doing?

Please do not feel that you must address each question each week. These are offered to prompt your thinking and reflection; they are not exam questions.

ibilities for acting within a morally problematic situation" (1993: 149). Service-learning helps students bridge that distance between theory and action by allowing them to discuss and explore alternatives with colleagues and faculty and then to take appropriate action in real situations.

Students realized that their choices are not always clear and usually not well defined. Conflicting needs must be met simultaneously, and creativity may be called for (Whitbeck 1992). One student wrote, "The topics of ethics and integrity keep coming into play. . . . I used to think a long time ago that accounting is a pretty clear-cut area." The situations students deal with also teach by presenting immediate ethical conflicts — such as how to deal with a client who wants to omit income from her tax return, or how to mediate a conflict between the client and the agency supervising the students. Students dealt with issues of professionalism: What should they do if they didn't have an immediate answer to a client's question? How should they weigh the importance of retaining the client's confidence against the possibility of providing incorrect advice? Who should pay — in lost time — if the students made a mistake in compiling the accounting records? How much time should they volunteer beyond the semester's end if they had not completed the agreed-upon tasks? These and other questions arose during the service-learning projects, providing some issues, as well as the opportunity to resolve those issues, that students will face as professionals.

# Pedagogical Issues

This section of the paper briefly reviews issues I encountered and issues that I have reflected on with the benefit of hindsight.

## Student Responses

Because ethics is not systematically integrated into the curriculum in my department, I felt it was essential to focus on that theme in the students' last semester. But because ethics was not stressed earlier in the curriculum, students found the shift from an emphasis on technical skill building rather unsettling. Some had expected and wanted a CPA review–type course. A student wrote on the course evaluation form, "I wanted a 'wrap-up, tie everything together' class. Some people have no trouble with 'liberal' ideas. But those are for social types of classes, and I don't think they belong in an accounting program." This student provides the legitimate caveat that faculty must avoid proselytizing their own beliefs, but also reinforces the need for faculty to help students understand that accounting cannot be divorced from its social role. As one colleague said to me, the more students resist this course, the more they show they need it.

Student objections centered on the provision of free services that are ordinarily provided at a fee, and on the mandatory nature of the assignment. All but one student who objected said that they felt community service was a good thing, but that it should not be mandated. One student described his reaction this way:

> I am approaching the service portion of this class with some trepidation. I am a little annoyed with the idea that I am being "forced" to provide volunteer service. To make matters worse, I have no real justification for feeling this way, because I am in complete agreement with the theory and concept behind this type of experience. Part of my reluctance can be attributed to fear. I know I have demonstrated knowledge of accounting in the classroom, but doing it in the "real world" is something else entirely.

A student who had been quite vocal in her opposition changed her mind entirely when her mother told her that this was comparable to student teaching, which she had found enormously useful. This student (who asked not to be quoted verbatim) said that she still felt that doing good should not be forced on people. The lone student who said community service was not desirable in any way characterized service-learning as a "taking," a legal term employed primarily when governments exercise eminent domain to buy land. He had never been in a class that required any type of field experience. Other students quickly listed many courses in which they had completed fieldwork, but he remained unconvinced. Rather than force him to work with a client, I assigned him an extensive research project on the definition and extent of service-learning in business colleges.

Students who were supportive gave reasons that reflected a functional self-interest in the opportunity to develop skills or spoke of their feelings about helping the community. One student, whose experience went smoothly, said, "It is enjoyable exercising some of my education to help others. I feel I have some responsibility to my community, and this experience helps me to see that I have something to contribute on a professional level." Two students who were employed by nonprofits evaluated service-learning through that prism. One, whose perspective was firmly in the tradition of personal voluntarism, said that "working for a nonprofit organization has made me very aware of the value of volunteer hours." The other student took the broader view that by helping others, students could improve their community. She said that service-learning

> . . . introduces students to the idea that their professional responsibility to the public interest goes beyond paying clients, creditors, employers, and investors to include members of their own community who cannot afford accounting services. Volunteering your accounting expertise benefits the community by helping its members who are unable to afford traditional services to become economically self-sufficient.

This student addressed a key issue — that the purpose of service-learning is not simply to reinforce notions of individualistic responsibility or a contract-based "paying back" of what one has benefited from society. Western morality tends to be highly individualistic and doesn't provide well-developed notions of community — hence our fascination with problems of free-riding and overconsumption of "free" public goods (Johnson 1993; Parks 1993). The next time I teach the course, I would focus more discussions explicitly on issues of community and the common good.

Interestingly, international students reacted somewhat differently from the U.S. students. While they were initially somewhat intimidated, early success gave them confidence, and they were very grateful for the opportunity to work as accountants, which their status as aliens had made difficult. One student said, "I was pleasantly surprised at my ability and knowledge to help other people," and when asked whether this experience had affected the likelihood of doing this sort of thing again, said, "Knowing that I have contributed in improving somebody's quality of life is worthwhile enough for me to do this." Another student expressed his lack of confidence as well: "I never imagined that there are small, just-started businesses that [could] use my help. I thought there are no businesses that would want the help from students. As far as I am concerned, I always feel that public service is everybody's responsibility, [and] anyone who has the capability of doing so should provide that service." Another student indicated that service-learning was the norm in her earlier education: "In my country, we were taught that our community is our big family. School education is connected closely with the community. We took part in community service each semester either voluntarily or involuntarily." She explicitly tied the benefits to the individuals to the benefits of the larger community:

> I feel that public service is the responsibility of everyone, including me, because a person living in the world is not independent. Everyone in the world interacts with each other and the society. . . . If professionals can provide some public service to those who need it and cannot afford the expenses, this will help not only the persons in need but also the community as a whole.

## Private (For-Profit) Versus Public (Nonprofit) Clients

Three students expressed concern about the for-profit nature of their client's business, but others said that without some help, these businesses wouldn't exist and they saw real social benefit for the individual business owners and for the community to have these businesses. One student who objected was already very active in promoting social causes and played a leadership role in several nonprofit organizations. A second student had a long history of involvement in nonprofit organizations, and, for him, service was integrally related to the notion of nonprofit businesses. The third student felt providing free services was a market imperfection in that it gave these businesses an unfair advantage. Nonetheless, she became very committed to her project and spent additional time on it after the semester ended.

Interestingly, the argument of whether service to for-profit businesses constitutes public service appears to drop out of consideration during times of crisis or catastrophe. Practicing accountants have often helped individuals and small private businesses after floods or hurricanes or earthquakes, and consider that assistance to be public service. One could, perhaps, extend the comparison to say that many small businesses are often in a state of financial crisis, given the high rate of failure of such businesses.

I would argue that there are features of small businesses that make them desirable members of one's community. Small businesses do not require large expenditures on infrastructure or demand significant tax abatements. Small businesses are more likely to stay in the area, to hire from the area, and to contribute to programs and other institutions in the area. That the nature of community is influenced by the local ownership of local businesses is evidenced by the fervor and tenacity with which people work to prevent the entrance of large (usually retail) firms into their small towns. The move from main street or downtown to outlying malls has been well documented. The effect on our sense of community is more difficult to quantify. A small business exemplifies the American dream; we like to believe anyone with a good idea can be successful in this country. Small businesses create the majority of new jobs in our economy and are an avenue increasingly taken by women and minorities. In this class, the client businesses were started primarily by people who were economically disadvantaged and for whom these businesses represented an alternative to continued government support. Thus, supporting these businesspeople was a way both to strengthen the local economy and to help these individuals become financially independent.

## Group Size and Time Constraints

One practical lesson that students quickly learned is that scheduling is a problem. Clients did not always keep appointments and did not always arrive with the necessary records. Students worked in teams of two. Larger groups would be more difficult to coordinate. If the assignments were more complex, then the student groups would have to be larger, but tasks would have to be broken down so that the entire student group and the client did not all have to meet on a regular basis.

In writing the syllabus for the course, I followed the rule of thumb of three hours outside of class for every hour in class, and I told students to plan to work five to six hours per week on their service-learning. Since the most frequent complaint the students made was excessive time spent on this class, I realized that most students do not expect to put in that much time, and that I underestimated the time needed to complete the reading and written assignments. Given the importance of service-learning, I will probably reduce the other assignments in the course and expand on the service journal and reflection aspect of the course.

## Student Evaluations

Faculty often observe that pedagogical innovation is not rewarded, either by their administration or by students. The overall rating for teaching effectiveness for this course was 3.4 on a 4-to-0 scale, which is slightly lower than I usually receive in a graduate course. However, the overall rating of the course was only 2.5, which is considerably lower than I usually receive. One student gave the overall course rating a 0 but answered the question "I learned a lot in this course" with a 4, the highest possible rating. The three students who rated the course as average (2) responded with 3s or 4s to the question regarding learning. In fact, the average response to that question was 3.5, which indicates that although this course was not what students expected, students believed it provided significant learning.

## Student Assessment

There are two important aspects of assessment — grades and outcomes. Grades are clearly very important to students. In this course, as in all courses at Iowa State, students receive a final letter grade. Grading the outcomes of service-learning is more complicated than grading a quantitative exam. One suggestion is that the faculty member and the students collaborate to devise a rubric or set of criteria for grading the project. Generally, the focus should be on what students have learned in relationship to the stated objectives, rather than on the project itself. While this might seem to mitigate students' sense of responsibility to perform well, the presence of real clients with very real needs invokes a powerful sense of obligation within students. The reason for not placing a focus on the outcome is that so much of the client situation is beyond the control of the students and the faculty. It is not likely that each student faces a client whose situation is equally complex, or whose records are equally confused, or who is equally amenable to receiving and understanding the students' services. Thus, too great a focus on the specific work completed in the project introduces an inevitable inequity. However, everyone has equal access to reflecting on his/her experience and to handling situations in a constructive, mature fashion.

Students received full points for the service-learning project if they met the goals established jointly with their clients. The community service representative monitored their work by meeting with the students and the clients, and reported back to me. Points for maintaining the service journal were slightly reduced if students included no reflective writing. The environmental reading sheets were graded as satisfactory or satisfactory plus, with students given the option of rewriting sheets that were not satisfactory. Finally, the environmental technical letter was submitted in draft form to provide students with the opportunity to improve the paper. Students reviewed another student's draft, using the grading guidelines that I would use for their finished papers. This helped students to understand the grading scale and also gave them insights about how to improve their own papers. I also reviewed the drafts. My overall approach to teaching and grading this course was in many ways a mastery-learning one, which tends to reduce variance in final grades. My intent was to provide the guidance and support to enable everyone to succeed at the assigned tasks.

As a faculty member, I am more concerned about outcomes than I am about grades. I did not take any formal survey or attitudinal measures of students' sense of civic obligation at the beginning and end of the course. That is one important change I plan to make. Based on reading I have done since the course, I can suggest the Markus, Howard, and King article (1993) or the Giles and Eyler article (1994) for an instrument that measures social outcomes. Deemer (1987) provides a list of issues that are important in assessing students' moral growth. In the accounting literature, the Rokeach Values Survey has been used to measure the balance between individual and social values (Ward, Ward, and Wilson 1995). Once a faculty member has clarified his or her purpose and objective(s) in using service-learning, then, given the relative novelty of this approach in accounting classes, it would be very useful to assess the effectiveness of service-learning with some measure of social attitudes or commitment.

## Arranging Service-Learning Projects

There are several sources of information on possible service-learning projects. First, one should contact offices within the university. The school may have a cocurriculum or student life office that may sponsor volunteer projects that could be used as service-learning opportunities. Another good source of information is Campus Compact, whose national office is at Brown University (Box 1975, Providence, RI 02912). Other possibilities are to call the local Accounting Aid Society, agencies working to train and develop nonprofits, or umbrella organizations such as United Way. If for-profit clients are desired, the local community development board (which I used), the local Chamber of Commerce, and other organizations, such as minority business consortia, could be helpful. Small projects could probably be found by offering to help the student organizations on campus with their financial reporting requirements. Based on my experience, I will arrange a mixture of profit and nonprofit organizations for students to work with.

## Pedagogy

Extensive service-learning projects inherently place much of the learning process beyond the control of the faculty member. Service-learning is a departure from the instructional paradigm that says teachers must be present for learning to occur (Barr and Tagg 1995). With service-learning, faculty must do a great deal of work to line up appropriate assignments, be available to help resolve problems and to provide technical and personal support to students, find relevant readings, and motivate students to reflect on their experience, but faculty will significantly reduce the amount of time spent on directive teaching. Faculty must also be very clear in their objectives in using service-learning in order to enable students to most beneficially incorporate the experience into their learning of related materials. This shift from direct teaching to less predictability must be one with which faculty feel comfortable if the experience is to be successful.

## The Benefits of Hindsight

As I prepare for another semester of teaching the same course, I see opportunities to improve the course. One is to explain more fully why I am using service-learning (see the handout at the end of this chapter). I also plan to have a Big Six manager, who is very enthusiastic about public service, come speak to the class the first day. I am considering asking for some student input on grading the service-learning portion of the course. Doing this could, I believe, lessen the sense of unfairness students may feel because of the inevitable differences across client situations and assignments. I also plan to do more to generate more reflection in student journals. I will also require more frequent journal entries and reports on progress toward completion of the goals for the semester. Finally, the section on environmental accounting was far too extensive, given the time I expected students to put in on service-learning. I realize that 50 hours tend to expand into much more, because the students tend to overestimate what they can accomplish in that amount of time. Instead, I will be using a less extensive set of readings and cases selected either because they help demonstrate the effect of accounting rules and principles on the allocation of social goods or because they explicitly address ethical issues in accounting.

# Conclusion

Service-learning affords faculty an opportunity to focus on teaching ethics beyond the limits of case-based courses. There are difficulties, and the use of service-learning requires new pedagogies and faculty may encounter student resistance. Faculty also will find great student enthusiasm. When service-learning is successful, significant cognitive learning occurs, and students have a greater understanding of and interest in their role in promoting the public interest. If real decisions and actions provide greater opportunity for and evidence of ethical development than do responses to dilemmas with forced-choice answers, educators should consider alternative pedagogies, such as service-learning, for teaching ethics. Both faculty and students can derive great satisfaction from participating as students develop a broader, more engaged definition of their communities and their responsibility within that community. As one student wrote on her evaluation, "It was a great experience and should be developed more. It is worthwhile for the student."

## References

Accounting Education Change Commission. (1990). "Objectives of Education for Accountants." Position Statement No. 1. *Issues in Accounting Education* 5(2): 307-312.

American Accounting Association, Committee on the Future Structure, Content, and Scope of Accounting Education. (1986). "Future Accounting Education: Preparing for the Expanding Profession." *Issues in Accounting Education* 1(1): 168-195.

American Institute of Certified Public Accountants. (1991a). *Accounting Recruiting Research: Survey of High School and College Students. Executive Summary and Synopsis.* New York: AICPA.

———— . (1991b). *Code of Professional Conduct.* New York: AICPA.

Armstrong, M.G. (1990). "Professional Ethics and Accounting Education: A Critique of the 8-Step Method." *Business & Professional Ethics Journal* 9: 181-191.

Barber, B.R. (1994). "A Proposal for Mandatory Citizen Education and Community Service." *Michigan Journal of Community Service–Learning* 1(1): 86-93.

Barr, R.B., and J. Tagg. (November/December 1995). "From Teaching to Learning: A New Paradigm for Undergraduate Education." *Change* 27(6): 12-25.

Bonwell, C.C., and J.A. Eison. (1991). *Active Learning: Creating Excitement in the Classroom.* ASHE-ERIC Higher Education Reports, no. 1. Washington, DC: George Washington University, Graduate School of Education and Human Development.

Boss, J.A. (1994). "The Effect of Community Service Work on the Moral Development of College Ethics Students." *Journal of Moral Education* 23(2): 183-197.

Camenisch, P.F. (1988). "On Being a Professional, Morally Speaking." In *Professional Ideals,* edited by A. Flores, pp. 14-26. Belmont, CA: Wadsworth Publishing.

Davis, T.M., and P.H. Murrell. (1993). *Turning Teaching Into Learning: The Role of Student Responsibility in the Collegiate Experience.* ASHE-ERIC Higher Education Reports, no. 8. Washington, DC: George Washington University, Graduate School of Education and Human Development.

Deemer, D. (1987). "Moral Judgment and Life Experience." Unpublished doctoral dissertation. Minneapolis, MN: University of Minnesota.

Derry, R., and R.M. Green. (1989). "Ethical Theory in Business Ethics: A Critical Assessment." *Journal of Business Ethics* 8(7): 521-533.

Fulmer, W.E., and B.R. Cargile. (1987). "Ethical Perceptions of Accounting Students: Does Exposure to a Code of Professional Ethics Help?" *Issues in Accounting Education* 2(2): 207-219.

Giles, D.E., Jr., and J. Eyler. (1994). "The Impact of a College Community Service Laboratory on Students' Personal, Social, and Cognitive Outcomes." *Journal of Adolescence* 17: 327-339.

Goldsmith, S. (1995). *Journal Reflection.* Washington, DC: American Alliance for Rights and Responsibilities.

Hiltebeitel, K.M., and S.K. Jones. (1991). "Initial Evidence on the Impact of Integrating Ethics Into Accounting Education." *Issues in Accounting Education* 6(2): 262-275.

Johnson, M. (1993). *Moral Imagination: Implications of Cognitive Science for Ethics.* Chicago, IL: University of Chicago.

Kerr, D.S., and L.M. Smith. (1995). "Importance of and Approaches to Incorporating Ethics in the Accounting Classroom." *Journal of Business Ethics* 14(12): 987-995.

Loeb, S.E. (1988). "Teaching Students Accounting Ethics: Some Crucial Issues." *Issues in Accounting Education* 3(2): 316-329.

Margolis, J. (1995). *Tipping Our Caps, Missing the Boat: Can We Make Business Ethics Relevant to Managers?* Proceedings of *From the Universities to the Market Place: The Business Ethics Journey,* pp. 283-293. Sponsored by St. John's University, New York, NY.

Markus, G.B., J.P.F. Howard, and D.C. King. (1993). "Integrating Community Service and Classroom Instruction Enhances Learning: Results From an Experiment." *Educational Evaluation and Policy Analysis* 15(4): 410-419.

Milam, E., and F. McNair. (1992). "An Examination of Accounting Faculty Perceptions of the Importance of Ethics Coverage in Accounting Courses." *Business & Professional Ethics Journal* 11(2): 57-71.

Newman, F. (1985). *Higher Education and the American Resurgence.* Princeton, NJ: Carnegie Foundation for the Advancement of Teaching.

Parks, S.D. (1993). "Is It Too Late? Young Adults and the Formation of Professional Ethics." In *Can Ethics Be Taught?* edited by T.R. Piper, M.C. Gentile, and S.D. Parks, pp. 13-72. Boston, MA: Harvard Business School.

Pascarella, E.T., C.A. Ethington, and J.C. Smart. (1988). "The Influence of College on Humanitarian/Civic Involvement Values." *Journal of Higher Education* 59(4): 412-437.

Piper, T.R. (1993a). "A Program to Integrate Leadership, Ethics, and Corporate Responsibility Into Management Education." In *Can Ethics Be Taught?* edited by T.R. Piper, M.C. Gentile, and S.D. Parks, pp. 117-149. Boston, MA: Harvard Business School.

————. (1993b). "Rediscovery of Purpose: The Genesis of the Leadership, Ethics, and Corporate Responsibility Initiative." In *Can Ethics Be Taught?* edited by T.R. Piper, M.C. Gentile, and S.D. Parks, pp. 1-12. Boston, MA: Harvard Business School.

Ponemon, L.A. (1993). "Can Ethics Be Taught in Accounting?" *Journal of Accounting Education* 11: 185-210.

Pritchard, M.S. (1992). "Good Works." *Professional Ethics* (1): 155-177.

Rest, J. (1986). *Moral Development: Advances in Research and Theory.* New York: Praeger.

S.A.S. (Spring 1996). Review of *Moral Development: A Compendium,* edited by B. Puka. Book Notes. *Harvard Educational Review* 66(1): 143-146.

Schine, J. (1995). "Community Service: When Theory and Practice Meet." *Educational Researcher* 24(2): 33-34.

Smith, M.W. (1994). "Community Service–Learning: Striking the Chord of Citizenship." *Michigan Journal of Community Service–Learning* 1(1): 37-43.

Solberg, J., K.C. Strong, and C. McGuire, Jr. (1995). "Living (Not Learning) Ethics." *Journal of Business Ethics* 14(1): 71-81.

Stanton, T.K. (1990). *Integrating Public Service With Academic Study: The Faculty Role.* A Report of Campus Compact. Providence, RI: Brown University.

Sullivan, W.M. (1988). "Calling or Career: The Tensions of Modern Professional Life." In *Professional Ideals,* edited by A. Flores, pp. 40-46. Belmont, CA: Wadsworth Publishing.

Ward, S.P., D.R. Ward, and T.E. Wilson, Jr. (1995). "University Accounting Professors: An Examination of Personal Values." *Accounting Educators' Journal* 7(1): 39-53.

Whitbeck, C. (1992). "The Trouble With Dilemmas: Rethinking Applied Ethics." *Professional Ethics* 1: 119-142.

# Syllabus

## ACCOUNTING 696
## Capstone Course for Master of Science in Accounting Program

REQUIRED TEXTS:

A coursepack has been prepared. But there will be many more readings that you will have to copy individually. The required readings that we will discuss in class as a group will be available to you for copying.

WHAT ARE THE OBJECTIVES OF THE COURSE?

This is a capstone course for MSA students and the course is being offered for the first time. The focus of the class will be on the role of accountants in society and clarification and exploration of your professional values. Put simply, the question we are asking is -- what should accountants do? We will explore those issues in three ways, through a series of personal essays on topics that encourage values clarification, through work in the community with a small business client, and through the process of writing a letter to an official body (e.g. the SEC, FASB, a Congressional committee, the EPA) arguing your support for a position on the question related to environmental accounting. I hope that through these exercises your technical appreciation of accounting will be enhanced, and that you will have a greater appreciation for the pervasive role that accounting has on businesses, as well as the profound, and often discounted, role that accounting has on social allocation of resources. In that process, you will, I hope, gain a better understanding of your reasons for choosing accounting and what you can do as an accountant.

HOW WILL CLASSES BE STRUCTURED?

We have a small group, and you will be working in teams with the business clients, so we should probably know each other pretty well by the end of the term. In addition to turning in a reflective journal on your public service, we will devote some class time to discussion of how your public service is progressing. We will have readings on environmental accounting that we will discuss. You will have reading sheets to prepare for class. You will also have to discuss the technical letter with the class, at several stages. (We want to avoid end of the term panic!).

HOW WILL GRADES BE ASSIGNED?

Grades will be based on the following weights:

| | |
|---|---|
| Personal essays | 10% |
| Service Learning | 45 |
| Environmental Acctg Letter | 25 |
| Reading sheets & Participation | 20 |

The Personal essays will not be graded; you will get full credit for submitting them and you will get feedback on them. Content is more important than grammar but spell checking on EVERY written assignment is a MUST!

Service learning will be evaluated on the basis of your records of how you spent time, your reflective journal discussing your experiences, and feedback from the Community Development Corporation. The focus is on learning from your experience, and on meeting the obligations that you establish with the client. In two weeks we will meet at the Community Development Corporation offices instead of in the usual classroom, and you will be given an orientation to the program and assigned a client(s), based on the answers you provide on the student information sheet.

The letter to an agency is the product of your research on environmental accounting. Two drafts will be submitted through the term, so you have lots of feedback and chances to improve the letter. The Accounting Department will pay the postage to mail the letter! These are going to be sent, so please do an excellent job.

Reading sheets should be typed and are based on questions asked the course readings. Most of the questions will not be of the look-it-up and copy the third paragraph kind; they will be more open-ended, won't always have right answers, and will require you to form and defend your opinions. Again, content is more important than grammar, but spell checking is required.

Because this is a capstone course, other faculty will be involved in the evaluation process. You will be asked to prepare a portfolio of all of your work throughout the term and that will be shared with other faculty for their input. Please note that the portfolio will not be used to determine your grade, but rather to assess the MSA program, and to evaluate how and whether we need to make adjustments in the program.

# Objectives of Service Learning

A significant portion of your time inside and outside of class will be spent in what is called academic service learning. You will be involved with an actual accounting client and will be responsible for developing a plan of action, carrying out and documenting that plan, reflecting on your experiences during that time, and presenting the results of your work to the group.

The clients will be a variety of profit and non-profit organizations and I will try to match your interests and skills with the needs of the clients. Working in this way with an actual client on real, complex accounting problems has several benefits:

- You will gain first-hand knowledge of the key importance of sound financial information to an organization's stability.

- You will gain first-hand knowledge of how the functional areas of accounting support and relate to one another. We teach tax separate from financial and from systems and from managerial, for instance. But in a real setting, users need all those systems and need to have them as integrated as possible.

- You will have a chance to consider your role and obligations as a professional accountant to use your expertise in your community. We will look at such questions as:
    What is my community?
    How do I define the "public interest" referred to in the AICPA Code of Conduct?
    Can and should I use my accounting expertise within my community?
    What is my responsibility to promote the good of my community?

- You will have a chance to face some of the ethical questions that arise in the course of executing one's professional duties. These could be the same or similar issues that you will face as a practicing professional after graduation.

- You will gain experience in the many details of being a professional accounting consultant:
    Making a plan of work
    Setting time lines
    Interviewing the client
    Having the appropriate information at the right time
    Documenting your work
    Follow-up with the client

# Student Consulting Organizations:
## An Alternative Approach to Service-Learning

by Timothy S. Mech

The articles in this volume reflect a growing consensus that direct experience enhances classroom learning. As D.V. Rama observes in her opening essay, it may not always be feasible to incorporate direct experience into the curriculum because of the large volume of specialized knowledge that must be taught. In such instances, students can obtain many of the benefits of direct experience through extracurricular activities. This chapter describes Project Empowerment, a student organization at Boston College that reinforces classroom learning by giving students the opportunity to provide short-term management services to not-for-profits. After providing some institutional background and sketching the origin of Project Empowerment, I describe how the organization operates and offer some observations about the strengths and weaknesses of this approach to active learning.

## Institutional Background

Because of the large number of required courses in Boston College's undergraduate accounting program, some have felt it impractical to incorporate direct experience into the formal curriculum. AACSB guidelines require undergraduate students to complete at least half their coursework in areas other than management. This leaves students with 60 credit hours to devote to management courses. Accounting students must take 37 hours of required management core classes,[1] followed by an additional 18 hours of advanced accounting classes. Many accounting students also wish to take supplementary classes in related management disciplines, such as finance and computer information systems. Little time remains for classes that provide direct experience. Some accounting students bridge the gap between classroom instruction and the workplace with part-time or summer jobs. These jobs frequently provide meaningful experiences, but offer few chances to discuss the work with professors or other students.

This article would not have been possible without Sylvain Fey, Alexander Wit, and Katherine Moran, the student founders of Project Empowerment, and Brian Fitzsimons of the Dec-Tam Corporation, which sponsored our initial project. I also appreciate the helpful comments of the editors of this volume.

Because the curriculum is tight, some of the objectives of Boston College's Carroll School of Management (CSOM) cannot be implemented fully through classes. Project Empowerment achieves a number of these goals outside the formal curriculum. Here are a few examples:

1. The official mission of the CSOM is "to educate future managers and decision makers who carry forth excellence in their professional lives in the mission of service to others." Project Empowerment gets future managers involved serving their community.

2. The CSOM seeks students with the "potential for humane leadership." Project Empowerment helps to train humane leaders by providing opportunities for students to use their management skills to help not-for-profits.

3. The CSOM mission statement encourages interaction between the university and the community. "Private, public, and not-for-profit practitioner interaction is sought and valued. . . ." Project Empowerment brings together Boston College's students and faculty, privately owned businesses, public officials, and not-for-profits.

4. The CSOM faculty has endorsed the idea of "active learning," through which students learn by doing. Project Empowerment gives hands-on experience to students.

In these and other ways, Project Empowerment contributes to the broader educational goals of the school, achieving what classroom instruction does not.

## Origins

Project Empowerment began in the classroom in fall 1993. As an experiment, I encouraged my students to discuss and to write about some of the broader issues facing managers. On one occasion, I told students about a homeless shelter that would have to be closed because it violated state lead paint laws. I suggested that students could work with private businesses and local government to rescue the not-for-profit.

One of our students expressed interest in this project. First, he found a lead abatement company that agreed to donate the labor for removing lead from the shelter. Next, a city official offered to apply for a grant to cover the cost of the materials. Within a few weeks, we were confident that the problem was well on its way to being resolved. We were pleased that such modest efforts on our part could achieve such significant results. We were wrong.

In January 1994, the student working on this project moved to Chile to study for a semester abroad. At about the same time, the director of the shelter was hospitalized, and the city official lost her job. The lead abatement company lost interest after its phone calls to the city official were left unanswered. No one on the city staff returned the departed official's calls or had the courtesy to explain that she had left!

When I learned how plans were derailed, I asked two other students to get things back on track. After dealing with a dozen government offices and contacting numerous businesses for help, we finally arranged to get the shelter de-leaded for only a few thousand dollars, without any government aid. Thanks to the lead abatement company and a local window manufacturer that supplied windows at cost, the homeless shelter saved more than $20,000.

We learned several important lessons from this project. First, we learned that developing a plan is much easier than implementing change. Second, we learned that things take time. The homeless shelter wasn't de-leaded until a year and a half after we began. Third, we found that small businesses can be effective partners. In our experience, managers of small businesses are accessible and willing to make decisions without long delays or excessive paperwork.

Shortly after we started working with the shelter, the students decided to establish an organization to provide this sort of service on an ongoing basis. In March 1994, we submitted our proposal to the Office of the Dean for Student Development and received approval to begin operating as an official student organization the following fall.

# The Constitution

Project Empowerment's original constitution, as written by the student founders, appears at the end of this chapter. With a few exceptions, noted below, this would be a good model for other groups that wish to start this type of organization. A few of its features deserve special attention.

## Membership

Even though the students who started Project Empowerment were from the School of Management, they wanted the organization to be open to students from all schools of the university. Not-for-profits frequently need help in areas such as graphic arts, multimedia presentations, and foreign language translations, as well as the traditional management disciplines. Also, students from different disciplines can teach one another. The official purpose of Project Empowerment (Article 2) and its membership requirements (Article 3) are general enough to welcome students from all parts of the university. In practice, however, Project Empowerment consists primarily of management students. Last year, all three officers were accounting majors.

It's important for students to take their commitments to Project Empowerment seriously. The organization's reputation suffers when a student fails to deliver promised services. The requirements in Article 3.D that active members attend at least half the meetings and participate in at least one project help to weed out unreliable and apathetic students.

## Officers

Project Empowerment's executive board consists of three student officers and a faculty adviser. In addition to the duties outlined in the constitution, the board exercises control by deciding the agendas of the meetings. The executive board operates on consensus; all decisions must be unanimous. At Boston College, it never has been a problem for the board members to agree.

According to the constitution, the executive board meets monthly. In practice, the student officers have almost daily contact with each other; the meetings keep the faculty adviser informed. In my opinion, the faculty adviser should try to meet with student officers at least every other week, either on the weeks without full membership meetings, or a day or two before each general meeting.

## Elections

Officers are elected at the end of the spring semester for the next academic year. The election procedures in the constitution are inefficient in several respects. First, it's awkward to have separate votes for each of the three positions. If everyone aspires to be president, no one runs for the other two offices. Given the egalitarian nature of the executive board, a person suited for one office would be well suited to serve in other capacities as well. Consequently, a single election could be held for all three positions. This could be handled in a number of ways. One approach would be to have each member rank his/her top three candidates. A candidate would receive one, two, or three points, depending on whether the member ranks the candidate third, second, or first. The president, vice president, and secretary-treasurer would be the people with the highest, next-highest, and third-highest total vote count.

Another awkward feature of the election procedure is that nominees address the members one week before the election. Because meetings are biweekly, this requires an extra meeting. Members in attendance at the election may not have been present when the nominees spoke. It would be much more convenient to have the nominees speak at the beginning of the meeting in which the election takes place.

# Implementation

The constitution leaves many questions unanswered about the daily operation of Project Empowerment. This section describes the recruitment of members, the role of the faculty adviser, project selection, and other topics about the operation of Project Empowerment.

## Recruitment of Members

Because student organizations don't appear in official course listings, student leaders must make efforts to inform prospective members about their groups. Methods differ from one campus to another, but they include posters, articles in campus newspapers, and word of mouth. Some colleges have student activities days near the beginning of the fall semesters, when student groups can recruit new members. The officers, elected in the previous spring, should meet before the fall term to prepare for recruitment.

Dates and locations of biweekly meetings should be determined well in advance and published in campus newspapers. In addition, campus papers are frequently willing to print articles about interesting projects or recently completed work. This serves as an important recruitment tool.

For Project Empowerment, the most important single source of new members has been referrals from faculty, administrators, and other members. Enthusiasm for current and potential projects is contagious. Interesting, relevant projects help the organization to attract and to retain members.

To maintain continuity from one year to the next, recruitment efforts should be directed toward freshmen and sophomores. If the organization consists mostly of juniors and seniors, membership changes too radically from year to year.

## The Role of the Faculty Adviser

Students bring certain characteristic strengths and weaknesses to the organization. On the one hand, college students are often idealistic and willing to work for a good cause. Many students are action-oriented, and willing to take constructive risks. Full-time undergraduate students frequently have time to volunteer, unencumbered by family demands and full-time employment. In addition, students have substantial talents and a willingness to share them. Students are a source of tremendous creative energy.

On the other hand, few 20-year-old students have the maturity and experience of a typical faculty member. Some students begin a task with great vigor, only to lose enthusiasm and quit. Others don't see the importance of procedures and paperwork, preferring to keep things informal and loose. Students sometimes have difficulty saying no to clients, and accept projects that don't meet the goals of the organization. Finally, some students tend to defer difficult issues from one meeting to the next, rather than resolving them. The faculty adviser should know the students well enough to help them channel their particular strengths, while working with them to overcome their weaknesses. In my experience, students welcome the faculty adviser's input and efforts to keep things on track. Strong faculty oversight is especially important for student consulting groups, because of the complexity of the tasks and the commitments to clients outside the university.

From an educational point of view, the faculty adviser has a responsibility to try to steer the group away from mindless tasks and to projects that have educational value and/or develop job skills. Not-for-profits that simply need free labor can be referred to student service organizations having a different focus. The adviser also has a responsibility to listen to students about projects under way and to offer constructive ideas. Because of the faculty member's greater experience, a few minutes of faculty time can spare students hours of frustration.

Obviously, the faculty adviser must set limits. His or her role should be to encourage and to guide, rather than to do the work for the students. The faculty adviser can remind student officers to type minutes of the meetings, for example, but shouldn't fall into the trap of actually doing the paperwork. Finally, the faculty adviser must not forget that friendships keep student organizations alive. The faculty adviser should exercise leadership in a way that boosts, rather than damages, student morale.

## Project Selection

A student consulting organization is only as worthwhile as the tasks it accomplishes. Interesting and useful projects attract motivated students and other necessary resources. Project Empowerment evaluates prospective projects according to the following standards:

1. *Members agree that the project will help the community.* This standard eliminates work for political groups and organizations that provide controversial services.

2. *The project is feasible.* It has a clear objective that can be completed with available resources. Rather than becoming involved in the ongoing operation of a not-for-profit, Project Empowerment focuses on short-term projects that leave an organization better equipped to serve the community. The name "Project Empowerment" reflects this last point: The objective is to *empower* not-for-profits to serve better.

3. *The work is interesting to the students.* A priority should be given to projects that teach students something that they can apply in the workplace after graduation.

4. *The client is committed to working with the students.* Because Project Empowerment doesn't charge for its services, not-for-profits sometimes ask for help without giving the matter much thought. This leads to discouragement when students find the clients are unavailable, or complete tasks only

to find the clients have changed their plans. Good paperwork, including project descriptions signed by the clients, is one way to reduce this risk. For accepted projects, if clients become unavailable or otherwise signal lack of interest, it's appropriate to ask them politely whether their plans have changed, before pouring more resources into a project.

Students should give project selection as much effort and professional care as they would give external clients. I would recommend mass mailings to potential clients at the beginning of each academic year to solicit proposals. Because only a fraction of the proposals will have significant pedagogical value, it is better to generate a large number of ideas, so the group can be selective.

Project Empowerment's list of potential clients includes not-for-profits that work with other Boston College groups, United Way agencies, and referrals from faculty and staff. Representatives of Project Empowerment invite potential clients to submit proposals. Members evaluate new proposals at each meeting, in accord with the standards listed above. Because the success of a project depends on the enthusiasm of the students, the final test for a proposal is whether enough members volunteer for the project.

Given the time and effort required to recruit new members, identify worthwhile projects, and effectively manage an organization, the officers of a student consulting group should view their own organization as their chief client, and take on additional projects only if they have extra time.

## Project Teams and Advisers

Each project has a team consisting of three to six interested students. Theoretically, each team appoints one of its members team leader, and finds a faculty member or MBA student to serve as project adviser. In practice, it has been difficult to find people willing to serve as advisers, so teams have operated with a minimum of faculty assistance. Some students volunteer for more than one project and belong to more than one team.

Each team schedules its own meetings and works with the not-for-profit to accomplish the proposed task. After the team begins its work on a project, the team and not-for-profit frequently redefine the objectives. We try to maintain a balance between flexibility and focus.

At any given time, Project Empowerment has about five projects under way. These projects vary widely in difficulty and scope. Some projects have a very explicit focus on management skills. For example, students created a donor database and accounting system for a soup kitchen, helped an incipient not-for-profit write a business plan, and assisted an organization that serves Boston's immigrant population with multilingual advertising. Because Project Empowerment includes nonmanagement students, other projects do not emphasize specialized business skills. For example, students provided artwork and wrote a brochure for a social service organization for senior citizens, organized a raffle for an organization that provides free child care for poor working families, and created a logo for an organization that helps AIDS care givers. In the spirit of the Rama essay and the Accounting Education Change Commission Issues Statement No. 4, even the projects that do not focus explicitly on traditional management skills teach students general skills, such as communication and organizational skills, that are broadly relevant to careers in management.

## Meetings

In addition to team meetings, Project Empowerment holds full-membership meetings every two weeks. At these meetings, members discuss current projects and evaluate new ones. Each team gives a progress report and describes difficulties relating to the project, then listens to ideas and recommendations from other group members.

These meetings achieve a number of important objectives. First, they make the group more cohesive. Because the teams work on different tasks at different locations, there would be a tendency for the group to become fragmented without these times to meet together. Second, the general meetings help teams to maintain momentum. Teams have an extra incentive to make progress, so they will have something to report at the next meeting. Third, the discussions of projects usually generate a number of useful ideas and suggestions that improve the quality of work. Given the limited faculty participation, these meetings give some teams the only faculty input they will receive. Finally, the meetings give students an informal opportunity to reflect about their experiences.

At its first few meetings, Project Empowerment had professional consultants speak to students about consulting skills and the structure of the organization. I would recommend this as a good way to start an academic year.

## Facilities

The location of the meetings has a significant effect on the dynamics. Large lecture halls make students feel like spectators rather than participants. This discourages students from contributing ideas, and leaves them with the impression that their attendance is unnecessary. For groups of 20 students or fewer, I would recommend arranging chairs in a circle to encourage discussion. Simple refreshments before the meetings and name tags are useful in helping members to get to know each other.

Because a great deal of the work happens over the telephone, students should have access to answering machines or voice mail. At Boston College, office space was helpful but unnecessary; students preferred meeting in their residence halls. At universities with large commuter populations, office space would be much more important.

## Institutional Support

Project Empowerment has negligible cash expenses (about $50 per year); funding comes from the Office of the Dean for Student Development. The group shares office space with the management school's Honors Program. Boston College administrators and faculty appreciate the contributions of a well-run student consulting organization. Significant funding could be attracted, if the need existed. It has been easy for Project Empowerment to get publicity in the school newspapers, when students take the initiative to contact the editors.

Faculty time is one of the scarcest resources. Project Empowerment has tried to recruit faculty through articles in the campus papers, announcements at faculty meetings, and personal contacts by the students and faculty adviser, with little success. One reason for the limited faculty involvement is that Project Empowerment competes with other community service organizations for faculty attention. Also, overseeing a student consulting group takes time from activities that have a much greater impact on promotion and tenure, such as research and publication.

# Advantages and Disadvantages of Extracurricular Active Learning

Student consulting organizations, such as Project Empowerment, have several advantages relative to classes that offer credit for service-learning. First, student organizations have more flexibility than formal classes. Very busy students can help with modest assignments and still gain valuable insights and skills. Students with more time can tackle difficult assignments or several smaller projects in the same semester. Second, students benefit from operating the organization. Besides helping external clients, students also recruit members, identify new projects, handle the publicity, communicate with the university administration, and manage funds. As Rama points out, this is consistent with the AECC's suggestion that students can gain business skills by serving in campus organizations.

Project Empowerment has helped students to learn about project management, client relationships, and working with local government and businesses. In addition, students have learned to relate to people from other socioeconomic backgrounds, developed perseverance in the face of unexpected problems, and acquired confidence. Clearly, these lessons will serve students well in their professional careers.

These and other benefits are possible from an extracurricular organization. Notwithstanding, there are significant advantages to making direct experience part of the formal curriculum. First, the ability to assign grades gives the faculty leverage to monitor projects more closely and to ensure better-quality work. Second, students have an incentive to complete projects punctually, so they will be able to complete the course on schedule. Third, students can be required to write papers summarizing and integrating their experiences. Fourth, the student's transcript would certify that the student has completed the active learning experience. Finally, more students would participate in this sort of experience if it were a formal part of the curriculum.

In my opinion, a formal course is a better method of providing direct experience than a student organization, if the curriculum can accommodate it. A second-best solution would be to reduce the faculty adviser's course load to give him or her time to oversee the extracurricular consulting group. Our experience at Boston College, however, shows that motivated students can get the benefits of a formal service-learning course when neither of these conditions holds.

### Note

1. A few of the management core classes are offered by departments outside the School of Management and don't count toward the 60-credit limit.

Project Empowerment

# Constitution

ARTICLE 1: The name of the organization will be PROJECT EMPOWERMENT.

ARTICLE 2: The purpose of this club is to provide Boston College students with the opportunities to apply the knowledge they acquire in college to help the community.

The goal is to identify needs in the community and to provide not-for-profit organizations with short term consulting support, such as help with grant writing, artwork/publicity, finding financial support, management services, and special needs.

ARTICLE 3: A) Membership is open to any Boston College undergraduate or graduate students full-time or part-time.
B) Each member shall have one vote in matters subject to a general vote.
C) There shall be no discrimination against any individual due to race, age, religion, color, sex, national origin, mental or medical handicaps, marital status, sexual orientation, Vietnam Veteran status.
D) In order to be considered an active member a student must attend 50% of the meetings and participate in one ongoing project, as projects become available.

ARTICLE 4: There shall be an executive board consisting of four members: the President, the Vice President, the Secretary/Treasurer and the Faculty Advisor. The duties of the Executive board shall be to schedule meetings, call emergency meetings, and coordinate fund-raising.

The responsibilities of the officers are as follows:
President: Schedule and preside over the meetings, organize agendas for each meeting, keep in regular contact with the Assistant Dean for non-funded clubs in ODSD, and attend the club officers meeting in September. Serves as principal liaison with community organizations.
Vice President: Shall assist the President with his/her duties as needed, and will assume responsibility if President is absent.
Secretary/Treasurer: Will monitor all financial activities of the club, keep in regular contact with the Budget Manager in the ODSD, and attend the club treasurer meeting in September. Takes minutes of meetings and submits them to Assistant Dean for non-funded clubs.
Faculty Advisor: Will aid the club in its involvement with University Officials. He/She will also be in the executive board.

The officers for the 1994-95 academic year will be:
Sylvain Fey (President), Alexander Wit (Vice President), Katy Moran (Secretary/Treasurer), and Professor Timothy Mech (Faculty Advisor).

Page 1

ARTICLE 5:   A) Officers meetings will be held monthly. Full membership meetings will be held biweekly throughout the academic year. Informal meetings may be scheduled by the faculty advisor to discuss projects taking place in the summer.
B) All decisions of the executive board shall be finalized only with a unanimous vote by the members of the executive board.

ARTICLE 6:   Anyone wishing to run for an officer position must have been an active member of the club for a minimum of two semesters. (Refer to Article 3.D.) Nominations will be taken two weeks prior to the election date.

▸   Members may either be nominated by another member or may nominate themselves.

▸   Officers of the club must be full-time undergraduate students.

▸   A week before elections, each nominee will be given the opportunity to address the club to advocate her/his candidacy.

▸   Outgoing officers will not vote unless there is a tie. In the event of a tie, the President, Vice President and Secretary/Treasurer will cast their votes.

▸   Voting will be done by secret ballot with each member receiving one vote for each available position. Ballots will be tallied by the faculty advisor.

Any member of the club wishing to have an officer impeached must first present the reasons to the executive board. In the event that the matter is not resolved, it will become the first item on the agenda of the next meeting with at least one half of the members present. At this time, the officer against whom charges were brought will have their duties as an executive member suspended and distributed among the remaining members of the executive board until a vote on the matter takes place. The vote will take place at the next meeting. The impeachment must be approved by two-thirds of the club members with each member having one vote. If the officer is impeached, nominations for his or her replacement will take place immediately. Elections to replace the impeached officers will take place the following meeting with the terms of the office beginning immediately after the elections.

ARTICLE 7:   Amendments to the constitution must be approved by two-thirds of the members of the club present at the meeting. At this meeting, at least one-half of the members must be present. The proposed amendment shall be submitted in writing to each member of the club at least one week prior to the vote on the amendment. Amendments must be approved by the ODSD before going into effect.

ARTICLE 8:   This constitution shall go into effect upon approval of registration from ODSD. It shall be reviewed on a yearly basis, and revised accordingly.

# Service-Learning Projects in Accounting:
## Implementation Strategies

by D.V. Rama

Prior essays in this volume have focused on the rationale for integrating service-learning and the goals of service-learning projects in accounting. These essays present examples of different ways in which service-learning can be integrated into the accounting curriculum. Each implementation involves numerous questions about integration of the project with course content, design of reflection mechanisms, grading, etc. This concluding article summarizes some of the key implementation decisions that must be made when integrating service-learning projects in the accounting curriculum. The advantages and disadvantages of different choices are also discussed. The objective of this discussion is to provide a starting point for instructors in making decisions about how to integrate service-learning into the accounting curriculum.

## Establishing Goals

Before attempting to integrate service projects into the accounting curriculum, accounting educators must first decide on their goals for such projects. Decisions regarding goals drive the design of the service and reflection components. One important goal is to reinforce technical accounting knowledge. Implementations in this volume provide examples of how service-learning can be used to reinforce knowledge of the accounting cycle, accounting systems, and taxation. Service-learning can also help in achieving other goals suggested by accounting educators and professionals. Such goals are discussed throughout this volume. Examples include developing capabilities required for lifelong learning, developing oral and/or written communication skills, and developing teamwork skills.

It is also important to establish goals that are consistent with the overall mission of the university and the mission of the accounting department. In his chapter, Alfonso Oddo provides one example of how the department's service-learning activities fit with the university and department missions.

## Academic Credit

Bringle and Hatcher define service-learning as "a course-based, credit-bearing educational experience" (1995: 112). Several options may be available for offering service projects for credit. One option is to include it as a require-ment in accounting courses such as accounting systems or taxation. Curtis DeBerg integrates a service-learning component into his Principles of Accounting course for extra credit. Such course-linked experiences can improve students' understanding and retention of the course content by providing them with an opportunity to apply material learned from lectures and readings to solve unstructured problems in real-world situations. In my chapter, I defined "reflection" as the critical examination of the service expe-rience in the light of specific learning objectives. In course-linked projects, the course learning objectives can readily be used in structuring the reflec-tion component. However, one difficulty with course-based projects is that technical projects may require a significant time commitment, and students may find it difficult to spend a large amount of time on a project that rep-resents only one part of a course's overall requirements.

Service-learning projects can also be implemented in a separate intern-ship course or capstone projects course (e.g., see James Woolley and Susan Ravenscroft elsewhere in this volume). Ken Milani's students participate in the VITA project by registering in a one-credit course. The major advantage of this approach is that since the course is dedicated to a comprehensive project, students can spend more time on the project than in a course such as intermediate accounting or taxation.

Finally, students may be able to participate in service projects through student organizations (e.g., through a student chapter of the Accountants for the Public Interest, as Wayne Bremser describes) and Project Empower-ment (see Timothy Mech's essay). This approach is consistent with the AECC (1993) suggestion that students "seek campus opportunities to build com-munication and business skills — for example, serve as an officer of a cam-pus organization" (433). This alternative is particularly attractive because the increasing complexity of accounting knowledge may limit the time available to integrate direct experiences in any given course. However, in adopting a cocurricular approach to service-learning, instructors must keep in mind the differences between community service and service-learning discussed in previous sections. To provide the educational benefits charac-terized by service-learning, such projects should be selected and designed so that they (1) meet a community need, (2) enhance understanding of mater-ial learned in accounting courses, (3) help in developing a broader apprecia-tion of the accounting profession, (4) help in promoting a sense of civic responsibility, and (5) develop communication, teamwork, and interperson-al skills. Faculty advisers have an important role to play in realizing the edu-cational potential of these community projects. One limitation of this approach, compared with course-based projects, is that it may be more difficult to implement structured reflection and to maintain quality control, given the fact that the sponsored projects are not for credit.

## Establishing Criteria for Project Selection

A third crucial decision relates to the type of service activities and selection of specific projects. Accounting service projects described in the implementation section involve working with individuals, nonprofits, and small businesses. It is critical that each program establish criteria for accepting service engagements. For example, which individuals are eligible for assistance under the VITA program? Bremser describes the criteria used by Accountants for the Public Interest in selecting projects involving projects with nonprofits, small businesses, and individuals. Bremser and Ravenscroft provide suggestions for gathering client information to help in selecting projects that meet their established criteria.

Several other issues must also be considered in making this decision. If service projects are to be integrated into a specific course, then the service activities must be structured around the curriculum for that course. For example, teaching fundamentals of accounting to middle school students can reinforce accounting concepts for students in an introductory accounting course. Similarly, service projects can be chosen to reinforce concepts in intermediate, managerial, cost, and tax courses. Another factor to be considered is the scope of the project. If the project is one part of a course with numerous other requirements, instructors have to select projects that do not involve a very large time commitment. More extensive projects are feasible if the course is an internship or capstone course. It is also important to consider student knowledge and skills during project selection. Thus, one important area in which information should be collected from potential clients relates to the complexity of the planned project and the expected time commitment it will entail.

## Institutional Support

Institutional support of service-learning is crucial to successful service-learning implementations. Faculty may be unwilling to spend time and effort in supervising service projects if these projects are not valued in tenure and promotion decisions. Institutions can also reward faculty in other ways — for example, by providing stipends or course release for designing/supervising service projects. Another useful form of support is organizing workshops and other faculty development opportunities related to service-learning.

Centralized service-learning programs within colleges and universities also have an important role to play. It is often difficult for faculty to communicate regularly with community agencies in order to identify potential projects. Service-learning programs can develop and maintain a list of opportunities to help faculty in identifying projects appropriate for their courses. There may also be other resources available to faculty. For example, the federal work-study program requires 5 percent of the work-study students at any given institution to be in community service positions. These work-study students can serve as liaisons with community agencies and help in managing projects at various sites. Faculty should consider such infrastructure issues before making their decisions on how to implement service-learning in their courses.

## Role of Professionals

Accounting professionals can often provide valuable assistance in service-learning projects. Many professionals participate in accounting projects involving accounting assistance to nonprofits. One approach for implementing projects is to have students work with professionals volunteering through organizations such as the Support Center of Massachusetts, Accounting Assistance Project. Such an approach can offer significant benefits to students, the faculty, and the community. Students benefit from the supervision of more experienced professionals; faculty have to spend less time monitoring and supervising each project; the community has the benefit of more professional attention.

Accounting professionals can also be involved to a more limited extent. For example, in this volume Janice Carr and Ken Milani discuss the role of CPAs in reviewing student work in the VITA program. Margarita Lenk describes another way in which professionals can be involved in such projects. Her students obtained funding from the Colorado Society of CPAs for conducting a study of internal control in nonprofit organizations as well as for disseminating these results.

## Student Issues

Student background and attitudes are critical to project success. Students must have the necessary knowledge and skills required to complete the project. Students who are working for 20 or more hours a week may have significant time constraints. In such cases, projects must be selected especially carefully. Extensive projects, such as implementing a database for an agency, may not be feasible. Another alternative is to make service-learning projects a course option rather than a course requirement.

Student attitudes must also be considered. As several essays in this section have noted, students sometimes have concerns about community-based projects. Their past experience, if any, is probably in very different settings, and they may be somewhat uncomfortable — at least initially — with this type of project. Student orientation and frequent faculty-student interaction are helpful in addressing such concerns.

## Project Planning, Supervision, and Evaluation

Several decisions must be made about the actual structuring of the project. The instructor plays an important role in establishing requirements for the service engagement. Often this involves preliminary discussion with outside agencies. The importance of this step cannot be overemphasized, for it is critical to the ultimate success of the project. It helps in ensuring that projects are useful to the community as well as useful in enhancing student course learning. If the college has a service-learning program or other, related programs (e.g., the federal work-study program), then the program staff may assist in this step. Such programs can work with the community to identify available projects. This list can then be reviewed by faculty members to see whether any potential projects are appropriate for their courses.

Frequent monitoring of the project is equally critical to its success. Both the faculty and outside agencies can play an important role in supervision and monitoring. Finally, instructors have to decide on the most appropriate evaluation process. Evaluation may be based on reports and oral presentations. For longer projects, it may be useful to require interim reports and consider these reports in assigning the overall grade. This approach enables instructors to manage the project better than would be the case if they require only a single, final report. Feedback from outside supervisors can also be factored in.

## Mandatory Versus Optional, Single Versus Multiple Projects

One especially important implementation issue to be considered in utilizing service projects in accounting courses is whether these projects should be mandatory or optional. If the projects are mandatory in required courses with a large number of students, it may be difficult for faculty to supervise so much fieldwork. Furthermore, some students may resist the idea of "forced" service. On the other hand, if the projects are optional, instructors face a different set of challenges. For example, in one semester I initiated service projects with two organizations. Thus, only two or three groups out of 20 could select a service-learning project. The advantage of optional projects is that it is easier for instructors to manage two or three projects in a semester than to manage 20. Furthermore, only motivated students who are willing to commit the time needed for such projects may become involved. However, when service projects are optional, instructors must design alternative assignments/projects for the students not participating in service-learning. Alternatively, the project can be an extra-credit project, as in DeBerg's case.

As for the relative merits of involving a class in a single project or in several, it is clear that when students are working on a common project — or very similar projects — project requirements and expectations can be more easily communicated to the class. However, with different groups working on projects with different requirements and schedules, it may become necessary to have separate discussions with the teams involved in the various projects. Such discussions involve a substantial time commitment for faculty. On the other hand, multiple projects allow for more student choice, and such choice can, in turn, affect student willingness to assume ownership of their work.

## Summary

This concluding essay has identified several implementation issues for faculty to consider before undertaking service-learning. While the list of issues discussed here is not exhaustive, several key issues that have been discussed include (1) establishing goals, (2) making decisions related to academic credit, (3) establishing criteria for project selection, (4) assessing institutional support, (5) getting external support from accounting professionals, (6) preparing students, (7) establishing project requirements, and (8) monitoring and evaluating projects. Since the actual projects described in this section differ from each other in many of the above areas, they can provide readers with a variety of useful models with which to develop their own initiatives.

References

Accounting Education Change Commission. (Fall 1993). "Improving the Early Employment Experience of Accountants." Issues Statement No. 4. *Issues in Accounting Education* 8(2): 431-435.

Bringle, Robert, and Julie Hatcher. (Fall 1995). "A Service-Learning Curriculum for Faculty." *Michigan Journal of Community Service–Learning*: 112-122.

## Afterword

# Service-Learning in Accounting Education

by Paul Locatelli

The renowned philosopher and educator Mortimer J. Adler wrote, speaking for a number of educators: "The heart of the matter [teaching and learning] is the quality of the learning that goes on during the hours spent in class and during the time spent doing assigned homework" (1982: 49).

The senior partners of the Big Eight, now Big Six, professional accounting firms sent the following challenge to educators: "The use of new teaching methods will be a message in itself. Students learn by *doing* throughout their education much more effectively than they learn from experiencing an isolated course" (Big Eight 1989: 11). [emphasis added]

Juxtaposing these two statements crystallizes the debate around the purpose of a university. For academics, universities are places that promote knowledge and intellectual development; but for those who take an extreme view, knowledge is seen solely as an end in itself. For most accounting practitioners, universities are places where knowledge is created and discovered for use; knowledge has utility. Rather than locate the debate on the extremes, academics and practitioners would be wise to move the dialogue to common ground by focusing on learning. Universities, then, become places of learning that connect a set of elements: scholarly research in all forms, the creation and acquisition of knowledge, and the development of professional skills to use knowledge intelligently and effectively.

Fortuitously, education is moving toward more integrated learning: interdisciplinary courses, writing across the curriculum, team projects, studies abroad, internships, experiential learning, service-learning, to cite a few examples. Some skeptics continue to question the value of these pedagogies, but research studies confirm that "doing" — *using* knowledge as part of the learning process — can increase knowledge and understanding. Faculty who incorporate service-learning must be scholars who rigorously research the impact of service-learning on the acquisition and use of knowledge, and on the development of skills. In short, done properly, connecting academic pursuits with genuine service-learning leads to a better-educated professional accountant — public or private.

Let me suggest a framework for evaluating the benefits of service-learning.

Overall, the purpose of service-learning, and of each project, must be articulated. In my judgment, the primary purpose is twofold: to improve learning and to educate for responsible citizenship in the profession and society.

As with all learning, the depth of learning depends on at least three personal characteristics: intellectual talent, a desire to learn, and a commitment to scholarly methodology and professional competence. Nothing can substitute for these. Searching openly, persistently, and systematically for knowledge depends largely on the qualities of intellectual curiosity and talent; developing skills to use knowledge for judging wisely and acting responsibly advances scholarly and professional competence. Knowledge, learning, and competence have their own validity and inherent value, but they do not have their own finality. For ultimately, professionals have commitments to their profession and an even greater responsibility to society. The Accounting Education Change Commission (AECC) called this a *professional orientation* (1990: 2-3). The heart of the matter for service-learning, then, is the degree to which it contributes to learning and developing citizenship.

Second, the service-learning projects must seek to achieve educational objectives. The AECC, in its monograph *Objectives of Accounting Education*, draws on a number of sources to develop a composite profile of "desired capabilities" for accounting graduates.

The three areas of desired capabilities, the objectives "on which lifelong learning is built," are skills, knowledge, and professional orientation. Graduates are expected to possess intellectual, interpersonal, communication, and accounting skills. They are expected to have gained a certain level of general (arts and sciences, analysis of ideas) knowledge, and knowledge in the areas of organizations, business, and accounting. And their professional orientation aims toward understanding ethics and value-based judgments as well as addressing "issues with integrity, objectivity, competence, and concern for the public interest" (AECC 1990: 3). Service-learning projects should seek to further one or more of these educational objectives outlined by the Commission.

Third, rigorous inquiry and reflective analysis are integral to service-learning, as a number of articles in this book argue. Rigorous inquiry is critical in acquiring knowledge, and reflective analysis in guaranteeing academic quality.

Projects that deliberately structure rigorous inquiry and reflective analysis increase the knowledge students acquire and their ability to relate and use knowledge for solving simulated or real-world problems. Inquiry and reflective analysis also help to clarify the difference and the relationship between intellectual and professional development. Service-learning that does not incorporate these two important elements shifts the project toward the domain of community service. Those that do, enable students to understand the importance of lifelong learning.

Fourth, research must substantiate the impact service-learning has on achieving course or program objectives. The case for service-learning must be made on more than anecdotal stories. Measuring the knowledge acquired and the development of intellectual skills is essential for service-learning to have credibility. Publication of this research will ultimately lead to accepting the development of skills associated with *knowledge as doing* as part of a curriculum or program.

Service-learning projects require clarifying curricular objectives, followed by scholarly evidence that these objectives have been achieved. Choosing the proper research metric to measure the increase in learning is essential for the student and both accounting faculty and practitioners. A variety of research methodologies to measure the extent of learning exist. For example, Bloom's taxonomy measures the development of cognitive skills. And, thus, it serves as a useful framework to measure students' ability to question, organize data, connect concepts to prior learning or experience, reflect on content and process of learning, and create new solutions to unstructured problems (Francis, Mulder, and Stark 1995). In short, for academic credibility and validity, service-learning must itself be the object of scholarly research. This same point applies to other learning practices such as studies abroad, internships, and team projects.

Fifth, service-learning, as an academic pedagogy, should contribute value to the learning process, but its contribution should not be confused with other methods of learning such as interdisciplinary studies and internships.

Research studies on the impact of different out-of-classroom factors that positively affect learning contribute to the case for service-learning. One study reports that certain out-of-classroom experiences "contribute directly or indirectly to persistence [in learning] and to valued skills and competencies [development] . . . important outcomes of attending college" (Kuh et al. 1994: 42). For example, it found that living on campus, sense of community, social and academic integration, and new-student orientation positively correlated with improvement in learning. Further, gains in knowledge acquisition and application positively correlated with involvement in community service, academic themes in residential life, tutoring other students, and peer interaction focused on course content around racial issues. Based on findings like these, it is reasonable to hypothesize that service-learning, which directly connects academic and experiential learning, will enhance student learning.

Service-learning must also be differentiated from community service, as D. V. Rama indicates in the first chapter of this book. The former requires an academic and theoretical component, while the latter may or may not. One shorthand way to differentiate service-learning from community service, albeit an incomplete characterization of both, is to see them as *serving-to-learn* and *learning-to-serve,* respectively.

Finally, a personal comment. This book covers a range of projects. By and large, they reveal that service-learning increases knowledge, enhances understanding, improves skills, and develops a sense of citizenship. Any one of these gives service-learning a role in a university. And all improve the quality of education and consequently benefit students and universities, the profession, and society.

I am encouraged by faculty who incorporate service-learning projects in their courses and programs (it is hard work), and I encourage others to experiment. I hope this book will inspire faculty and students to use these — or better, to generate their own ideas for *serving-to-learn*. I also suggest as references the two AAA/AECC monographs *Intentional Learning* (Francis, Mulder, and Stark 1995) and *Assessment for the New Curriculum* (Gainen and Locatelli 1995); they define the larger context in which service-learning exists.

I congratulate the authors of this book for their commitment to their students, universities and colleges, and society. Students and society have benefited or will benefit from these efforts.

## References

Accounting Education Change Commission. (September 1990). "Objectives of Education for Accountants." Position Statement No. 1. *Issues in Accounting Education* 5(2): 307-312.

Adler, Mortimer J. (1982). *The Paideia Proposal: An Educational Manifesto*. Institute for Philosophical Research. New York: Macmillan.

Big Eight Accounting Firms. (April 1989). *Perspectives on Education: Capabilities for Success in the Accounting Profession*. New York: Author.

Francis, Marlene C., Timothy C. Mulder, and Joan S. Stark. (1995). *Intentional Learning: A Process for Learning to Learn in the Accounting Curriculum*. Accounting Education Series, no. 12. Sarasota, FL: American Accounting Association.

Gainen, Joanne, and Paul Locatelli. (1995). *Assessment for the New Curriculum: A Guide for Professional Accounting Programs*. Accounting Education Series, no. 11. Sarasota, FL: American Accounting Association.

Kuh, George D., Katie Branch Douglas, Jon P. Lund, and Jackie Ramin-Gyurnek. (1994). *Student Learning Outside the Classroom: Transcending Artificial Boundaries*. ASHE-ERIC Higher Education Reports, no. 8. Washington, DC: The George Washington University, Graduate School of Education and Human Development.

# Appendix

# Annotated Bibliography

Astin, Alexander. (1993). *What Matters in College? Four Critical Years Revisited.* San Francisco: Jossey-Bass.

This book provides convincing evidence that the "traditional" educational model of higher education should be revised because:

• The kinds of colleges and college experiences that favorably affect the student's performance are quite different from those that enhance retention and other cognitive and affective outcomes.

• Being in a particular type of institution does not necessarily limit the effectiveness of undergraduate education. It is the environment created by the faculty and the students that really seems to matter.

• The single most important environmental influence on student development is the peer group; by judicious and imaginative use of peer groups, any college or university can substantially strengthen its impact on student learning and personal development.

Astin found that the relevance of the "peer group effect" is in the underlying principle: Students in similar circumstances and with common needs and interests have been afforded an opportunity to interact and learn together.

Barr, Robert, and John Tagg. (November/December 1995). "From Teaching to Learning: A New Paradigm for Undergraduate Education." *Change* 27(6): 12-25.

The authors advocate a change from an "instruction" paradigm to a "learning" paradigm. In the instruction paradigm, many faculty are more interested in providing instruction and doing research than focusing on student learning. College is atomistic in this paradigm. In its universe, the "atom" is the 50- or 75-minute lecture, and the "molecule" is the one-teacher, one-classroom, three-credit-hour course. From these basic units, the physical architecture, the administrative structure, and the daily schedules of faculty and students are built. The resulting structure is powerful and rigid; it is antithetical to creating almost any other kind of course.

In the learning paradigm college, the structure of courses and lectures becomes dispensable and negotiable. Semesters and quarters, lectures, labs, syllabi — indeed, classes themselves — become options rather than received structures or mandatory activities. The learning theory of the instruction paradigm reflects deeply rooted societal assumptions about talent, relationships, and accomplishment: That which is valuable is scarce, life is a win-lose proposition, and success is an individual achievement. The learning paradigm of learning reverses these assumptions. Under the learning paradigm, faculty and everyone else are unambiguously committed to each student's success.

Batchelder, Thomas H., and Susan Root. (1994). "Effects of an Undergraduate Program to Integrate Academic Learning and Service: Cognitive, Prosocial Cognitive, and Identity Outcomes." *Journal of Adolescence* 17: 341-355.
  The authors used a combination of quantitative and qualitative measures to examine the effect of service-learning on civic involvement, social responsibility, and social conscience. Several new instruments were developed for the study that allowed researchers to investigate the effect of service-learning instruction and on-site supervision. Additionally, researchers compared service-learning students with students not enrolled in such a course. Student journals were reviewed to assess changes in prosocial decision making and prosocial reasoning using Eisenberg's methodology to assess moral reasoning. Researchers determined that students in service-learning courses experienced significant increases in prosocial decision making and reasoning along with cognitive gains related to multidimensionality. Of interest here, as well, is the positive relation between the quality of instruction and both prosocial reasoning and higher-order thinking. Structured, guided reflection appears to be a key element in enhancing student gains.

Boyer, Ernest L. (Spring 1992). "Scholarship Reconsidered: Priorities of the Professoriate." *Issues in Accounting Education* 7(1): 87-91.
  The author describes highlights from the 1990 Carnegie report *Scholarship Reconsidered,* and addresses how this report can be applied to accounting professors. Boyer proposes a new paradigm of scholarship with four interlocking parts: scholarships of discovery, integration, application, and teaching. Service-learning most aptly falls under scholarship of application in order to relate theory and research to the realities of life.
  Boyer is convinced that there is now an urgent new service agenda to be considered. Today, our shorelines are polluted, the ozone layer may be threatened, our schools are dangerously deficient, our cities are imperiled. He believes that university scholars urgently need to respond to the crises of this century, just as they responded to the needs of agriculture and industry a century ago. How can we justify a

university that is surrounded by pressing human needs and essentially ignores them? It's a failure not only intellectually but ethically as well. The good news is that professional schools — from architecture, to medicine, to journalism, to education, and accounting — increasingly are linking scholarship to real life. They are demonstrating that not only can knowledge be applied but theory can in fact emerge from practice and scholarship can occur in hospitals, gyms, and in the schools, as well.

Bremser, Wayne G. (April 1990). "Volunteering Your Know-How." *New Accountant* 5(8): 42-45.

This article describes how accountants volunteer their services to the community. It encourages accounting majors to seek opportunities to volunteer their services while in school and in the early stages of their careers. Service-learning benefits are described.

————, and Stanley Kligman. (March 1979). "All of Us Should Be Public Interest Accountants." *The CPA Journal* 49(3): 56-57.

Why should accountants volunteer services? This article is a call for volunteer accountants. It presents an argument for responsibility to give back to the community.

Bringle, Robert G., and Julie A. Hatcher. (March/April 1996). "Implementing Service Learning in Higher Education." *Journal of Higher Education* 67(2): 221-239.

The authors come up with a preferable definition for service-learning as "a credit-bearing educational experience in which students participate in an organized service activity that meets identified community needs and reflect on the service activity in such a way as to gain a further understanding of course content, and an enhanced sense of civic responsibility." Unlike extracurricular voluntary service, service-learning is a course-based service experience that produces the best outcomes when meaningful service activities are related to course material through reflection activities as directed writings, small-group discussions, and class presentations.

Buckley, William F., Jr. (1990). *Gratitude: Reflections on What We Owe to Our Country*. New York: Random House.

There is a growing debate in the United States as to whether the young should be encouraged or even compelled to give a year on "national service" to help the nation cope with its social problems, e.g., health care and illiteracy. Buckley does not advocate compulsory service, but he does argue that the young should be encouraged, through various rewards and sanctions, to give a year of service out of gratitude for civil liberties inherited and protected.

Cha, Stephen, and Michael Rothman. (1994). *Service Matters: Campus Compact's Sourcebook for Community Service in Higher Education.* Boulder, CO: Education Commission of the States.
    Includes statistics and trends on campus service programs, documents stages involved in program development, and lists service organizations across the country, and more than 500 model programs and institutional initiatives.

Collins, Dennis. (1996). "Serving the Homeless and Low-Income Communities Through Business & Society/Business Ethics Class Projects: The University of Wisconsin–Madison Plan." *Journal of Business Ethics* 15: 67-85.
    Collins describes his MBA students' projects, which included starting a grocery co-op, day-care center, and a transportation business. Student groups also developed networks to link low-income communities with student organizations, university professors, and United Way volunteers. The projects exposed the students to the living conditions of the disenfranchised and allowed them to explore ways in which the government can effectuate change. The projects also allowed students to work as teams in applying business theory to social services. Collins provides a very complete summary of these projects and discusses student reactions, project outcomes, obstacles, grading, professorial time commitments, and organizational issues.

Duley, John. (1982). *Learning Outcomes: Measuring and Evaluating Experiential Learning.* Panel Resource Paper No. 6. Raleigh, NC: National Society for Experiential Education.
    The focus of this paper is on measuring and evaluating the learning acquired by students in field experience education. This resource paper also includes a booklet entitled "Efficient Evaluation of Individual Performance in Field Placement." The goal of this guide is to answer the questions, What and how much should be evaluated? How should students be prepared for evaluation? How should students be evaluated? Who should evaluate the students? and How should feedback be provided to students?

Ehrlich, Thomas. (March 1995). "Taking Service Seriously." *AAHE Bulletin* 47(7): 8-10.
    The author subscribes to John Dewey's belief that individuals should

be trained not for narrow professions alone but for life, and that learning in practical arenas should constantly interact — lest we be unable to learn from our experiences or to link those experiences to our intellectual inquiries. Ehrlich provides several reasons for service-learning in academic courses: enhanced learning, enrichment of moral character of students, and civic education. The last two are closely related to another perspective: Community service as a regular part of an undergraduate course in the humanities or social sciences can link classroom learning to the professional and personal lives of students after graduation.

The role of service-learning fits well within the larger picture of current changes in undergraduate education. An expanded use of internships, an enhanced focus on problems that cut across disciplines, and an increased emphasis on collaborative learning are all examples of shifts in higher education that complement service-learning. As educators, learning is our mission. Involvement in community service can be key to achieving that mission.

Elliot, R. (June 1992). "The Third Wave Breaks on the Shores of Accounting." *Accounting Horizons:* 61-85.

Market conditions will force higher education — just as it has forced other service providers and industrial concerns — to stop looking only inward at the product, and look outward at the value created for the consumers. This means focusing on curriculum design, teaching methods, and learning materials. The national interest can no longer tolerate what the Bedford Committee found: 50 years with no significant change in the accounting curriculum. It's not enough to redesign the curriculum and say, "That's it, we have the new one, and it's optimal," and disband the curriculum renovation process. From now on, it's a full-time job.

The Accounting Education Change Commission (AECC) is best evidence of the emerging consumerism and of the cooperation among interested parties that can bring about needed change. The AECC originated in a call by a consumer group, the (then) eight largest accounting firms, who are major employers of accounting graduates. Higher education must also look to its suppliers. Universities frequently complain that the quality of K-12 education in America is so poor that the university is reduced to remediation. Higher education in the United States cannot just sit around wringing its hands about K-12 and do nothing about it. It must participate in solving the problem.

Gamson, Zelda. (January/February 1995). "Faculty & Service." Editorial. *Change* 27(1): 4.

The focus of the service-learning dialogue has been on the student as the one engaged in service. But what about faculty themselves as providers of service? Gamson describes faculty service in two areas: professional service (academic outreach), which is external, and internal service. External service draws on disciplinary and professional expertise; the expertise is useful in the service, rather than civic service. The author provides several reasons why academic leaders should be interested in emphasizing external service for faculty.

Giles, Dwight, Jr., Ellen Porter Honnet, and Sally Migliore. (1991). *Research Agenda for Combining Service and Learning in the 1990s.* Raleigh, NC: National Society for Experiential Education.

This booklet, based on the discussions of the Wingspread Conference in March 1991, gives a general description of the questions that need to be addressed about service-learning research, the participants involved in service-learning research, and the practices that must be implemented for such research. Includes a listing of "Helpful Resources."

Greenleaf, Robert K. (1991). *Servant Leadership: A Journey Into the Nature of Legitimate Power and Greatness.* Mahwah, NJ: Paulist Press. The Robert Greenleaf Center. ISBN 0-8091-2527-7.

This book is a philosophical treatise on the societal and personal benefits of leading efforts of service. A beautiful collection, including stories of historic service leaders, motivating poems, and ethical questions concerning the purpose of service and the related responsibilities of U.S. citizens that arise from the U.S. political and economic structures.

Guskin, Alan E. (September/October 1994). "Reducing Student Costs & Enhancing Student Learning: Part II, Restructuring the Role of Faculty." *Change* 26(5): 16-25.

Restructuring the role of faculty will, at first, prove to be a monumental undertaking. All of the incentives seem against doing so — except, in the end, survival. The alternative to the present role of faculty states the problem and challenge: To create learning environments focused directly on activities that enhance student learning, we must restructure the role of faculty to maximize essential faculty-student interaction, integrate new technologies fully into the student learning process, and enhance student learning through peer interaction.

Guskin believes that faculty spend precious little time involved in the activities that are unique to faculty and that have major impact on student learning — namely, direct, individual faculty-student interaction, intense small-group discussions, mentoring, and advising — and in encouraging students to be involved in activities that are important for student learning but do not involve faculty — peer-group, team-oriented settings, peer tutoring and coaching, and experiential learning outside the institution. The growth of student interest in community service activities provides settings in which ideas can be tested through direct experience. Such off-campus activities, which enable students to apply ideas or experience new environments, are important but do not necessarily emphasize reflection and conceptual development. What converts these experiences into a setting for conceptual development is reflecting on the experience itself through the written word and/or presentation to, and reflection with, others.

Linking experiential learning in real-life settings with student reflection, through written reports and presentations, while faculty act as mentors/advisers, is learning in its broadest sense. Since the experiences occur beyond the campus, their actual institutional costs are small; substantial costs do occur, however, in the faculty-student interactions focused on encouraging students to reflect on their experiences. Implications: (1) Students must be more active and more independent learners; (2) the academic calendar must be changed to become more flexible; (3) the undergraduate curriculum must change from focus on faculty disciplinary interests to focus on student learning; (4) assessment procedures must change, with an emphasis on student learning contracts (assessment of service-learning may become a primary area of faculty-student interaction — an interaction that could possibly have considerable positive impact on students).

Hirsch, Deborah. (May 1996). "An Agenda for Involving Faculty in Service." *AAHE Bulletin* 48(9): 7-9.
Student service-learning and faculty professional service share a common problem of nomenclature. The term "service" presents difficulties because of the various meanings associated with it.

Hogner, Robert H. (1996). "Speaking in Poetry: Community Service–Based Business Education." *Journal of Business Ethics* 15: 33-43.
Hogner provides a detailed description of community service projects, including a program to feed Miami's homeless. Business school community service is modeled using the theoretical context of Whyte's

Participatory Action Research. Hogner also discusses project goals and outcomes, including excerpts from students' self-reflections.

Jackson, Jesse. (Fall 1993). Abstract of plenary address at 1993 AACSB Annual Meeting. *Newsline* 24(1): 2-7.

Rev. Jesse Jackson talks about healing and rebuilding America. Just as there is a plan to capitalize and rebuild Russia, we should have a plan to rebuild America. Minorities are no longer minorities; in fact, 55 percent of south central Los Angelenos are Latino. Therefore, there should be a plan to uplift not just the minorities but also majorities who happen to be the minorities now. Jackson says, "Let's not argue black-white. Let's talk work–don't work, practical-impractical. Let's talk about how to offset the impact of a red line, how to build a green line." His focus is on the defects in the economics of urban America. His point is to make a plan to provide technology, and form programs that train students, businesspeople, scientists, and officials in ways of the free market in their formative years. Rationale: national security and economic interest.

Jackson, Katherine, ed. (1994). *Redesigning Curricula: Models of Service Learning Syllabi*. Boulder, CO: Campus Compact.

Consists of about 20 syllabi and commentaries to demonstrate how faculty have integrated service-learning in a range of disciplines and courses.

Kendall, Jane C., and Associates, eds. (1990). *Combining Service and Learning: A Resource Book for Community and Public Service*. 3 vols. Raleigh, NC: National Society for Internships and Experiential Education.

Volume I summarizes service-learning theories, research, and principles of good practice for institutional issues and implementation. The programs described in this volume support the development of moral and ethical views concerning multicultural awareness, civic responsibilities, and leadership skills. Volume II contains many practical curriculum ideas and models. Pre- and postservice organization and evaluation tools are provided as well as a discussion of related legal issues. Volume III contains an annotated bibliography of service-learning literature from the past 30 years. These volumes contain more than 1,300 pages of important resource material for interested community service–learning partners.

Kolenko, Thomas A., Gayle Porter, Walt Wheatley, and Marvelle Colby. (1996). "A Critique of Service Learning Projects in Management Education: Pedagogical Foundations, Barriers, and Guidelines." *Journal of Business Ethics* 15: 133-142.

> The authors critique nine service-learning projects within schools of business. Service-learning goals, pedagogical foundations, service-learning component themes, course curriculum issues, barriers to service-learning, and guidelines to maximizing service-learning success are discussed.

Lane, Michael S., et al. (1988). "Pygmalion Effect: An Issue for Business Education and Ethics." *Journal of Business Ethics* 7: 223-229.

> Reports the results of a survey designed to assess the impact of business education on the ethical beliefs of business students. The study examines the beliefs of graduate and undergraduate students about ethical behavior in educational settings. The investigation indicates that the behavior students learn or perceive is required to succeed in business schools may run counter to the ethical sanctions of society and the business community. Essentially finds that business students believe that winning is everything and that grades are what matter most, although they don't feel it necessary to resort to politics or "dirty tactics" or to sacrifice their own beliefs to be successful in their business programs.

Lempert, David H. (1996). *Escape From the Ivory Tower: Student Adventures in Democratic Experiential Education.* San Francisco: Jossey-Bass.

> This author offers an experiential Freirean alternative to the traditional U.S. textbook-only approach to education for the purpose of promoting an ideal democratic society. Student-initiated learning, with teachers facilitating contractual methods of evaluation, accountability to the community, support of diversity and multiculturalism, the identification and development of community values and ethics, and the promotion of self-activating potential are but some of the key elements of this new approach to education.

Meek, Joseph C. (Winter 1973-74). "Education Through a Tax Clinic." *Collegiate News and Views:* 19-20.

> A volunteer effort in St. Louis, Missouri, is described and appraised by the author, a partner in a CPA firm. Viewing the program from a student, practitioner, and faculty perspective, the author concludes that benefits are generated for all of these groups, plus for the taxpayers who are being helped.

Schön, Donald. (1983). *The Reflective Practitioner.* New York: Basic Books.
A study of professionals in five disciplines — engineering, architecture, management, psychotherapy, and town planning. Studies the unpredictable problems practicing professionals typically face and looks at their resolutions. These solutions are more than just applications of the knowledge learned in school and are, in fact, "informal improvisation that [is] the essence of professional knowledge" — knowledge that is acquired through what the author describes as "reflection in action." The author also suggests that it might be applied to training future professionals, but saved the "education for reflective practice" piece for a follow-on book.

——— . (1987). *Educating the Reflective Practitioner.* San Francisco: Jossey-Bass.
Believes professional education should be redesigned to combine the teaching of applied science with coaching "reflection in action" as discussed in his earlier work. Learning by doing develops the individual's ability to continue learning through problem solving, which should carry over to his/her professional career. Discusses techniques for the teacher to become a coach to maximize the benefits of reflection — much like a music or art teacher. When the educator and students engage in reciprocal reflection, the students learn how to reflect, and the educator practices "reflection in action."

Sims, Ronald R., and Serbrina J. Sims. (1991). "Increasing Applied Business Ethics Courses in Business School Curricula." *Journal of Business Ethics* 10: 211-219.
The purpose of this article is to take a background and historical look at reasons for the new emphasis on ethical coursework in business schools. The article suggests a prescription for undergraduate and graduate education in applied business ethics and explores in detail the need to increase applied business ethics courses in business schools to enhance the ethical development of students. Specifically, this prescription for applied business ethics includes (1) allowing the students to form their own personal values and moral ideas, (2) giving the students exposure to moral problems and issues of the day, (3) exposing them to ethical theories and moral traditions, and (4) allowing students to address both personal and professional applications of business ethics.

Swift, John S., Jr. (1990). *Social Consciousness and Career Awareness: Emerging Link in Higher Education.* ASHE-ERIC Higher Education Reports, no. 8. Washington, DC: The George Washington University, Graduate School of Education and Human Development.

>Reports on the shift in attitudes of college freshmen from 1970 to 1989 toward the pursuit of business and engineering degrees and away from education and the arts and humanities. The shift was, not surprisingly, coupled with a decrease in community service, voluntarism, and concern for the environment. Despite this shift, the students did feel that participating in the community would provide positive rewards, but they felt unable to find ways to serve without some kind of service program. Swift calls on the federal government to provide such a program (much like today's AmeriCorps program), and also feels colleges and universities should take the lead in establishing service programs linked with higher learning.

Troppe, Marie, ed. (1995). *Connecting Cognition and Action: Evaluation of Student Performance in Service Learning Courses.* Boulder, CO: Campus Compact.

>Addresses the importance of ensuring academic integrity in service-learning courses, and suggests how to measure the extent to which students connect their service experience (and the learning that results) to course content.

Unseem, Michael. (1986). "What the Research Shows." In *Educating Managers: Executive Effectiveness Through Liberal Learning,* pp. 70-101. San Francisco: Jossey-Bass.

>Correlates a shift in education from liberal arts to more technical coursework because of a shift in job opportunities from 50/50 government/private industry split in 1970 to 25/75 split by 1980. Author studied the makeup of the workforce at different levels and found the technically educated dominated the lower levels of management, the liberally educated were slightly more successful middle managers, and executive ranks were split evenly between the two disciplines. Unseem stresses more liberal learning as part of the curriculum, arguing that possession of specialized knowledge and technical skills is of moderate importance compared with other character elements, and that students should be educated for their career, not their first job. Found that liberally educated managers tended to be more concerned about the stakeholders of the company (not just the shareholders), and they maintained a more thorough understanding of the social/political forces impacting the corporation.

Varma, Kavita. (April 8, 1996). "Turning a Taxing Job Into College Credit." *USA Today.*

> This article describes a Volunteer Income Tax Assistance program at Baldwin-Wallace College. It explains some of the basics, benefits, and burdens of operating a tax return preparation program for low-income taxpayers using college students as the major source of human talent.

Williams, Doyle Z. (August 1993). "Reforming Accounting Education." *Journal of Accountancy:* 76-82.

> The increased complexity of the accounting profession, the CPA's broader role in the organization, standards proliferation, and technology have all required changes in accounting education. Many business programs are reforming their curricula from a more traditional approach (i.e., "the right" solutions, highly technical memorization, CPA exam preparation, etc.) to a more modern approach that integrates the accounting courses (tax, financial accounting, auditing, etc.), and emphasizes unstructured solutions to problems, active learning, and decision making. These changes in accounting education were proposed by the profession, and are quickly becoming adopted by educators.

Wingspread Group on Higher Education. (1993). "An American Imperative: Higher Expectations for Higher Education." Racine, WI: The Johnson Foundation.

> There is no substitute for experience. Academic work should be complemented by the kinds of knowledge derived from firsthand experience, such as contributing to the well-being of others, participating in political campaigns, and working with the enterprises that create wealth in our society.

Wyer, Jean C. (January/February 1993). "Accounting Education: Change Where You Might Least Expect It." *Change* 25(1): 12-17.

> The discipline of accounting, which "does not seem like a likely candidate for innovation," is facing pressure from the profession (namely, the Big Six CPA firms) to change the fundamental framework of learning. The new emphasis is on improved communications, teamwork, and active learning in order to "help students learn to reason from context instead of practicing the application of rules to narrow, stilted fact patterns." There is also a decreased emphasis on preparing the students to pass the CPA exam. In order to "fit" these fundamental changes into the rigid curriculum, educators are experimenting with

requiring a fifth year of undergraduate education (an additional 30 credit hours). Response of students to experimental programs is positive.

Zlotkowski, Edward. (January 1996). "Opportunity for All: Linking Service-Learning and Business Education." *Journal of Business Ethics* 14(1): 5-19.
   The service-learning movement offers business faculty an excellent opportunity to expand the education breadth of business students regarding the external environment of business. By developing curriculum projects linked to community needs, faculty can further their students' technical skills while helping them simultaneously develop greater interpersonal, intercultural, and ethical sensitivity.

Appendix

# Contributors to This Volume

## Volume Editor

**Dasaratha V. Rama** is a professor of accounting and information systems in the Earle P. Charlton College of Business & Industry at the University of Massachusetts-Dartmouth.

## Other Contributors

**Wayne G. Bremser** (PhD, CPA) is a professor of accountancy at Villanova University.

**Janice L. Carr** is an associate professor of accounting in the College of Business at California Polytechnic State University, San Luis Obispo.

**Curtis L. DeBerg** is a professor of accounting and Samuel M. Walton Free Enterprise Fellow at California State University, Chico.

**Martha Doran** teaches a variety of accounting courses at San Diego State University and specializes in "active learning."

**Margarita Maria Lenk** (PhD, CMA), an associate professor in the Department of Accounting at Colorado State University, is very active in community service-learning and experiential education.

**Paul Locatelli** is the president of Santa Clara University and a former member of the Accounting Education Change Commission (AECC).

**Timothy S. Mech** is an assistant professor of finance at the Frank Sawyer School of Management at Suffolk University.

**Alfred R. Michenzi** is an associate professor of accounting in the Sellinger School of Business and Management at Loyola College in Maryland.

**Ken Milani** is a professor of accountancy at the University of Notre Dame.

**Alfonso R. Oddo** is an associate professor of accounting at Niagara University.

**Nathan Oestreich** is a professor of accounting specializing in taxation at San Diego State University.

**Lynn M. Pringle** is the director of the Master of Accountancy Program at the University of Iowa.

**Susan P. Ravenscroft** is an associate professor in the Department of Accounting at Iowa State University.

**Carol Venable** is an associate professor in the School of Accountancy at San Diego State University.

**William L. Weis** is a professor of accounting and management and the director of the MBA Program in the Albers School of Business and Economics at Seattle University.

**James W. Woolley** is an associate professor of accounting in the Devid Eccles School of Business at the University of Utah.

## Series Editor

**Edward Zlotkowski** is professor of English and founding director of the Service-Learning Project at Bentley College. He also is senior associate at the American Association for Higher Education.